PREFACE

TRADEMARKS & COPYRIGHT

Yamaha® is the registered trademark of Yamaha Motor Corp. This publication is not sponsored by or endorsed by the trademark owner. We recognize that some words, model names and designations, for example, mentioned herein are the property of the trademark holder. We use them for identification purposes only. This is not an official publication however; it may include non-copyright works of the trademark holder.

INTRODUCTION

Welcome to the world of digital publishing ~ the book you now hold in your hand was printed using the latest state of the art digital technology. The advent of print-on-demand has forever changed the publishing process, never has information been so accessible and it is our hope that this book serves your informational needs for years to come. If this is your first exposure to digital publishing, we hope that you are pleased with the results. Many more titles of interest to the classic automobile and motorcycle enthusiast, collector and restorer are available via our website at www.VelocePress.com. We hope that you find this title as interesting as we do.

NOTE FROM THE PUBLISHER

The information presented is true and complete to the best of our knowledge. All recommendations are made without any guarantees on the part of the author or the publisher, who also disclaim all liability incurred with the use of this information.

INFORMATION ON THE USE OF THIS PUBLICATION

This manual is an invaluable resource for those interested in performing their own maintenance. However, in today's information age we are constantly subject to changes in common practice, new technology, availability of improved materials and increased awareness of chemical toxicity. As such, it is advised that the user consult with an experienced professional prior to undertaking any procedure described herein. While every care has been taken to ensure correctness of information, it is obviously not possible to guarantee complete freedom from errors or omissions or to accept liability arising from such errors or omissions. Therefore, any individual that uses the information contained within, or elects to perform or participate in do-it-yourself repairs or modifications acknowledges that there is a risk factor involved and that the publisher or its associates cannot be held responsible for personal injury or property damage resulting from the use of the information or the outcome of such procedures.

WARNING!

One final word of advice, this publication is intended to be used as a reference guide, and when in doubt the reader should consult with a qualified technician.

CONTENTS

CHAPTER ONE

GENERAL INFORMATION 1

    Service hints   Special tools
    Safety first   Periodic maintenance
    Model identification

CHAPTER TWO

TROUBLESHOOTING 5

    Operating requirements   Engine noises
    Starting difficulties   Piston seizure
    Poor idling   Excessive vibration
    Misfiring   Clutch slip or drag
    Flat spots   Poor handling
    Power loss   Brake problems
    Overheating   Lighting problems
    Backfiring   Troubleshooting guide

CHAPTER THREE

ENGINE 10

    Removal   Rotary valve
    Installation   Drive sprocket
    Cylinder head   Splitting the crankcase
    Cylinder   Crankshaft
    Piston, pin, and rings   Bearings and oil seals
    Piston/cylinder clearance   Kickstarter
    Crankcase cover   Autolube service

CHAPTER FOUR

TRANSMISSION AND CLUTCH 33

    Gearshifter mechanism   Clutch inspection
    U5 series clutch   Clutch adjustment
    YJ1/2, 80cc, and 100cc series clutch   Primary drive gear
    JT1 and JT2 clutch   Transmission
    MJ1 and MJ2 clutch   Transmission assembly
    MJ2T clutch

FLOYD CLYMER - 2025 EDITION
YAMAHA
ROTARY VALVE SINGLES
50cc - 55cc - 60cc - 80cc - 100cc
WORKSHOP MANUAL
1962 to 1976
ALL MODELS - U5 - YJ - MJ
JT - YG - G5 to G7 - YL - L5

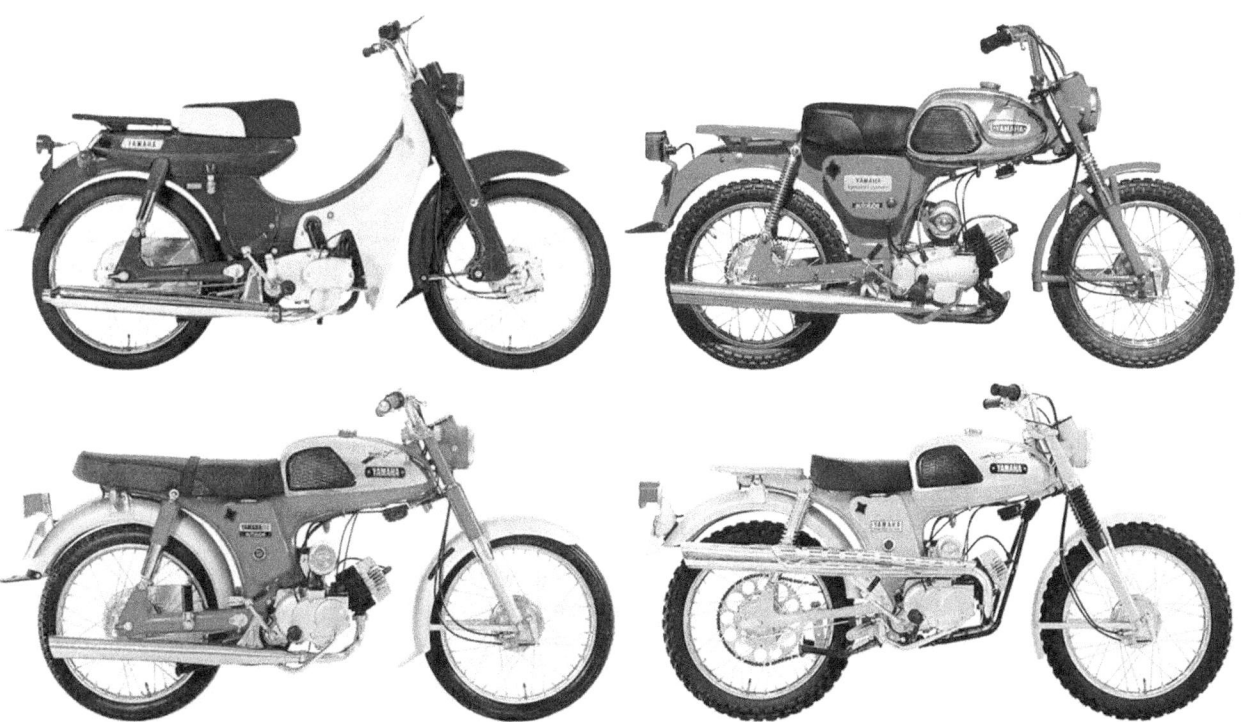

A Floyd Clymer Publication - 2025 VelocePress.com

CHAPTER FIVE

FUEL SYSTEM 60

    Basic principles
    Periodic maintenance
    Teikei Y16P carburetor
    Mikuni VM carburetor
    Carburetor adjustments
    Air filter
    Fuel tank

CHAPTER SIX

ELECTRICAL SYSTEM 73

    Magneto ignition system
    Battery/coil ignition system
    Lighting/charging system (magneto)
    Lighting/charging system (generator)
    Wiring diagrams

CHAPTER SEVEN

CHASSIS 90

    Front wheel
    Front brake
    Front forks (JT1/2, 80cc, 100cc, and YJ1/2)
    Front forks (U5 series)
    Front forks (MJ1/2)
    Front end (MJ1/2)
    Steering head
    Rear wheel
    Rear brake
    Tires and tubes
    Rear sprocket
    Rear sprocket assembly
    Chain
    Rear shocks (U5 series)
    Rear shock absorbers (JT1/2, 80cc, 100cc, YJ1/2)
    Rear shocks (MJ1/2)
    Rear swing arm
    Rear swing arm (MJ1/2)
    Frame (JT1/2)
    Frame (MF2/MJ2)
    Frame (YJ1/2)

CHAPTER EIGHT

SPECIFICATIONS 125

INDEX 137

YAMAHA SERVICE & REPAIR WORKSHOP MANUAL
ROTARY VALVE SINGLES • 1962-1976

U5	50cc
U5E	50cc
U5L	50cc
YJ1	55cc
YJ1K	55cc
MJ1	55cc
YJ2	60cc
YJ2S	60cc
MJ2	60cc
MJ2T	60cc
JT1	60cc
JT1L	60cc
JT2	60cc
JT2M	60cc
YG1 (S&T)	80cc
YG1K (S&T)	80cc
YG5T	80cc
G5S	80cc
G6S	80cc
G6SB	80cc
G7S	80cc
YL2	100cc
YL2C	100cc
L5T	100cc
L5TA	100cc

CHAPTER ONE

GENERAL INFORMATION

Repairing your motorcycle should be a pleasure. You should get a lot of satisfaction from doing the work yourself and knowing it has been done right. Generally, the correct way is the easy way. Correct procedures and correct tools are very important.

SERVICE HINTS

Start every job on a clean motorcycle. Try to find a clean place to work and keep it that way as you go along. Keep your tools in good condition and laid out so they are easily found when needed. Keep a can of fresh solvent around for cleaning parts and tools when necessary. *Don't* use gasoline for this purpose; it's too hazardous. Solvent is cheap and does a good job.

Before beginning a service procedure, read the entire section in this manual pertaining to the job you are undertaking. Get an idea of what will be involved and what special tools you will need. Some jobs cannot be completed without special tools. These tools are available from Yamaha dealers and reasonably priced for the most part.

If you think you will only be doing a particular operation one time and it requires a special tool, you may be better off trying to borrow or rent the tool overnight from a friendly dealer.

You may also consider bringing the assembly into a service department to have the work done. Labor charges on repairs are often considerably lower if the dealer or mechanic only performs essential work, but doesn't have to charge you for time-consuming preparation you can do at home with no special tools.

Precision measuring tools like inside and outside micrometers and dial gauges need care in their use and few dealers would trust them out of their sight. You'd probably be better off letting an experienced mechanic do crankshaft and cylinder wear checking, for example.

Simple wiring checks are easily made at home; but knowledge of electronics is almost a necessity for performing tests with complicated electronic testing gear.

During disassembly of parts keep a few general cautions in mind. Force is rarely needed to get things apart. If parts are a tight fit, like a magneto on a crankshaft, there is usually a tool designed to separate them. Never use a screwdriver to pry parts with machined surfaces such as crankcase halves, covers, and rotary valve covers. You'll mar the surfaces and end up with leaks.

Clean parts as you go along and keep them separated into subassemblies. The use of trays, jars, or cans will make reassembly that much easier.

Make diagrams wherever similar-appearing parts are found. For instance, case cover screws are often not the same length. You may *think* you can remember where everything came from—but mistakes are costly. There is also the possibility you may be sidetracked and not return to work for days or even weeks—in which interval carefully laid out parts may have become disturbed.

Wiring should be tagged with masking tape and marked as each wire is removed. Again, don't rely on memory alone.

When reassembling parts, be sure all shims and washers are replaced exactly as they came out. Whenever a rotating part butts against a stationary part, look for a shim or washer. Use new gaskets if there is any doubt about the condition of old ones. Generally, you should apply gasket cement to only one mating surface so the parts may be easily disassembled in the future. A thin coat of oil on gaskets helps them seal effectively.

Heavy grease can be used to hold small parts in place if they tend to fall out during assembly. However, keep grease and oil away from electrical components and brake shoes and drums.

High spots may be sanded off a piston with sandpaper, but emery cloth and oil do a much more professional job.

Carburetors are best cleaned by disassembling them and soaking the parts in a commercial carburetor cleaner. Never soak gaskets and rubber parts in these cleaners. Never use wire to clean out jets and air passages; they are easily damaged. Use compressed air to blow out the carburetor only if the float has been removed first.

Note that Autolube service for all models is covered in Chapter Three.

A baby bottle makes a good measuring device for adding oil to forks and transmissions. Get one that is graduated in ounces and cubic centimeters.

Take your time and do the job right. Don't forget that a newly rebuilt motorcycle engine must be broken in the same as a new one. Keep rpm's within the limits given in your owner's manual when you get back on the road.

SAFETY FIRST

Professional motorcycle mechanics can work for years and never sustain a serious injury. If you observe the following rules of common sense and safety, you can also enjoy many safe hours servicing your own bike. You can also hurt yourself or damage the machine if you ignore these rules.

1. Never use gasoline as a cleaning solvent.
2. Never smoke or use a torch in the area of flammable liquids, such as cleaning solvent in open containers.
3. Never smoke or use a torch in an area where batteries are charging. Highly explosive hydrogen gas is formed during the charging process.
4. If welding or brazing is required, remove the fuel tank to a safe distance—at least 50 feet away.
5. Be sure to use properly sized wrenches.
6. If a nut is tight, think for a moment what would happen to your hand should the wrench slip. Be guided accordingly.
7. Keep your work area clean and uncluttered.
8. Wear safety goggles in all operations involving drilling, grinding, or use of a chisel.
9. Do not use worn tools.
10. Keep a fire extinguisher handy. Be sure that it is rated for gasoline and electrical fires.

MODEL IDENTIFICATION

Table 1 lists all models covered in this manual. All models are stamped with an engine identification number specifying model and serial (production) number. This number is important when requesting information, identifying your model, or buying replacement parts.

The number is stamped on top of the left case half as shown in **Figure 1**. The first 3 numbers (or letters) specify the model, and the remaining numbers can be decoded to determine serial number and year of manufacture.

SPECIAL TOOLS

Additional tools besides normal hand tools are needed for various service procedures. **Table 2** identifies tools needed, their identification number, and intended use.

PERIODIC SERVICE

To ensure good performance, dependability, and safety, regular preventive maintenance is necessary. **Table 3** outlines required periodic maintenance.

Table 1   MODELS COVERED

Model	Year Introduced	Displacement
U5	1967	50cc
U5E	1967	50cc
U5L	1967	50cc
YJ1	1964	55cc
YJ1K	1965	55cc
MJ1	1965	55cc
YJ2, YJ2S	1966	60cc
MJ2	1965	60cc
MJ2T	1965	60cc
JT1	1971	60cc
JT1L	1972	60cc
JT2, JT2M	1972	60cc
YG1 (S&T)	1965	80cc
YG1K (S&T)	1966	80cc
YG5T	1968	80cc
G5S	1969	80cc
G6S	1970	80cc
G6SB	1972	80cc
G7S	1973	80cc
YL2	1967	100cc
YL2C	1967	100cc
L5T	1969	100cc
L5TA	1970	100cc

Table 2   SPECIAL YAMAHA TOOLS

Tool	Yamaha Part No.	Use
Point checker	908-90030-31-00	Measure ignition point opening and closing
Dial indicator	908-90030-03-00	Measure piston location when setting ignition timing
Dial gauge stand	908-90010-39-00	Mount for dial indicator
Clutch holding tool	908-90010-23-00	Hold clutch
Flywheel puller	908-90010-33-00	Pull flywheel off crankshaft
Slide hammer	908-90010-31-00	Hold magneto during nut removal
Exhaust ring nut wrench	908-90010-40-00	Loosen muffler pipe nut
Crankcase separating tool	908-90010-11-00	Separate crankcase
Crankshaft installer	See dealer	Pull crankshaft into case

Table 3   PERIODIC MAINTENANCE

Parts to be Lubricated	Type of lubricant	Initial Maintenance (Miles)	Periodic Maintenance
Steering wheel race	Multipurpose grease	At disassembly or repair	
Brake cable	Multipurpose grease	1,000	Every 2,000
Meter unit	Multipurpose grease	4,000	Every 4,000
Front brake cam	Multipurpose grease	1,000	Every 2,000
Front hub bearing	Multipurpose grease	4,000	Every 4,000
Brake pedal	Multipurpose grease	1,000	Every 2,000
Kick shaft	Multipurpose grease	1,000	Every 2,000
Change shaft	Multipurpose grease	1,000	Every 2,000
Rear arm shaft	Multipurpose grease	1,000	Every 2,000
Secondary chain	Engine oil	300	Every 1,000
Rear brake cam	Multipurpose grease	1,000	Every 2,000
Rear hub bearing	Multipurpose grease	4,000	Every 4,000
Accelerator grip	Multipurpose grease	4,000	Every 4,000
Dynamo lubricator felt		1,000	Every 2,000
Transmission oil	Motor oil	300	Every 1,000

CHAPTER TWO

TROUBLESHOOTING

Diagnosing motorcycle ills is relatively simple if you use orderly procedures and keep a few basic principles in mind.

Never assume anything. Don't overlook the obvious. If you are riding along and the bike suddenly quits, check the easiest, most accessible problem spots first. Is there gasoline in the tank? Is the gas petcock in the ON or RESERVE position? Has a spark plug wire fallen off? Check the ignition switch. Sometimes the weight of keys on a key ring may turn the ignition off suddenly.

If nothing obvious turns up in a cursory check, look a little further. Learning to recognize and describe symptoms will make repairs easier for you or a mechanic at the shop. Describe problems accurately and fully. Saying that "it won't run" isn't the same as saying "it quit on the highway at high speed and wouldn't start", or that "it sat in my garage for 3 months and then wouldn't start".

Gather as many symptoms together as possible to aid in diagnosis. Note whether the engine lost power gradually or all at once, what color smoke (if any) came from the exhaust, and so on. Remember that the more complicated a machine is, the easier it is to troubleshoot because symptoms point to specific problems.

You don't need fancy equipment or complicated test gear to determine whether repairs can be attempted at home. A few simple checks could save a large repair bill and time lost while the bike sits in a dealer's service department. On the other hand, be realistic and don't attempt repairs beyond your abilities. Service departments tend to charge heavily for putting together a disassembled engine that may have been abused. Some won't even take on such a job—use common sense, and and don't get involved over your head.

OPERATING REQUIREMENTS

An engine needs 3 basics to run properly: correct gas/air mixture, compression, and a spark at the right time. If one or more are missing, the engine won't run. The electrical system is the weakest link. More problems result from electrical breakdowns than from any other source. Keep that in mind before you begin tampering with carburetor adjustments and the like.

If a bike has been sitting for any length of time and refuses to start, check the battery if the machine is so equipped, for a charged condition first, and then look to the gasoline delivery system. This includes the tank, fuel petcocks, lines, and the carburetor. Rust may have formed in the tank, obstructing fuel flow. Gasoline deposits may have gummed up carburetor jets and air passages. Gasoline tends to lose its potency after standing for long periods. Condensation may contaminate it with water. Drain old gas and try starting with a fresh tankful.

Compression, or the lack of it, usually enters the picture only in the case of older machines. Worn or broken pistons, rings, and cylinder bores could prevent starting. Generally, a gradual power loss and harder and harder starting will be readily apparent in this case.

STARTING DIFFICULTIES

Check gas flow first. Remove the gas cap and look into the tank. If gas is present, pull off a fuel line at the carburetor and see if gas flows freely. If none comes out, the fuel tap may be shut off, blocked by rust or foreign matter, or the fuel line may be stopped up or kinked. If the carburetor is getting usable fuel, turn to the electrical system next.

For generator models, check that the battery is charged by turning on the lights or by beeping the horn. Refer to your owner's manual for starting procedures with a dead battery. Have the battery recharged if necessary.

Pull off the spark plug cap, remove the spark plug, and reconnect the cap. Lay the plug against the cylinder head so its base makes a good connection, and turn the engine over with the kickstarter. A fat, blue spark should jump across the electrodes. If there is no spark, or a weak one, you have electrical system trouble. Check for a defective plug by replacing it with a known good one. Don't assume a plug is good just because it's new.

Once the plug has been cleared of guilt, but there's still no spark, start backtracking through the system. If the contact at the end of the spark plug wire can be exposed, it can be held about 1/8 in. from the head while the engine is turned over to check for a spark. Remember to hold the wire only by its insulation to avoid a nasty shock. If the plug wires are dirty, greasy, or wet, wrap a rag around them so you don't get shocked. If you do feel a shock or see sparks along the wire, clean the wire and/or its connections.

If there's no spark at the plug wire, look for loose connections at the coil and battery. If all seems in order there, check next for oily or dirty contact points. Clean points with electrical contact cleaner, or a strip of paper. On battery ignition models, with the ignition switch turned on, open and close the points manually with a screwdriver.

No spark at the points with this test indicates a failure in the ignition system. Refer to Chapter Six (*Electrical System*) for checkout procedures for the entire system and individual components. Refer to the same chapter for checking and setting ignition timing.

Note that spark plugs of an incorrect heat range (too cold) may cause hard starting. Set gap to specifications. If you have just ridden through a puddle or washed the bike and it won't start, dry off plug and plug wire. Water may have entered the carburetor and fouled the fuel under these conditions, but a wet plug and wire is the more likely problem.

If a healthy spark occurs at the right time, and there is adequate gas flow to the carburetor, check the carburetor itself at this time. Make sure all jets and air passages are clean, check float level, and adjust if necessary. Shake the float to check for gasoline inside it and replace or repair as required. Check that the carburetor is mounted snugly and no air is leaking past the mounting flange. Check for a clogged air filter.

Compression may be checked in the field by turning the kickstarter by hand and noting that an adequate resistance is felt, or by removing the spark plug and placing a finger over the plug hole and feeling for pressure.

An accurate compression check gives a good idea of the condition of the basic working parts of the engine. To perform this test, you need a compression gauge. The motor should be warm.

1. Remove the plug on the cylinder to be tested and clean out any dirt or grease.

2. Insert the tip of the gauge into the hole, making sure it's seated correctly.

3. Open the throttle all the way.

4. Crank the engine several times and record the highest pressure reading on the gauge.

POOR IDLING

Poor idling may be caused by incorrect carburetor adjustment, incorrect timing, or ignition system defects. Check the gas cap vent for any obstruction. Also check for loose carburetor mounting bolts or a poor carburetor flange gasket.

MISFIRING

Misfiring can be caused by a weak spark or dirty plugs. Check for fuel contamination. Run the machine at night or in a darkened garage to check for spark leaks along the plug wires and under the spark plug cap. If misfiring occurs only at certain throttle settings, refer to the carburetor chapter for the specific carburetor circuits involved. Misfiring under heavy load, as when climbing hills or accelerating, is usually caused by bad spark plugs.

FLAT SPOTS

If the engine seems to die momentarily when the throttle is opened and then recovers, check for a dirty main jet in the carburetor, water in the fuel, or an excessively lean mixture.

POWER LOSS

Poor condition of rings, pistons, or cylinders will cause a lack of power and speed. Ignition timing should be checked.

OVERHEATING

If the engine seems to run too hot all the time, be sure you are not idling it for long periods. Air-cooled engines are not designed to operate at a standstill for any length of time. Heavy stop-and-go traffic is hard on a motorcycle engine. Spark plugs of the wrong heat range can burn pistons. An excessively lean gas mixture may cause overheating. Check ignition timing. Don't ride in too high a gear. Broken or worn rings may permit compression gases to leak past them, heating heads and cylinders excessively. Check oil level and use the proper grade lubricants.

BACKFIRING

Check that the timing is not advanced too far. Check fuel for contamination.

ENGINE NOISES

Experience is needed to diagnose accurately in this area. Noises are hard to differentiate and harder yet to describe. Deep knocking noises usually mean main bearing failure. A slapping noise generally comes from loose pistons. A light knocking noise during acceleration may be a bad connecting rod bearing. Pinging, which sounds like marbles being shaken in a tin can, is caused by ignition advanced too far or gasoline with too low an octane rating. Pinging should be corrected immediately or piston damage will result. Compression leaks at the head/cylinder joint will sound like a rapid on-and-off squeal.

PISTON SEIZURE

Piston seizure is caused by incorrect piston clearances when fitted, fitting rings with improper end gap, too thin an oil being used, incorrect spark plug heat range, or incorrect ignition timing. Overheating from any cause may result in seizure.

EXCESSIVE VIBRATION

Excessive vibration may be caused by loose motor mounts, worn engine or transmission bearings, loose wheels, worn swinging arm bushings, a generally poor running engine, broken or cracked frame, or one that has been damaged in a collision. See also *Poor Handling*.

CLUTCH SLIP OR DRAG

Clutch slip may be due to worn plates, improper adjustment, or glazed plates. A dragging clutch could result from damaged or bent plates, improper adjustment, or uneven clutch spring pressure.

POOR HANDLING

Poor handling may be caused by improper tire pressures, a damaged frame or swinging arm, worn shocks or front forks, weak fork springs, a bent or broken steering stem, misaligned wheels, loose or missing spokes, worn tires, bent handlebars, worn wheel bearings, or dragging brakes.

BRAKE PROBLEMS

Sticking brakes may be caused by broken or weak return springs, improper cable or rod adjustment, or dry pivot and cam bushings. Grabbing brakes may be caused by greasy linings (which must be replaced). Brake grab may also be due to out-of-round drums or linings which have broken loose from the brake shoes. Glazed linings will cause loss of stopping power.

LIGHTING PROBLEMS

Bulbs which continuously burn out may be caused by excessive vibration, loose connections that permit sudden current surges, poor battery connections, or the wrong type bulb.

A dead battery or one which discharges quickly may be caused by a faulty generator or rectifier. Check for loose or corroded terminals. Shorted battery cells or broken terminals will keep a battery from charging. Low water level will decrease a battery's capacity. A battery left uncharged after installation will sulphate, rendering it useless.

A majority of light and horn or other electrical accessory problems are caused by loose or corroded ground connections. Check those first, and then substitute known good units for easier troubleshooting.

TROUBLESHOOTING GUIDE

The following "quick reference" guide summarizes the troubleshooting process. Use it to outline possible problem areas, then refer to the specific chapter or section involved.

LOSS OF POWER

Cause	Things to check
Poor Compression	Piston rings and cylinders Head gaskets Crankcase leaks
Overheated engine	Lubricating oil supply Clogged cooling fins Ignition timing Slipping clutch Carbon in combustion chamber

Cause	Things to check
Improper mixture	Dirty air cleaner Restricted fuel flow Gas cap vent holes
Miscellaneous	Dragging brakes Tight wheel bearings Defective chain Clogged exhaust system

GEARSHIFTING DIFFICULTIES

Cause	Things to check
Clutch	Adjustment Springs Friction plates Steel plates Oil quantity

Cause	Things to check
Transmission	Oil quantity Oil grade Shift adjustment Shift drum Shift forks

STEERING PROBLEMS

Problem	Things to check
Hard steering	Tire pressure Steering damper adjustment Steering stem head Steering head bearings
Pulls to one side	Unbalanced shock absorbers Drive chain adjustment Front/rear wheel alignment Unbalanced tires

Cause	Things to check
Pulls to one side (contd.)	Defective swinging arm Defective steering head Defective steering oil damper
Shimmy	Drive chain adjustment Loose or missing spokes Deformed rims Worn wheel bearings Wheel balance

BRAKE TROUBLES

Problem	Things to check
Poor brakes	Worn linings Brake adjustment Oil or water on brake linings Loose linkage or cables

Cause	Things to check
Noisy brakes	Worn or scratched lining Scratched brake drums Dirt in brake housing
Unadjustable brakes	Worn linings Worn drums Worn brake cams

CHAPTER THREE

ENGINE

Service procedures for these Yamaha models are virtually identical. Where differences exist, they are identified.

Engine, tools, and working area should be as clean as possible. Read the entire procedure before beginning work to determine if you will need any special tools. Some jobs require special Yamaha tools.

ENGINE REMOVAL

1. Warm the engine for a few minutes, shut down, and drain the transmission oil as shown in **Figure 1**.

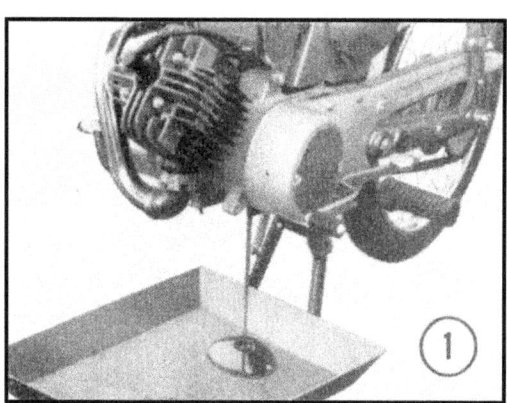

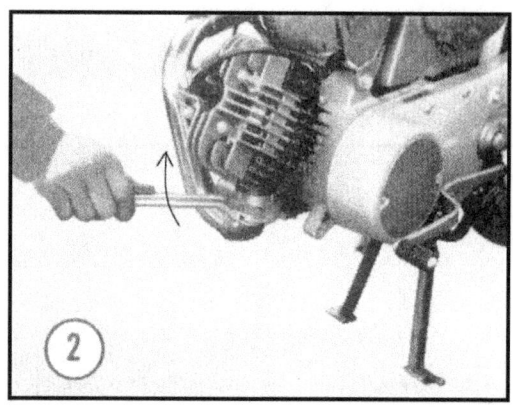

2. Remove the muffler and exhaust pipe. **Figures 2 and 3** identify the ring nut and bolts that must be loosened.

3. Remove the gearshift pedal as shown in **Figure 4**.

4. Remove the left-side crankcase cover as shown in **Figure 5**.

5. On U5E, U5L, MJ2, YG5T, L5T, L5TA, YL2, and YL2C models, remove the through

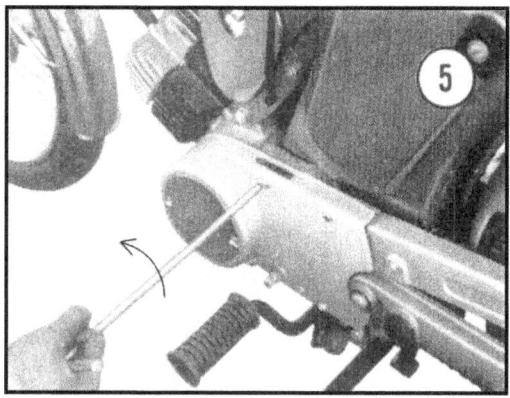

bolt, then slip off the point cam (or ignition advance unit, if electric start). Refer to **Figures 6 and 7**.

NOTE: *The following 3 steps apply only to generator/electric start models.*

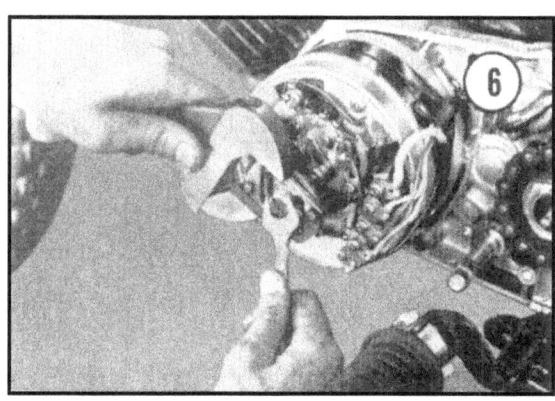

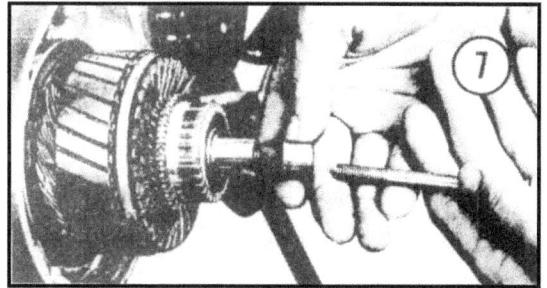

6. Disconnect all wiring at the junction points on the generator yoke assembly. See **Figure 8**.

NOTE: *When reconnecting wires, match the wire color code with color identification band pasted above each Phillips screw. This ensures correct hook-up.*

7. Remove the yoke. Loosen and remove both long screws shown in **Figure 9**. Pull back the carbon brushes, then pull the yoke off.

8. Remove the armature. Use a slide hammer. Slide the long bolt through the weight and screw it into the threaded center of the armature until it bottoms. Slide the weight back sharply to jar the armature loose.

NOTE: *The next 2 steps apply to magneto equipped models.*

9. Remove the magneto locknut as shown in **Figure 10**.

10. Remove the magneto flywheel as shown in **Figure 11**. Use the magneto puller which has a left-hand thread. Hold the puller body with a wrench and turn the push-type handle. If the flywheel refuses to come off easily, keep pressure

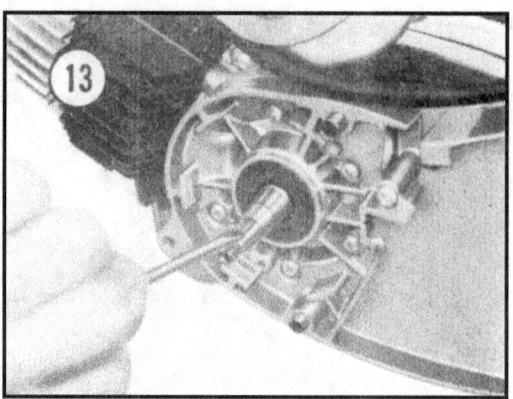

on the push screw and tap the end of the push screw. This shock force should pop the flywheel off. Take care not to bend the push screw.

11. Remove magneto backing plate and swing it out of the way. Secure it to the frame as shown in **Figure 12** to avoid damaging the wires.

14. Remove the carburetor cover shown in **Figure 15**.

15. Shut off the gas at the gas tank petcock and remove the carburetor.

12. Pry out the Woodruff key on the crankshaft with a screwdriver. See **Figure 13**.

13. Remove the drive chain by disconnecting the master link. Refer to **Figure 14**.

> NOTE: *If you plan to remove the drive sprocket later, loosen it now with the chain attached. With the rear brake applied, the chain will lock the drive sprocket in place.*

NOTE: *A pinch bolt secures the carburetor. Loosen the screw shown in* **Figure 16,** *then pull the carburetor out while twisting it carefully. If cocked, it will bind and probably refuse to slide off.*

16. Disconnect the oil line. Plug it with a screw of the appropriate size. See **Figure 17**.

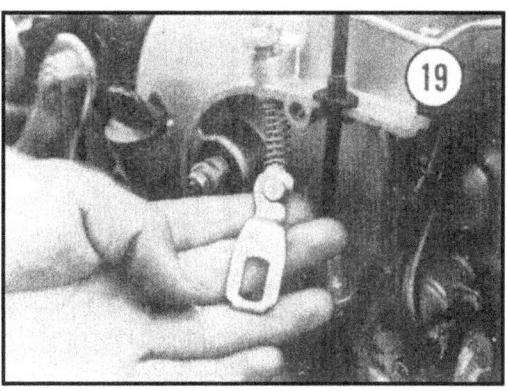

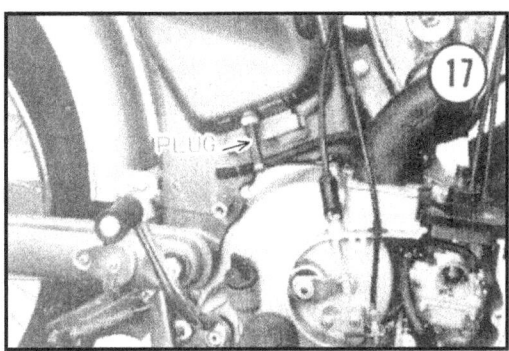

17. On models with Autolube pumps, disconnect the pump cable and adjusting holder. See **Figure 18**.

> NOTE: *After attaching the cable and laying it in the pulley channel, operate the throttle to make sure you have wound the wire around the pulley in the proper direction.*

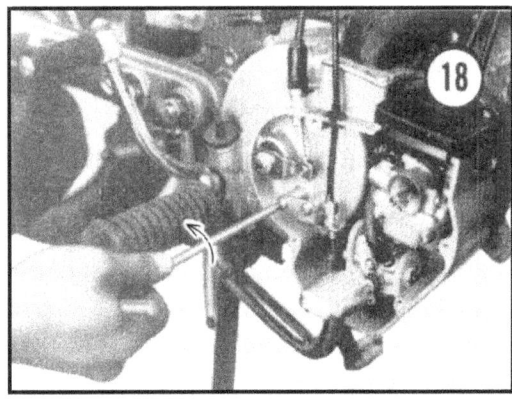

18. Disconnect the clutch cable. See **Figure 19**. The left case must be removed on all except JT1/2 series bikes.

19. Remove the air cleaner as shown in **Figure 20** (except JT1/2 series).

20. Disconnect the spark plug wire.

21. Remove the 2 upper engine mounting bolts and loosen the footrest mounting bolt. The engine is free to tilt forward (**Figures 21 and 22**).

> NOTE: *The YG5T and L5T series have a detachable frame member/engine protection plate. This must be removed to allow the engine to tilt forward. The foot peg/kickstand unit must also be removed. Lean the bike against something to continue engine removal.*

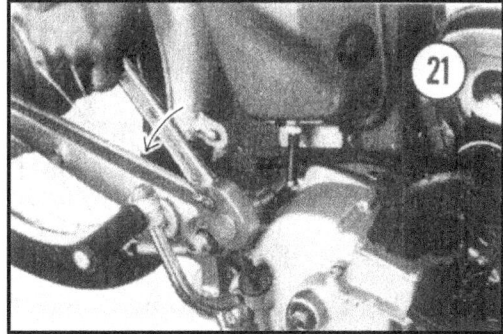

> NOTE: *The JT series has an enclosed frame. Simply remove all 4 engine mounting bolts in the manner shown in* **Figure 23** *and lift out the engine from the side.*

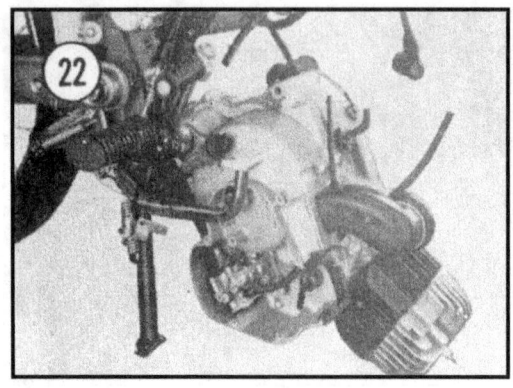

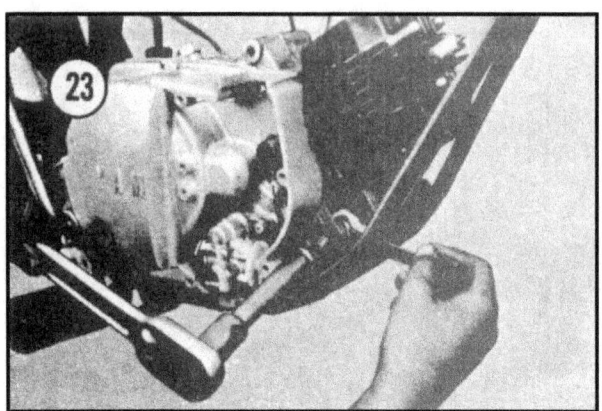

Table 1   TRANSMISSION OIL QUANTITY

Model	Amount*
50 and 60cc (except JT)	400-450cc
JT series	800-850cc
YG1 series	400-450cc
YG5T, G5S	600-650cc
G6S, G6SB, G7S, 100cc	600-650cc

* 10W/30 Type SE oil

4. Autolube cable adjustment (if applicable).
5. Drive chain adjustment.
6. Engine mounting bolt tightness.
7. Ignition timing.

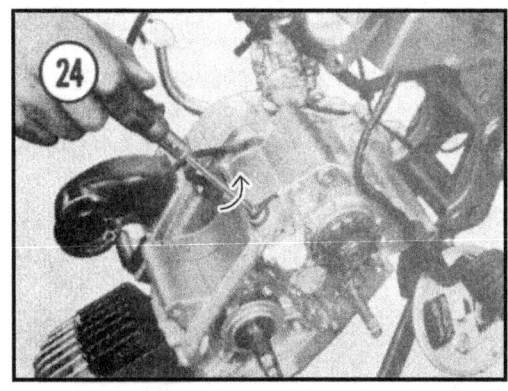

23. Pull out the footrest mounting bolt and remove the engine from the chassis (**Figure 25**).

ENGINE INSTALLATION

Reverse the removal procedure to install the engine. Be sure to check the following items before starting the engine.

1. Transmission oil level (**Table 1**).
2. Clutch adjustment.
3. Throttle cable adjustment.

CYLINDER HEAD

Removal/Installation

1. Remove the spark plug.
2. Loosen head nuts in a crisscross pattern, each ¼ turn at a time, until all are loose.
3. Lift off head. Discard head gasket (see **Figure 26**); always replace with a new gasket.
4. Carefully remove carbon from inside the cylinder head, using a screwdriver or the rounded end of a hacksaw blade (**Figure 27**).
5. Before head installation, clean stud threads first. Tighten each nut to 90 in-lb. in a crisscross pattern in 2 progressive stages. Torque head when cold; *never* when hot.

CYLINDER

Removal/Installation

1. Remove cylinder head as described earlier.
2. Tap cylinder lightly at exhaust port to loosen it. Lift cylinder high enough to plug up crank-

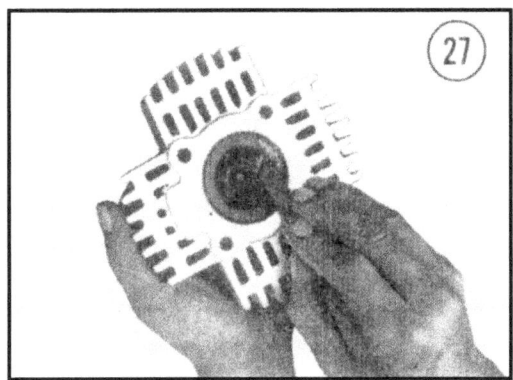

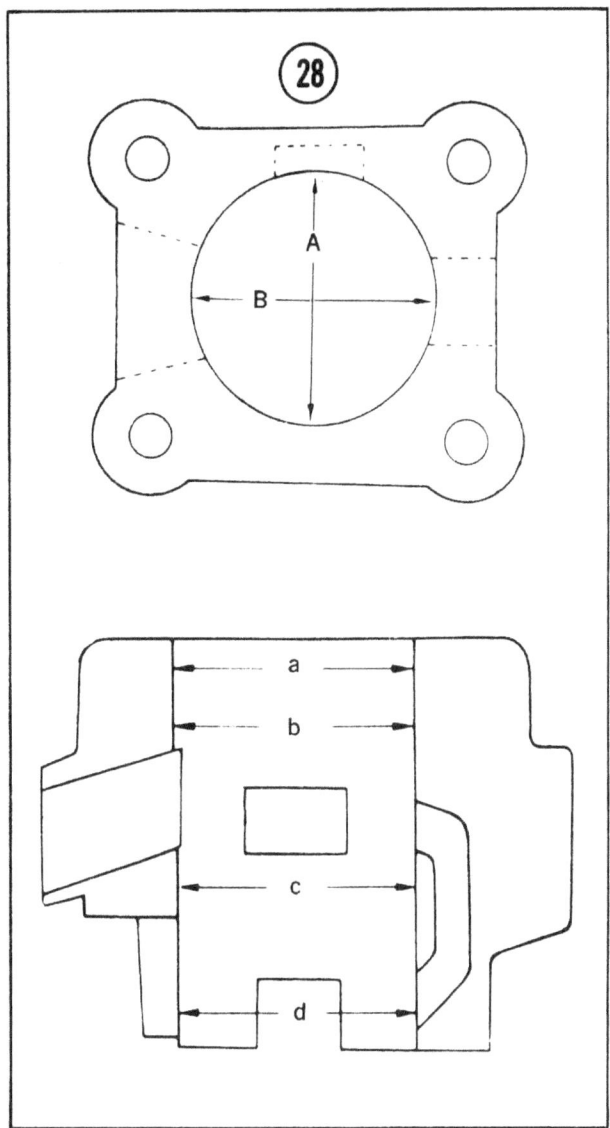

case opening by stuffing clean rags beneath piston. This prevents broken rings or contamination from entering. Remove cylinder.

3. Carefully scrape any gasket remnants from cylinder base and crankcase mating surfaces. Always replace base gasket to prevent leaks.

> NOTE: *When installing base gasket, check that gasket shape matches the irregularly-shaped transfer port channels on the case.*

Inspection

1. Carbon accumulations must be carefully removed from the cylinder exhaust port. A file can damage the port; use a carbon scraper.

2. Measure cylinder for wear using an inside micrometer or dial gauge. Measure bore diameter at 4 different depths and 2 directions as shown in **Figure 28**. If difference between maximum and minimum diameters exceeds 0.0019 in. (0.05mm), rebore and hone cylinder.

3. Pistons are available in 0.25 and 0.5mm oversizes. Cylinder should be bored to diameter of oversize piston plus standard clearance listed in **Table 2**. Error between maximum and minimum cylinder diameter after boring and honing should not exceed 0.0004 in. (0.01mm).

Table 2 PISTON CLEARANCE

Model	Clearance
U5 series	.030-.035mm
YJ1 & 2	.030-.035mm
MJ1 & 2	
80cc series	.040-.045mm
YL2, YL2C	.035-.040mm
L5T series	.040-.045mm

Installation

When installing the cylinder over the piston (**Figure 29**), squeeze the piston rings into their grooves using a piston ring compressor, your

fingers, or a radiator hose clamp. Apply a liberal quantity of clean motor oil to the rings and grooves to make the job easier. Note that the ring end gap fits around a pin in the piston grooves. Keep rags stuffed into the crankcase hole until the piston is inside the cylinder.

PISTON, PIN, AND RINGS

Piston Removal

1. Remove cylinder head and cylinder as described earlier.
2. Cover the crankcase opening with a clean rag before removing the piston pin clip. Use a pair of needle-nose pliers to pull out the clip; then push out the piston pin with a drift or screwdriver (**Figure 30**). Use new circlips during reassembly.

CAUTION
Eventually, a ridge of aluminum builds up around the circlip groove. This makes the pin hole smaller and pin removal sometimes impossible. DO NOT hammer the pin out. This could easily bend the rod. Protect the crankcase opening with rags, then carefully chamfer the raised circlip outer groove edge with a knife to scrape away this ridge. The pin should then slide out easily.

Piston Reconditioning

Pistons showing signs of seizure (see **Figure 31**) are noisy and keep the engine from developing full power. If a seized piston is used again without any correction, another seizure may occur at the same point. Lightly sand damaged areas with No. 400 sandpaper, or better, with fine emery cloth and oil (**Figure 32**).

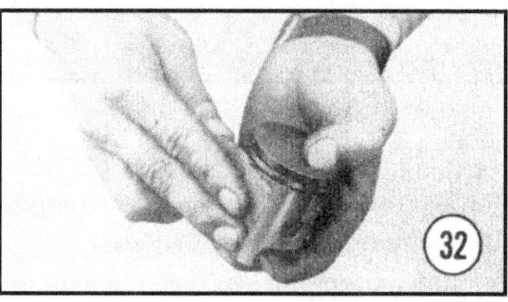

Replace the piston if the seizure marks cannot be removed with minimal polishing. If in doubt, replace the piston.

Carefully examine the entire piston surface. Check for cracks, partially melted piston crown, score marks, broken or deformed ring grooves, or any other damage. Replace the piston if any of these types of wear are noticed.

Scrape off carbon accumulations on the top of the piston with a carbon scraper or screwdriver blade. Use care to avoid scratching the piston (**Figure 33**).

PISTON/CYLINDER CLEARANCE

Piston clearance is the difference between the minimum cylinder bore and the maximum piston diameter. To determine maximum piston diameter, measure the piston with a micrometer at right angles to the pin bosses, 10mm from the piston bottom edge. See **Figure 34**.

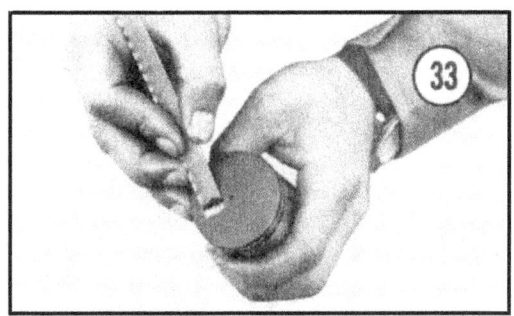

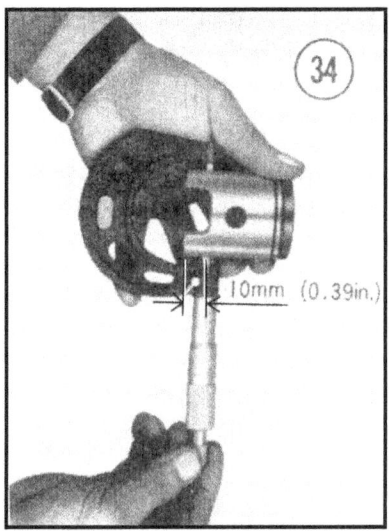

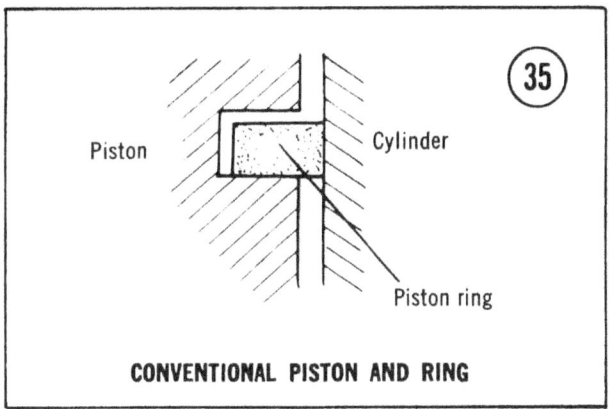

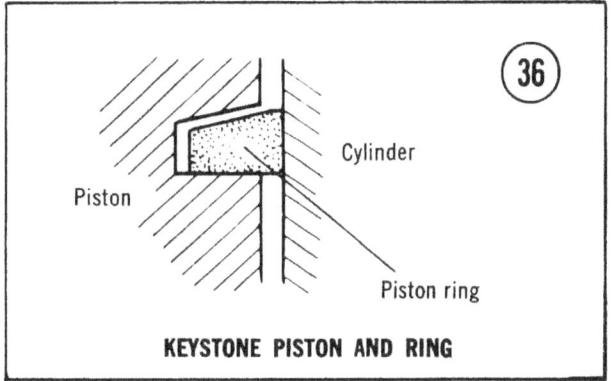

If a cylinder gauge and outside micrometer are not available to determine piston clearance, try this. Insert the piston into the cylinder, then slide the largest possible feeler gauge that will fit alongside the piston (not into a port). The feeler gauge size will be close to existing piston-to-cylinder clearance. Compare with the tolerances given in Table 2. If total clearance is 0.004 in. (0.1mm) or more, piston noise will most likely occur. Determine if piston or cylinder bore has worn. This piston skirt might have collapsed or the cylinder bore might be worn oversize or both conditions might exist.

> NOTE: *If the above wear conditions exist and you do not have precise measuring instruments, have a shop measure both cylinder and piston to decide which parts need replacement or reconditioning.*

Ring Identification

Two ring types are used: the *standard* design and the *Keystone* design. **Figures 35 and 36** illustrate the differences. The standard ring top and bottom surfaces are parallel. The Keystone top surface is angled 7° to permit a scrubbing motion as the ring moves; a letter "K" is stamped on these rings.

> CAUTION
> *The piston groove is cut to accept only one style of ring.* **The rings are not interchangeable.** *A standard ring put into a Keystone ring groove will bind. If cylinder installation is attempted, the piston will be damaged and possibly the cylinder wall.*

The Keystone rings are stamped to indicate position. The top ring is 1, the bottom ring is 2.

Ring Removal

To remove the rings, put your thumbs at each end of the ring and pull the ring ends apart. See **Figure 37**. Slide the ring out of the groove on the back side of the piston.

Ring Carbon Removal

Before assembling the piston and rings, clean all carbon and gum from the piston ring grooves. Use a broken piston ring with the sharp end edges filed off, but don't try to clean a standard piston with a Keystone ring or vice versa.

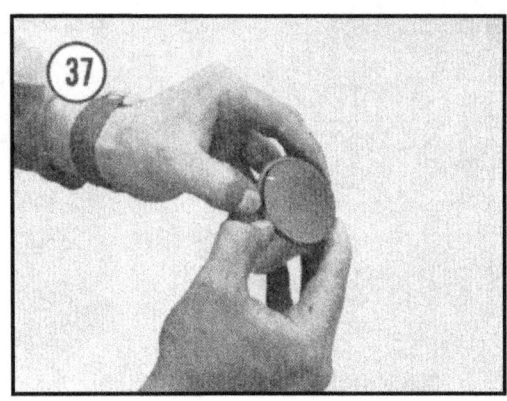

Ring End Gap Measurement

To measure the piston rings for wear, put the ring in the cylinder so that the ring is parallel with the bottom edge of the cylinder. Measure the gap between the ring ends with a feeler gauge. Normal end gap is 0.0059-0.014 in. (0.15-0.35mm) for both top and bottom rings, Keystone and regular rings alike.

Ring Side Gap Measurement

Measure side gap play after carbon has been removed. See **Figure 38**. The No. 1 ring should have 0.0016-0.0032 in. (0.04-0.08mm) clearance; the No. 2 ring should have 0.0012-0.0028 in. (0.03-0.07mm) clearance.

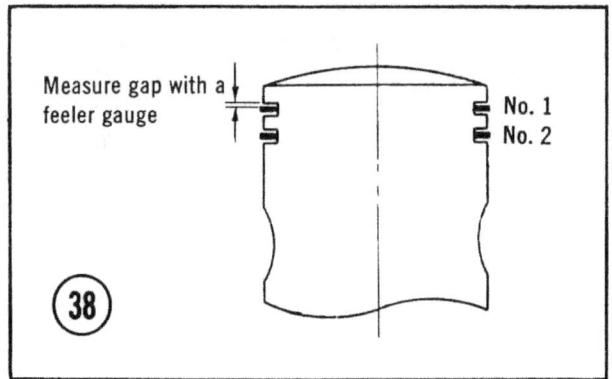

Ring Installation

When installing piston rings, first fit the No. 2 ring and then the No. 1 ring. Use a pair of piston ring pliers to spread the rings for installation, if available; if not, spread the rings carefully with your thumbs just enough to slip them over the piston. Align the end gaps with the locating pin in each ring groove, as shown in **Figure 39**. The printing on the rings must be toward the top of the piston.

Piston Pin Fit

The piston pin should fit snugly in the piston hole so that it drags slightly as you push it. If the pin is loose, the pin and/or piston should be replaced. Check the pin for wear at the point it rests inside the small end bearing. Check this by inserting the pin into the small end of the connecting rod. Excessive free-play indicates that replacement of the pin or bearing is necessary.

Piston Installation

Reinstall piston with the arrow marked on its head pointing toward the exhaust port. See **Figure 40**.

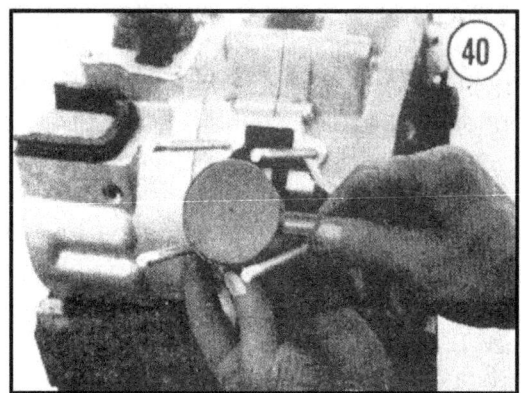

CRANKCASE COVER

1. Remove the kickstarter crank clamping bolt in **Figure 41** and remove the kickstarter lever.

2. If your model is equipped with Autolube, remove the banjo bolt from the pump delivery pipe valve cover shown in **Figure 42**.

3. Remove the Phillips screws from the crankcase cover and take off the cover. (The cover

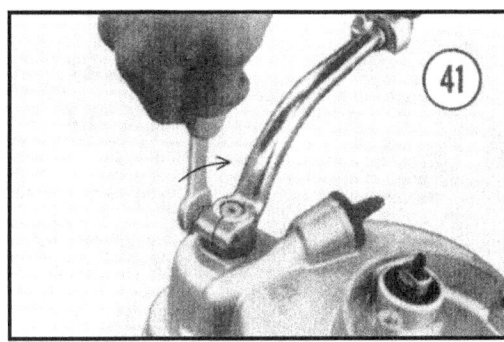

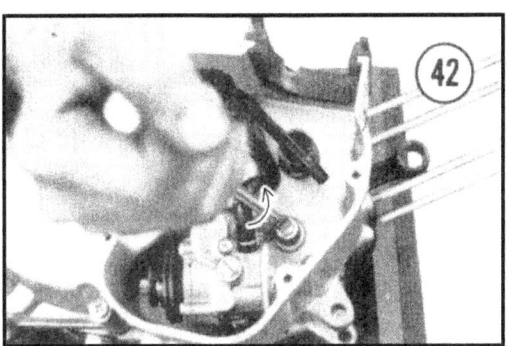

may be removed with the oil pump mounted to it.) See **Figures 43 and 44**.

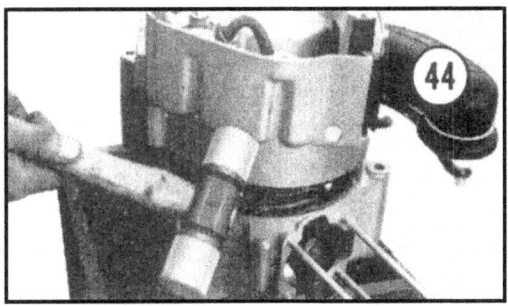

4. Remove crankcase cover gasket if it has been damaged. **Figure 45** shows its location.

5. When installing right-hand case cover, be sure all old gasket and sealer has been carefully scraped off both gasket mating surfaces.

6. Apply fresh Yamabond #5 (or equivalent gasket sealer) to case and crankcase gasket mat-

ing surfaces. Lay gasket into place, then install case cover. Don't let Yamabond dry.

7. During installation, check that Autolube (if equipped) pump drive gear is correctly meshed with primary drive gear. The case cover must slide on fully and easily. If it stops about ¼ inch short, the pump gear is not meshed.

8. Further right-hand case disassembly requires removal of all components. Other than the rotary valve, component disassembly steps are given on the following pages: *Clutch*, pages 42-51; *Shifter Mechanism*, pages 33-41; *Kickstarter*, pages 26-30.

ROTARY VALVE

1. Remove the valve cover mounting bolts and take off the valve cover (**Figure 46**).

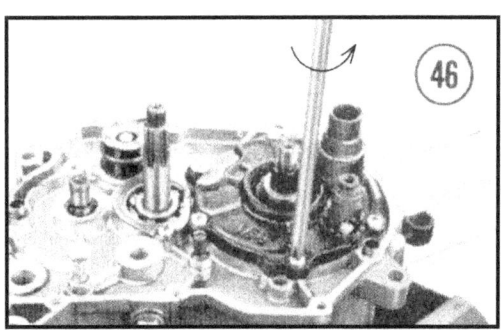

2. As shown in **Figure 47**, push out the valve knock pin with a nail or small punch. Do not damage the crankcase sealing surface.

3. Fit the valve identified in **Figure 48** over the valve unit collar and check for play. If play is excessive, replace the valve. If the collar shows wear from the locating pin (see **Figure 49**), replace the collar.

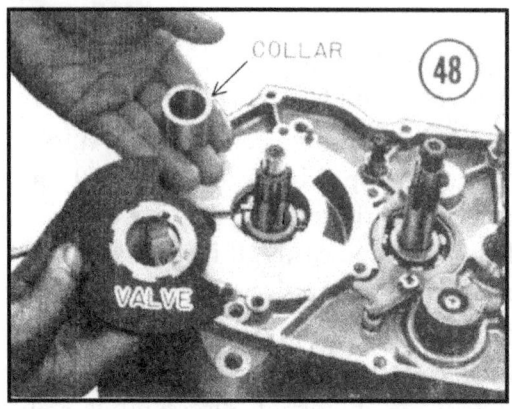

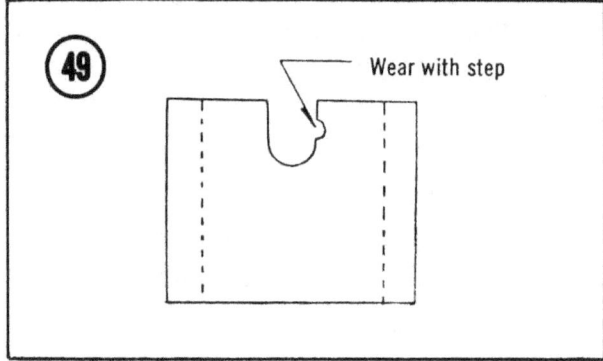

4. The valve cover O-ring (**Figure 50**) should be replaced if it shows any signs of stretching. Grease it to ease installation.

5. The crankshaft O-ring is easily damaged when the valve unit collar is installed. Grease the O-ring before installation (**Figure 51**).

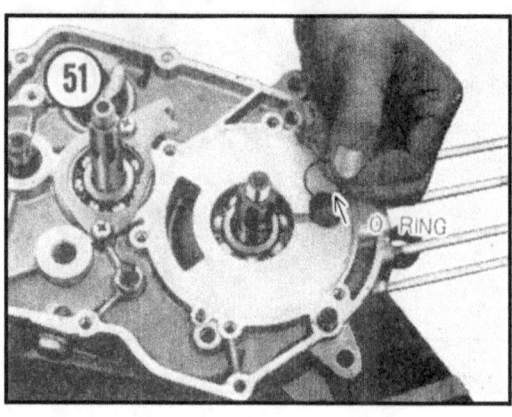

6. Apply good quality grease to the lip surface of the valve cover oil seals when installing the cover (**Figure 52**).

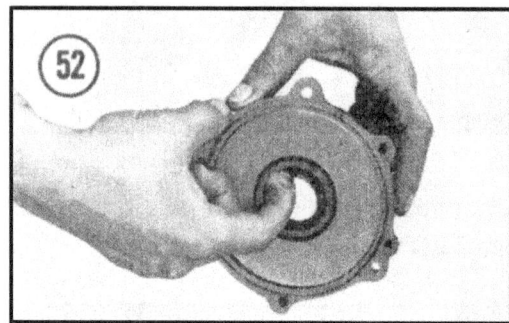

Rotary Valve Timing

Since the rotary valve can be installed 2 ways, it is possible to install the valve 180° out of correct alignment. To ensure correct installation, follow this procedure.

1. Rotate the crankshaft until the piston is at top dead center; remove the spark plug and lock, if need be.

2. The rotary valve should be installed so it is just about ready to close the intake hole into the crankcase (on JT series, valve must be right at edge of intake hole). Remember, the crankshaft turns in a clockwise direction when the engine is running. **Figure 53** shows correct and incorrect installation.

NOTE: *JT1 and 2 models have a collar whose outer splines engage the valve. To align this valve, find piston top dead center. Line up the end of the knock pin (in crankshaft) with 2 indentations found on the face of the valve. When both indentations and knock pin form a straight line, the valve is installed correctly.*

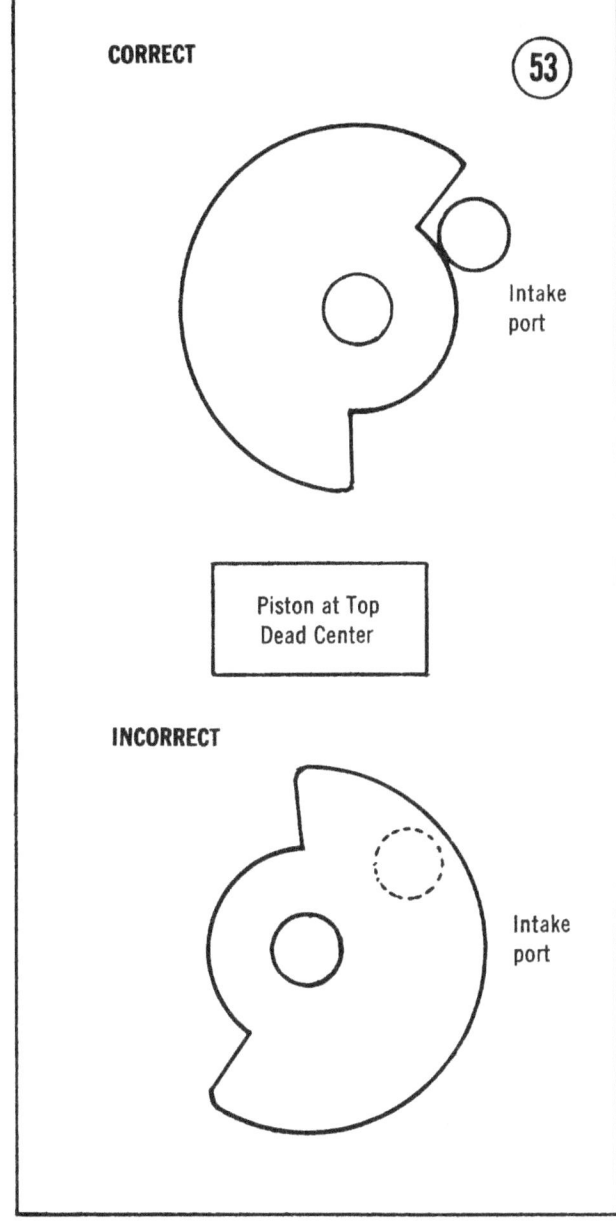

2. **Figure 55** shows how to keep the drive sprocket from turning with the flywheel magneto holding tool and loosening the sprocket nut. If no magneto tool is available, shift the transmission to first gear, fit a socket wrench on the sprocket nut, and tap the wrench handle with a hammer so the impact will loosen the nut.

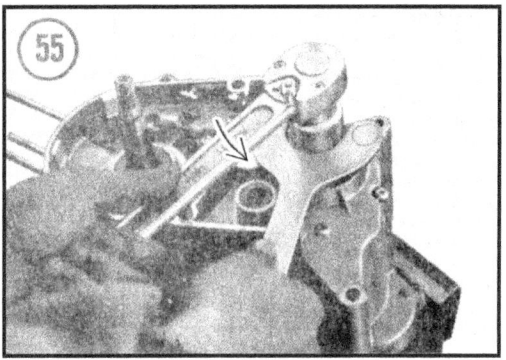

3. A worn drive sprocket may result in abnormal noise and can shoften the life of the chain. Check the sprocket teeth carefully, especially on older machines. A worn sprocket will quickly wear out a new drive chain so it may be false economy to overlook the sprocket. See **Figure 56** for comparison.

SPLITTING THE CRANKCASE

The crankcase may be split from either side, but the splitting tool should be installed on the right half of the crankcase.

The following procedure applies to all models.

NOTE: *Remove the neutral stopper on shift drum models.*

1. Remove all case securing screws. Loosen them in a crisscross pattern, ¼ turn each, to prevent warping. **Figure 57** shows typical locations; other models may differ.

NOTE: *To avoid losing the screws, and to ensure proper location during assembly, draw a case outline on cardboard, then punch holes to correspond with screw locations. Insert screws in their appropriate locations as they are removed.*

2. Install the case separating tool (Yamaha part No. 908-90010-11-00) as shown in **Figure 58**. Mount it on the right side, although it fits on

DRIVE SPROCKET

1. To remove the drive sprocket, straighten the bent edge of the locking washer with a chisel, as shown in **Figure 54**.

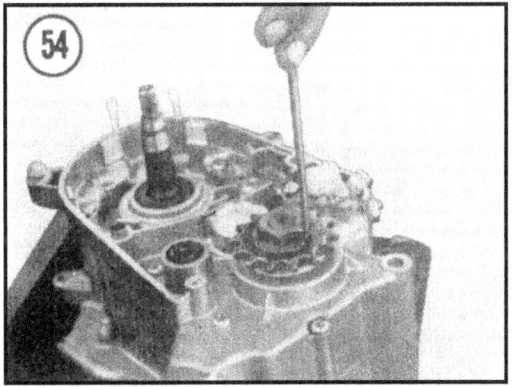

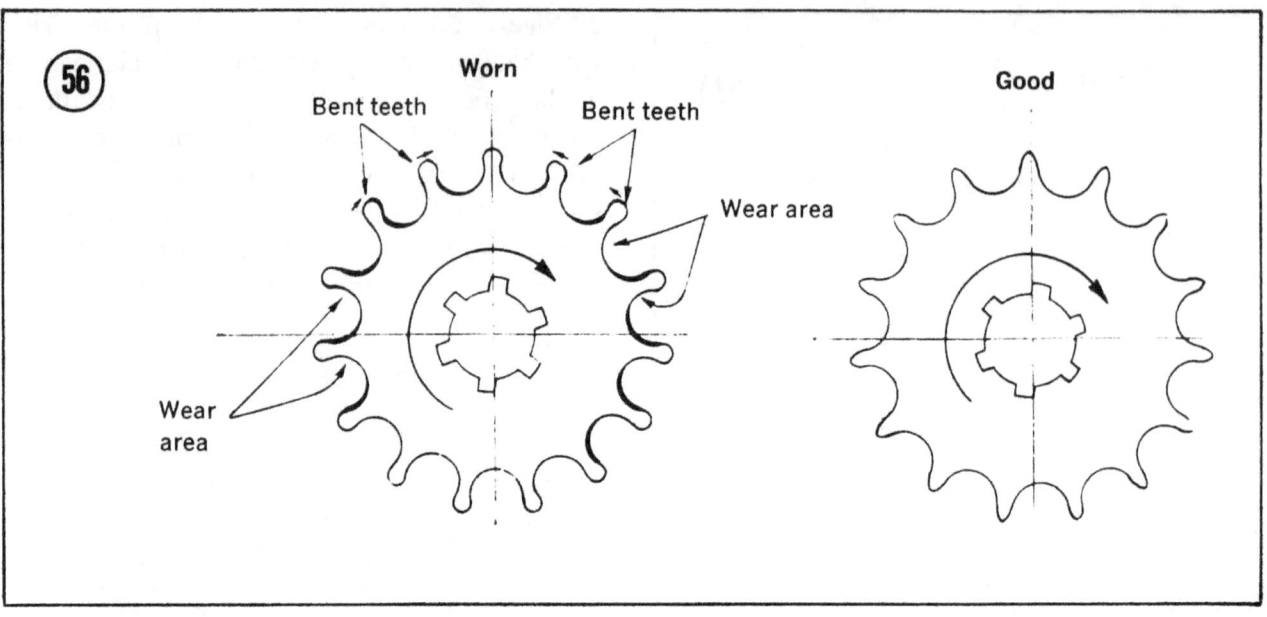

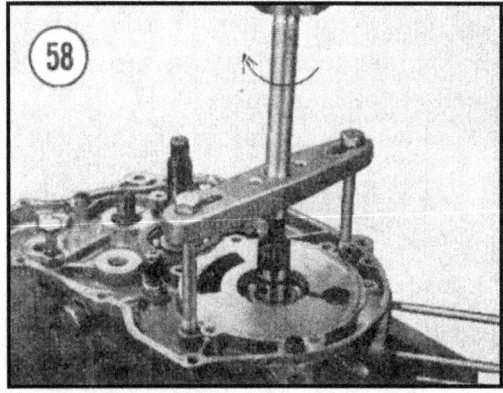

either side. The cross piece must be parallel to the case surface. One long bolt can be backed out to achieve this, but basically both bolts must be fully screwed in.

3. Move the piston to top dead center to prevent connecting rod damage, then tighten the push screw so the right case half starts to lift off the crankshaft and transmission shafts.

4. Tap front and back case sections to make sure the case lifts without tilting at either end. If needed, tap the transmission shafts back down if they hang up during case removal (**Figure 59**).

CAUTION
a. Splitting the case requires only hand twisting pressure on the push bolt. If extreme pressure is needed, STOP. Check for screws still attached, part of shift linkage left attached, or transmission shafts temporarily hung up in bearings. Relieve push screw pressure immediately and check.

b. Never place a prying tool between the case halves to assist in splitting the case. This can easily destroy the seal on both case halves.

c. Only use rawhide or a rubber hammer when tapping on case or transmission shafts.

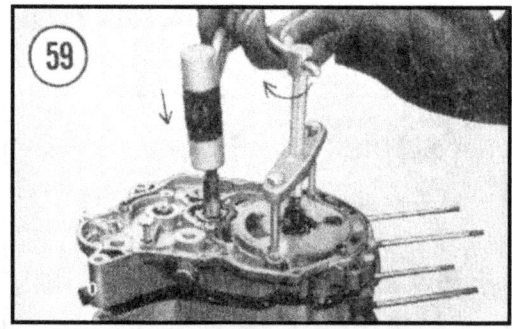

5. As you lift off the separated case, immediately check inside for transmission shims that may stick to the transmission bearings.

Case Maintenance

1. Clean both case halves thoroughly with solvent to remove oil, dirt residue, metal particles, and to make inspection easier. Rinse out all bearings carefully.

2. Examine the case mating surfaces for any dents or nicks that would result in lost crankcase compression. Major dents or gouges on sealing surfaces would require case replacement. Minor case mating surface deformation at the transmission chamber will result in oil leaks, but does not automatically require case replacement. If in doubt, ask a dealer mechanic.

3. One case half has at least 2 hollow dowel pins to make sure both case halves line up with each other and to prevent shifting. Check that they are in the case mating surfaces.

Case Assembly

1. Thoroughly clean both cases, then install transmission unit (and shift drum/shift forks, if equipped) and crankshaft into the left case (see following sections on transmission and crankshaft for installation procedures).

2. Install all transmission and crankshaft shims.

3. Make sure all case-locating dowel pins are installed, then place the right case half down over the crankshaft and transmission shafts.

4. Apply Yamabond #5 (or equivalent gasket sealer) to both case mating surfaces (**Figure 60**). Slide the right case half down until it mates with the left case half. Do not allow the Yamabond to dry. If needed, tap the right case half lightly to seat over the shafts. The right case half should slide down easily. If the case half stops within 1/16-1/8 in. of mating, but further efforts are not successful, do not force the case. Pull the case half off and check for incorrect shimming or improperly installed parts.

   NOTE: *Keep transmission in neutral during case assembly.*

5. Install case securing screws. If installed in proper locations, each screw should stick up about 1/4-3/8 in. above the case before tightening. Tighten the screws by hand in a crisscross pattern until snug, then repeat the procedure by hand until firmly hand-tight.

CRANKSHAFT

The following crankshaft information is applicable to all models covered in this manual. **Figure 61** provides an exploded view of a conventional crankshaft. Depending on your model, it may or may not have connecting rod shims (5, Figure 61). It may or may not have crankshaft shims (12, Figure 61), or it may have this shim only on one side. Take care during removal to check for the presence of these shims.

1. Remove the crankshaft assembly with the crankcase dividing tool shown in **Figure 62**. Tighten the dividing tool bolts into the crankcase and keep the crankcase horizontal. Pull the connecting rod up to top dead center so it will not hit the crankcase. Keep it there by inserting a thrust bearing between the end of the crankshaft and center bolt of the dividing tool.

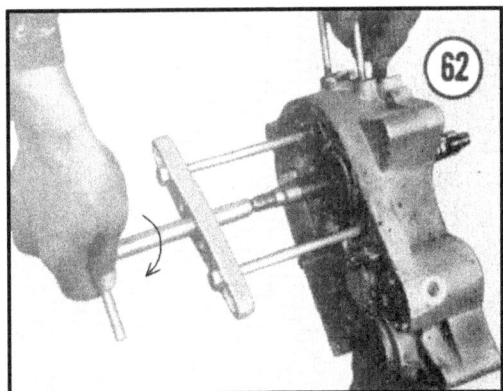

2. To install the crankshaft assembly, put shims on both ends of the crankshaft, if your model has them, and install the assembly by using the crankshaft installing tool shown in **Figure 63**. Hold the connecting rod at top dead center with one hand while turning the handle of the installation tool with the other.

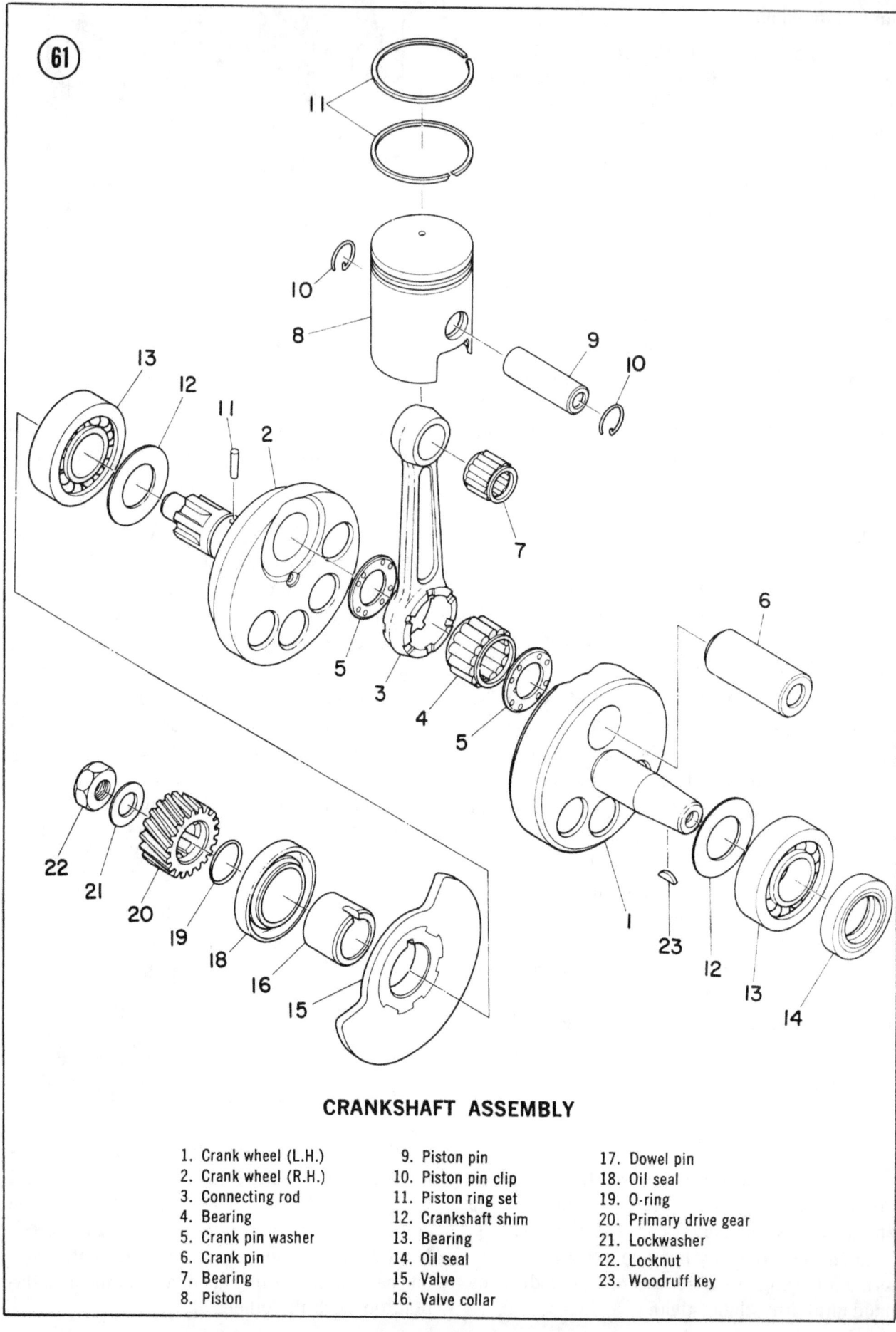

CRANKSHAFT ASSEMBLY

1. Crank wheel (L.H.)
2. Crank wheel (R.H.)
3. Connecting rod
4. Bearing
5. Crank pin washer
6. Crank pin
7. Bearing
8. Piston
9. Piston pin
10. Piston pin clip
11. Piston ring set
12. Crankshaft shim
13. Bearing
14. Oil seal
15. Valve
16. Valve collar
17. Dowel pin
18. Oil seal
19. O-ring
20. Primary drive gear
21. Lockwasher
22. Locknut
23. Woodruff key

NOTE: *Do not hammer the crankshaft into the case. If needed, let a shop install it with proper tools.*

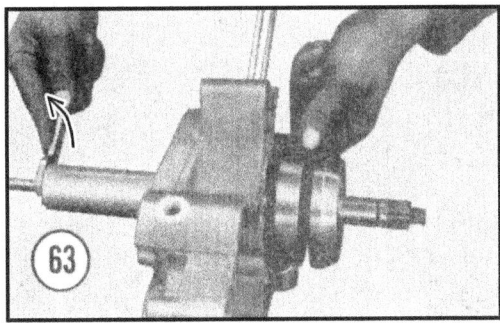

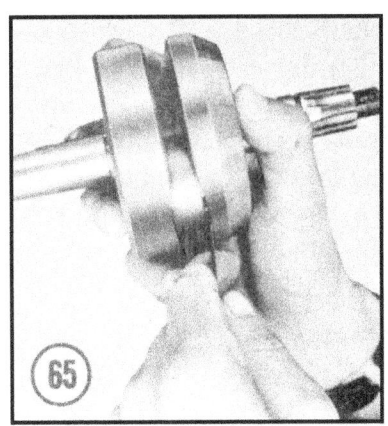

3. Several measurements must be made at this time to check the accuracy of the crankshaft assembly. Using a dial gauge, check the axial play in the large end of the connecting rod by measuring play at the small end. **Figure 64** illustrates this procedure. Play should be 0.079 in. (2mm) or less. After reconditioning, axial play should be 0.032-0.039 in. (0.8-1.0mm).

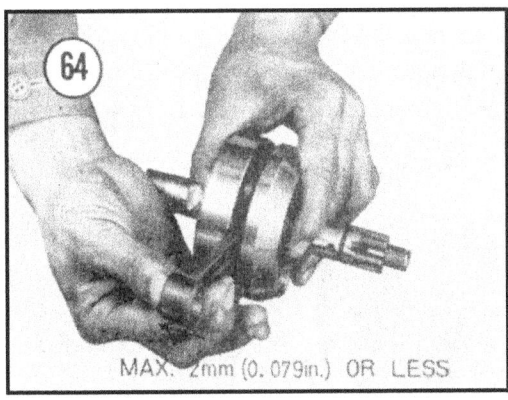

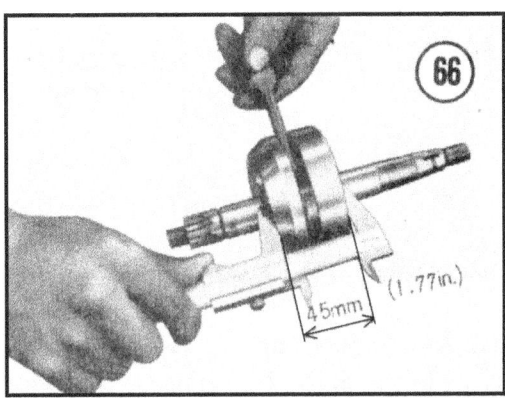

Table 3 CRANK WIDTH SPECIFICATIONS

Measurement*	Model
43.00mm	U5 series, YJ1/2 series, YG1 series
38.00mm	MJ1 & 2 series
45.00mm	YG5T, G5S, G6S, G6SB, B7S
50.00mm	YL2, YL2C, L5T series

*Plus .00mm   Minus 0.10mm

4. To check for connecting rod large end sideplay, hold the connecting rod to one side and insert a feeler gauge between the large end and crank wheel as shown in **Figure 65**. Side-play limits are 0.004-0.012 in. (0.1-0.3mm).

5. Overall length of the crankshaft assembly, as shown in **Figure 66**, should equal the amount listed in **Table 3**.

6. Runout of the crankshaft should not exceed 0.0012 in. (.03mm). Runout adjustment must be performed by an expert. See your shop mechanic.

BEARINGS AND OIL SEALS

1. Bearings are secured by circlips that fit into grooves in the bearing hole. Additionally, transmission bearings are held by bearing retainer plates located outside the case. Remove any circlips with circlip pliers.

2. Remove the bearing. Although bearings can be forced out of the case cold, it is better to heat the case evenly (in an oven, if possible) to 250°F for about 15 minutes. The bearings will fall out when the case is turned over.

CAUTION
This heat will destroy rubber seals or any plastic attached to the case. Be prepared to replace them.

3. Pry the oil seals out of place with a slot-head screwdriver.

4. To properly install a seal, lightly oil the outer seal edge that slips into the hole. Tap repeatedly around the seal edge to start it into the hole. See **Figure 67**. Once started, use a large socket slightly smaller than the seal and tap the seal in until seated. Do not allow the seal to get cocked during installation.

CAUTION
If a bearing has a seal on one side, always place the sealed side to the outside.

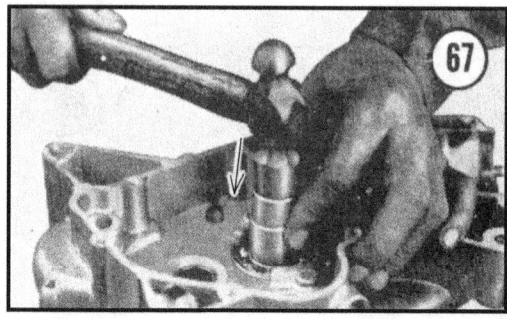

5. Install all bearings and oil seals with stamped manufacturer's mark or numbers facing outward. Lubricate all bearings with an adequate amount of oil before installation.

KICKSTARTER

This procedure applies to the following models:

- U5 series
- YG1 series
- YJ1 and YJ2 series
- MJ1 and MJ2 series

Figures 68 and 69 identify all parts of this kickstarter unit. Refer to them during the following procedures as needed for visual aid.

Removal/Installation

1. The kick gear assembly can be lifted out as a unit (**Figure 70**). Be careful not to lose the kick rollers when disassembling, and note the position of the washers.

2. Remove the kick idler gear by removing the circlip and lifting out the gear shown in **Figure 71**.

3. Note how washers for the top driven gear and kick idler are located. See **Figure 72**. The washer for the top driven gear is dark in color.

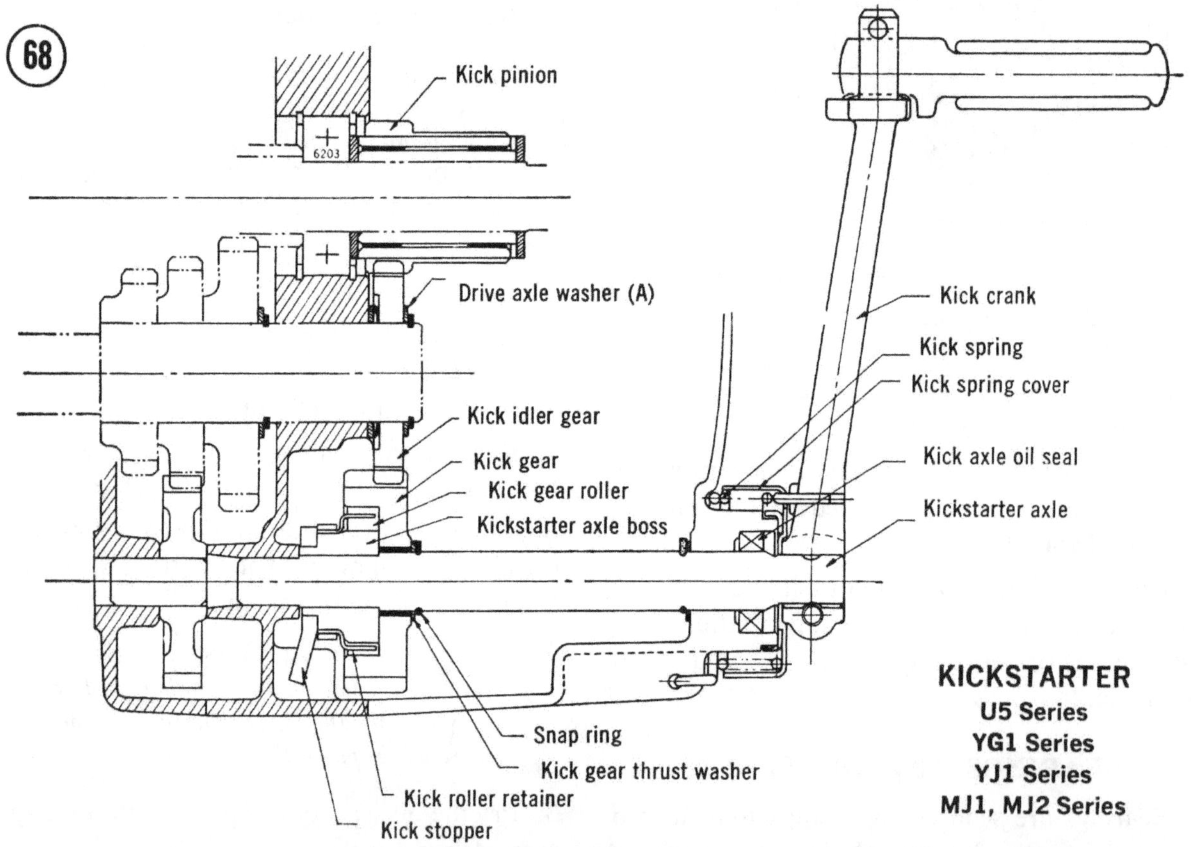

KICKSTARTER
U5 Series
YG1 Series
YJ1 Series
MJ1, MJ2 Series

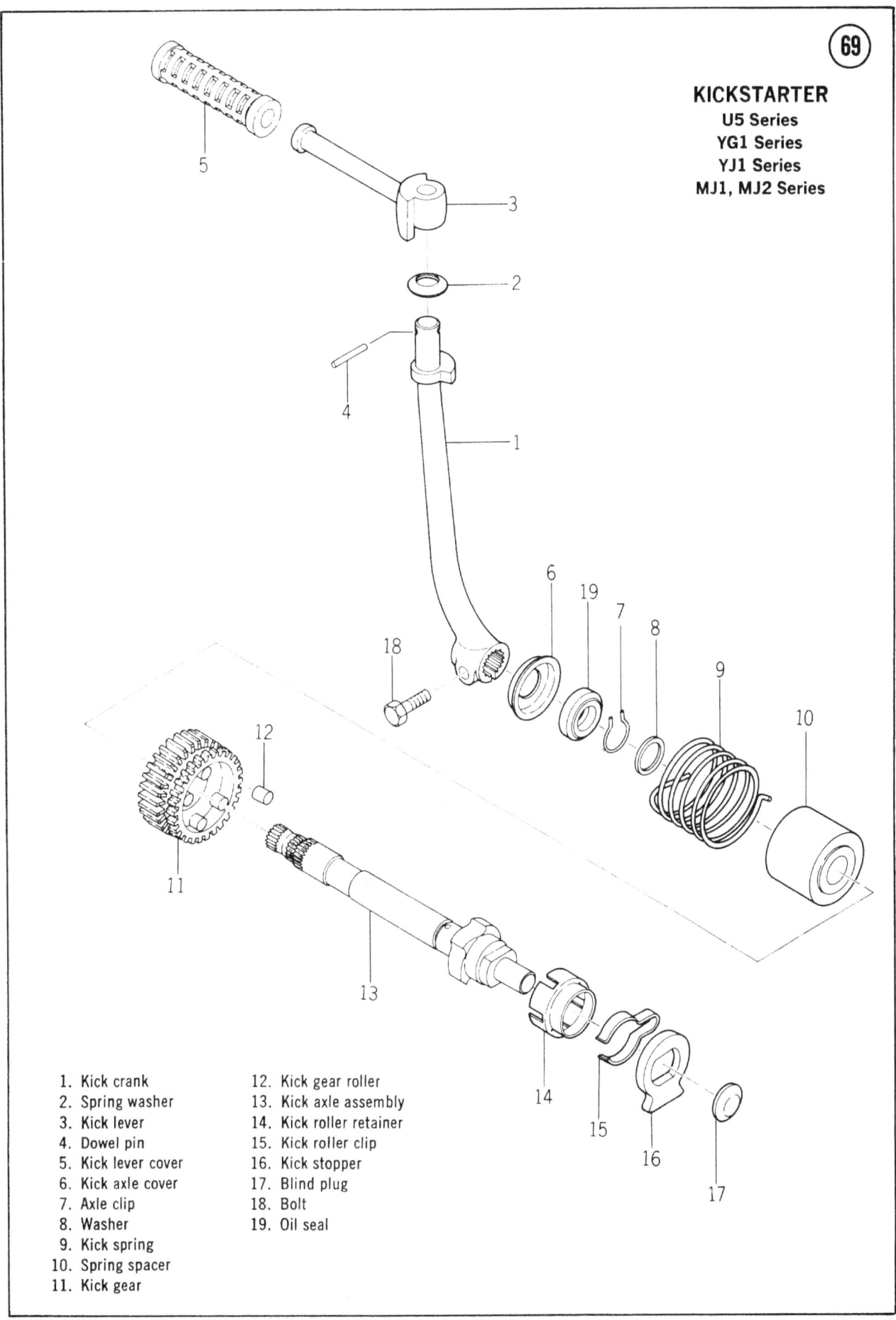

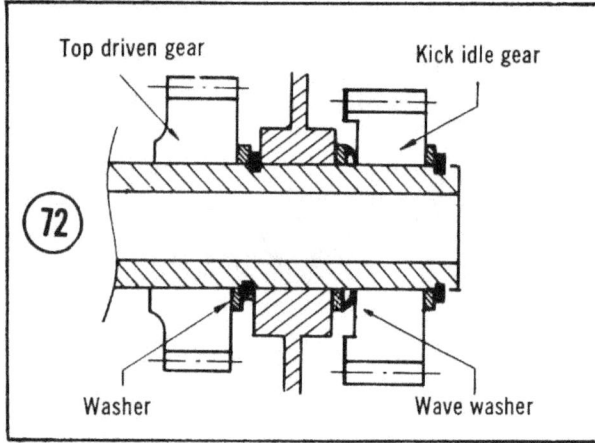

NOTE: *The U5 series kickstarter is located outside the right case. All others in this series are inside the cases with the transmission. The cases must be split for access to the kickstarter.*

KICKSTARTER

This procedure applies to the following models:

G5S	L5T
G6S	L5TA
G65B	JT1/2
G75	YG5T

The kickstarter in these models differs from most other systems in that it is engaged with the idler gear only when the kickstarter lever is operated. As the kickstarter axle is turned, the kick gear travels along the kick axle and engages the kick idle gear. When the 2 gears are completely meshed, the thrust load is imposed on the kick gear to rotate the crankshaft and turn over the engine. See **Figures 73 and 74**.

Removal/Installation

1. Remove the circlip and spring cover.
2. Detach the spring from kick axle and remove the spring.
3. Remove the kickstarter assembly as shown.
4. Unhook kick spring and lift the entire assembly out. See **Figures 75 and 76**.

5. To remove the kick idler gear, remove the circlip retaining the idler gear, take off the thrust washer, and then slide the gear off the drive axle. See **Figure 77**.

KICKSTARTER

This procedure applies to the YL2 series. **Figure 78** identifies all related parts and their positions.

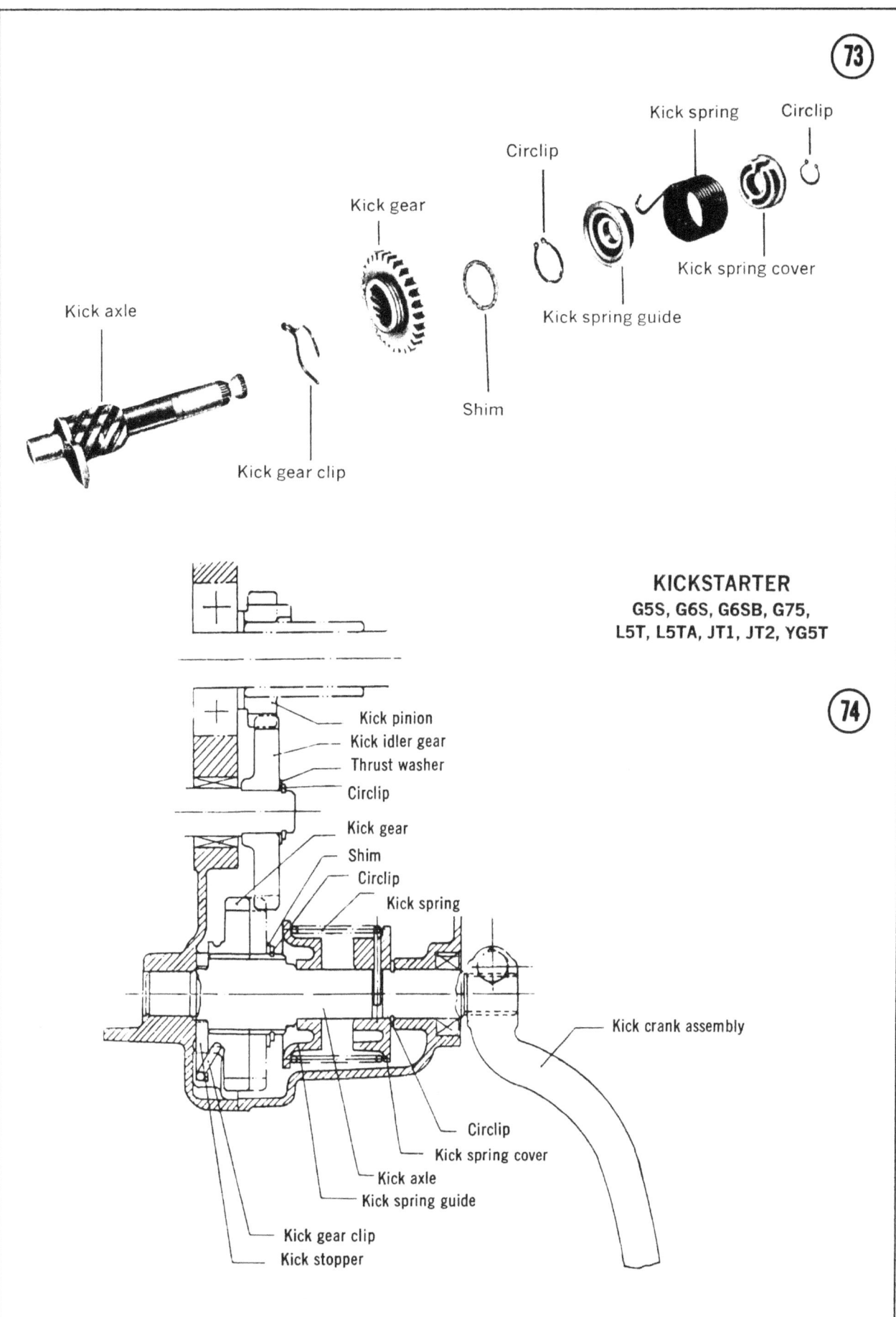

KICKSTARTER
G5S, G6S, G6SB, G75,
L5T, L5TA, JT1, JT2, YG5T

1. Remove the circlip and spring cover shown in **Figure 79**.

2. **Figure 80** shows how to detach the spring from the kick shaft and remove the spring.

3. Remove the kickstarter mechanism in the manner shown in **Figure 81**.

AUTOLUBE SERVICE

The Yamaha Autolube system is nearly identical on all models covered in this manual. Procedures and specifications are the same except for adjustment of pump stroke on the

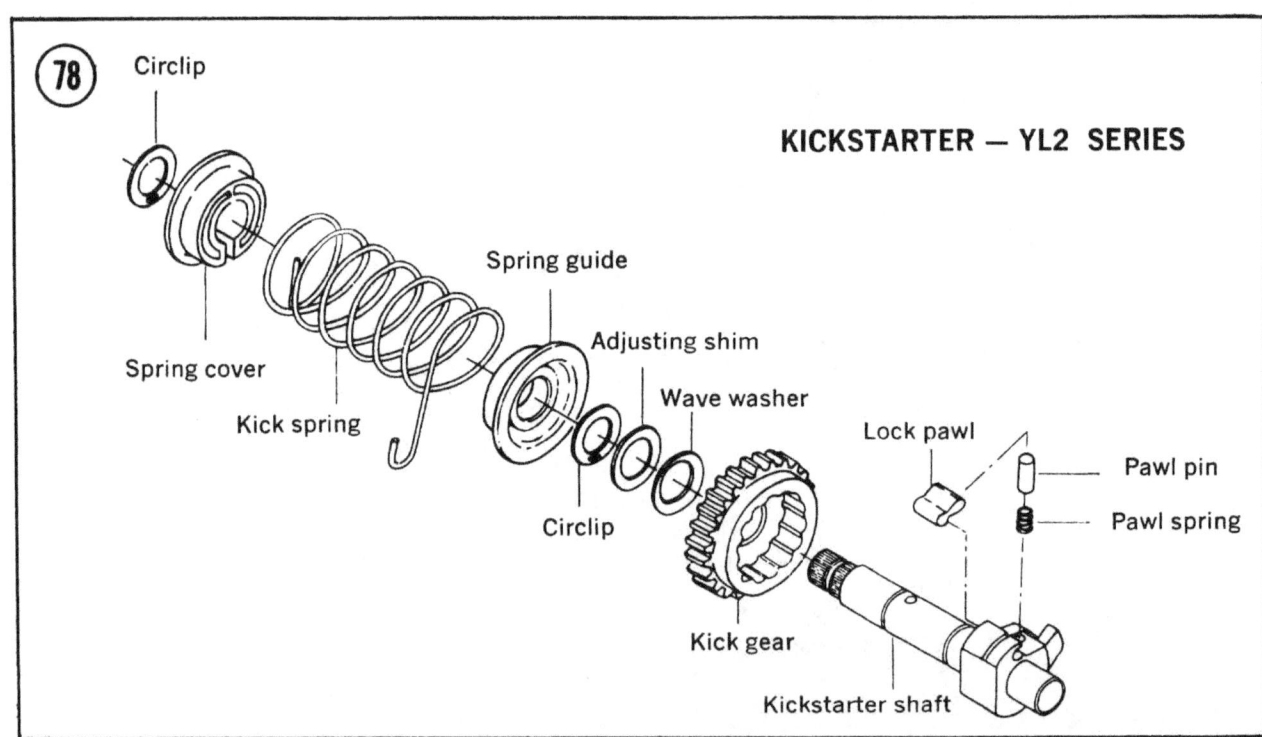

JT1/2 Mini-Enduro. The only difference is that the pump cable is adjusted at idle on the JT1/2 and at half throttle on all other models.

No attempt should be made to disassemble the oil pump. Just keep it clean and remember it must be bled and adjusted after reinstallation.

Minimum Pump Stroke

1. To check and adjust the minimum pump stroke, first set the throttle at closed position.

2. Turn the white oil pump starter plate in the direction of the arrow marked on the plate, creating a gap between the adjusting plate and adjusting pulley. See **Figure 82**. When the gap appears to be at its maximum (**Figure 83**), insert a feeler gauge (**Figure 84**). If a 0.006 in. (0.15mm) gauge can be inserted, then the gap will be slightly larger than this; it needs no adjustment. If it cannot be inserted, the gap will have to be adjusted.

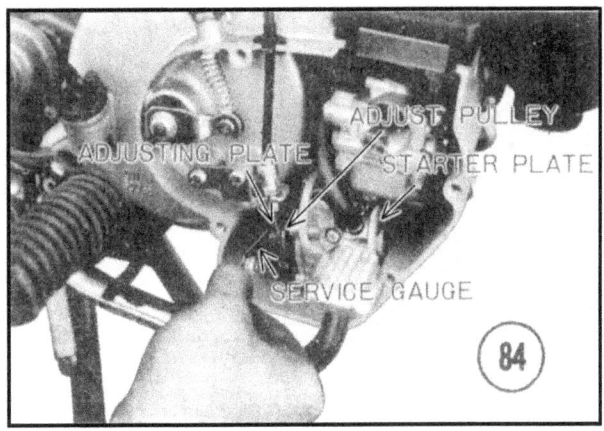

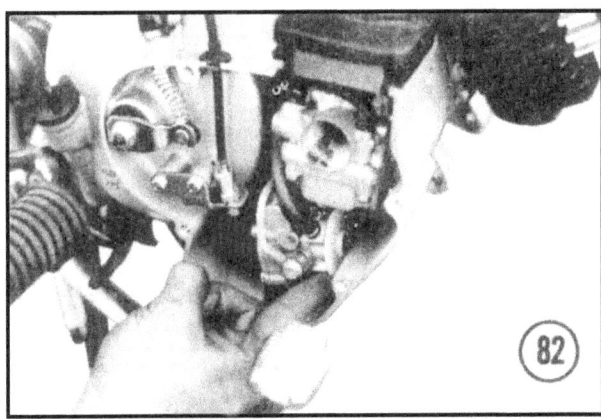

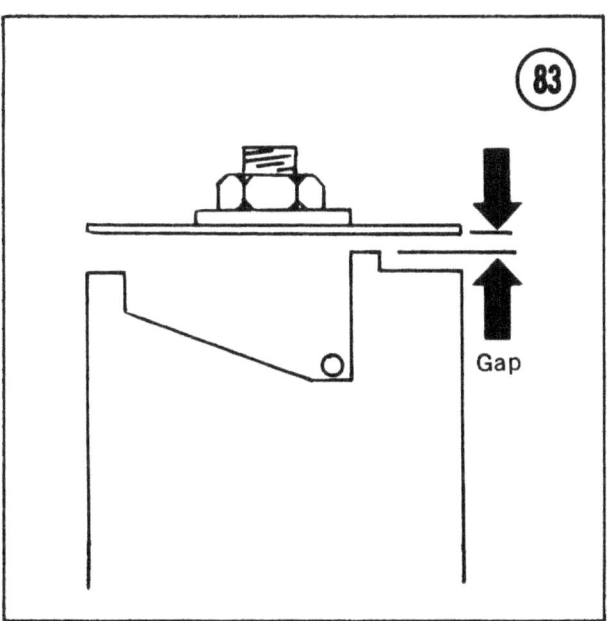

3. Remove the adjusting plate and insert the appropriate sized shim. Reinstall the adjusting plate and check the gap size again. The corrected gap should be from 0.008 to 0.010 in. (0.20-0.25mm).

Pump Cable Adjustment

After checking and/or adjusting the minimum pump stroke, set the carburetor and pump in the following manner.

1. Adjust the idle speed of the carburetor until it is satisfactory.

2. Adjust the free-play of the throttle cable at the carburetor end to 0.04 in. (1mm). See **Figure 85**.

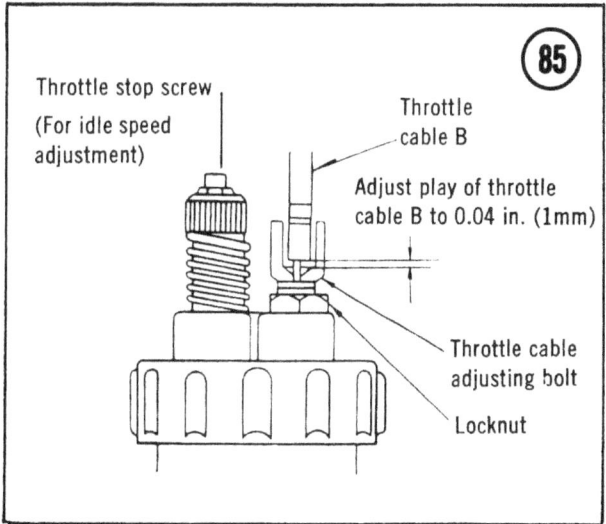

3. On the JT1/2, leave the throttle in the idle position; but on all other models, slowly turn the throttle until the stamped circular marking on the carburetor slide is just touching the main bore of the carburetor. Refer to **Figure 86**. This

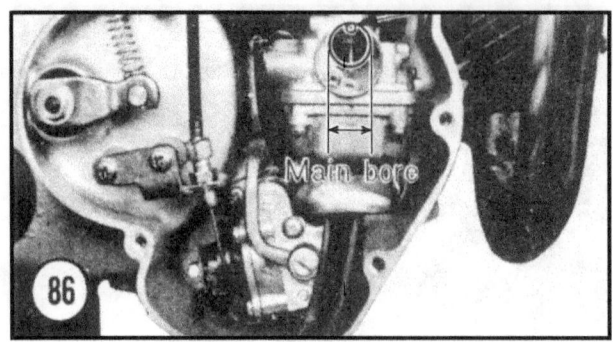

Bleeding the Autolube Pump

Whenever the pump has been removed or been allowed to run dry, it must be bled.

1. Remove the bleeder bolt (**Figure 88**).

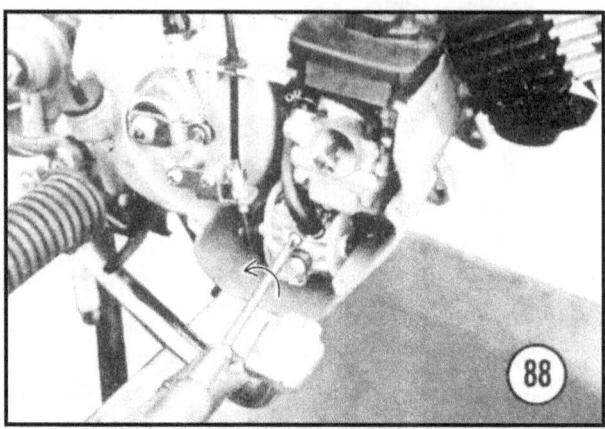

position represents half throttle. Hold the throttle at this opening and check to see if the pump guide pin is aligned with the mark on the adjusting pulley. If the pin and the mark are not aligned, loosen the locknut shown in **Figure 87** and turn the adjusting screw in or out to loosen or tighten the pump cable. Tighten the locknut after the mark and pin have been lined up.

2. Rotate the starter plate in the direction of the arrow marked on the plate (**Figure 89**). Continue turning the plate until a steady flow of oil comes out of the pump and no more air shows in the lines. To facilitate this process, hold the throttle open while rotating the plate, thus increasing the pump stroke. This process will normally take several minutes.

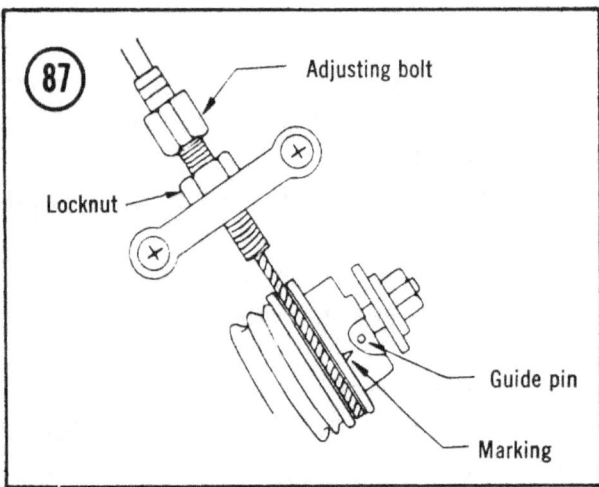

On the JT1/2 also check the pin position at full throttle and see that it doesn't hit the raised boss at the end of the pump.

CHAPTER FOUR

TRANSMISSION AND CLUTCH

This chapter describes repair and replacement procedures for the clutch, gearshift system, and transmission. Where model differences exist, they are pointed out.

GEARSHIFTER MECHANISM

This procedure applies to the following models:

YG5T	G7S
G5S	ST1/2
G6S	100cc series
G6SB	

Refer to **Figures 1 and 2** (pages 34 and 35). Operation of the gear changing mechanism is as follows: When the gearshift lever is depressed, gearshift arm B moves and this in turn moves gearshift arm A. The combined action pushes the gearshift drum pins mounted on the gearshift drum, turning the shift drum in the process.

The gearshift drum is equipped with 5 drum pins and is designed to make 1/5 of a turn each time the gearshift lever is depressed. One full turn of the drum would shift the transmission through 5 stages: neutral, first, second, third, and fourth.

The gearshift pins are held by the disc so that the stopped plate can secure the operation in any of the 5 stages.

The outer portion of the gearshift drum is provided with slots along which the shift forks travel back and forth when shifting gears.

Removal

1. To remove gearshift arms A and B, remove the circlip and washer as shown in **Figures 3 and 4**. Lift up gearshift arm from the shifter drum and remove it from the right side of the engine. See **Figure 5**.

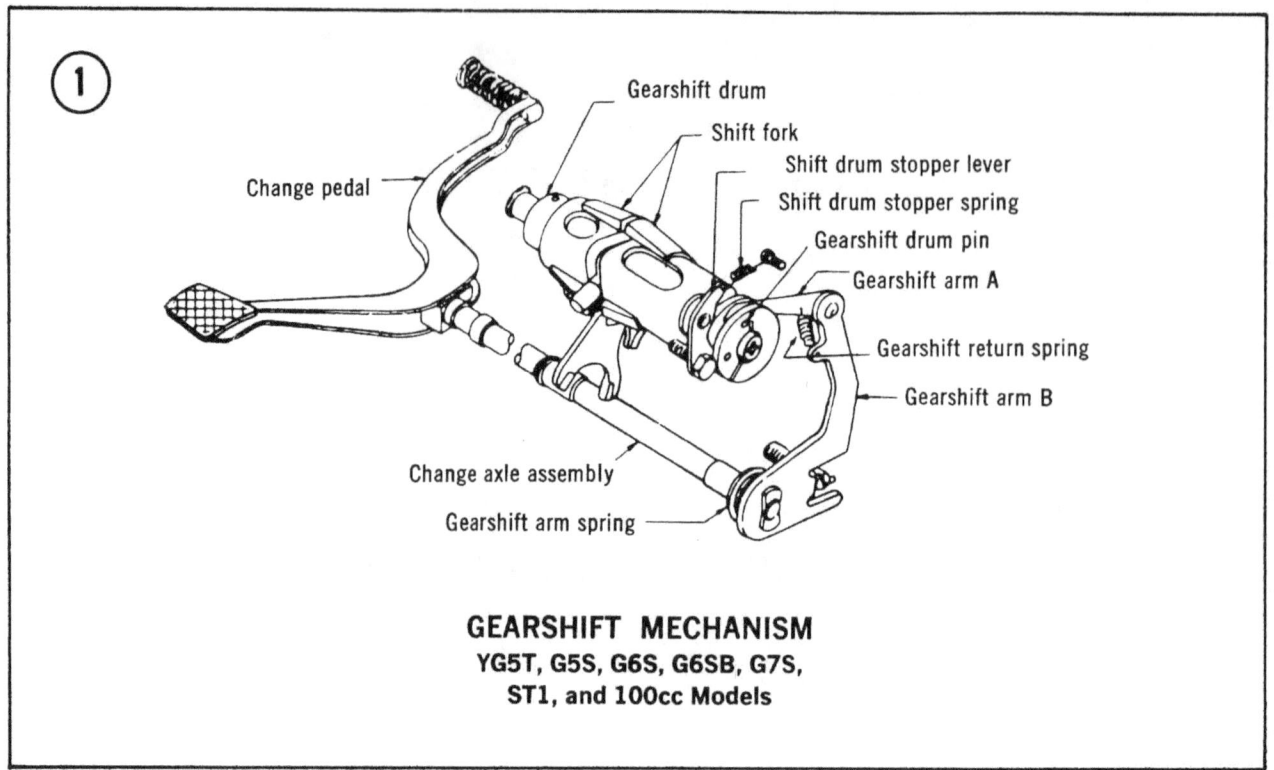

GEARSHIFT MECHANISM
YG5T, G5S, G6S, G6SB, G7S,
ST1, and 100cc Models

2. Remove the mounting bolt and remove the 2 springs (**Figure 6**). A weak or broken stopper spring may let the lever slip from one shifter drum pin to another.

3. Remove the clip cover (**Figure 7**), then the shift drum clip (**Figure 8**).

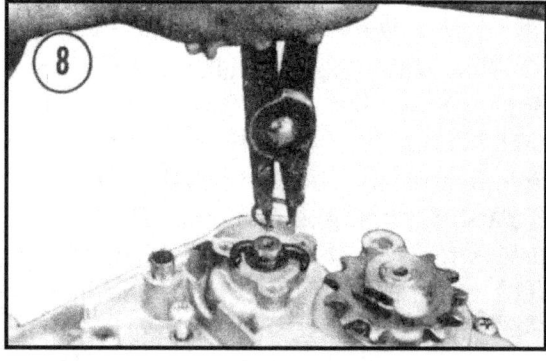

Inspection

Check the gearshift return spring for fatigue or damage. A broken or fatigued spring will impair the return action of the shifting mechanism (**Figure 9**).

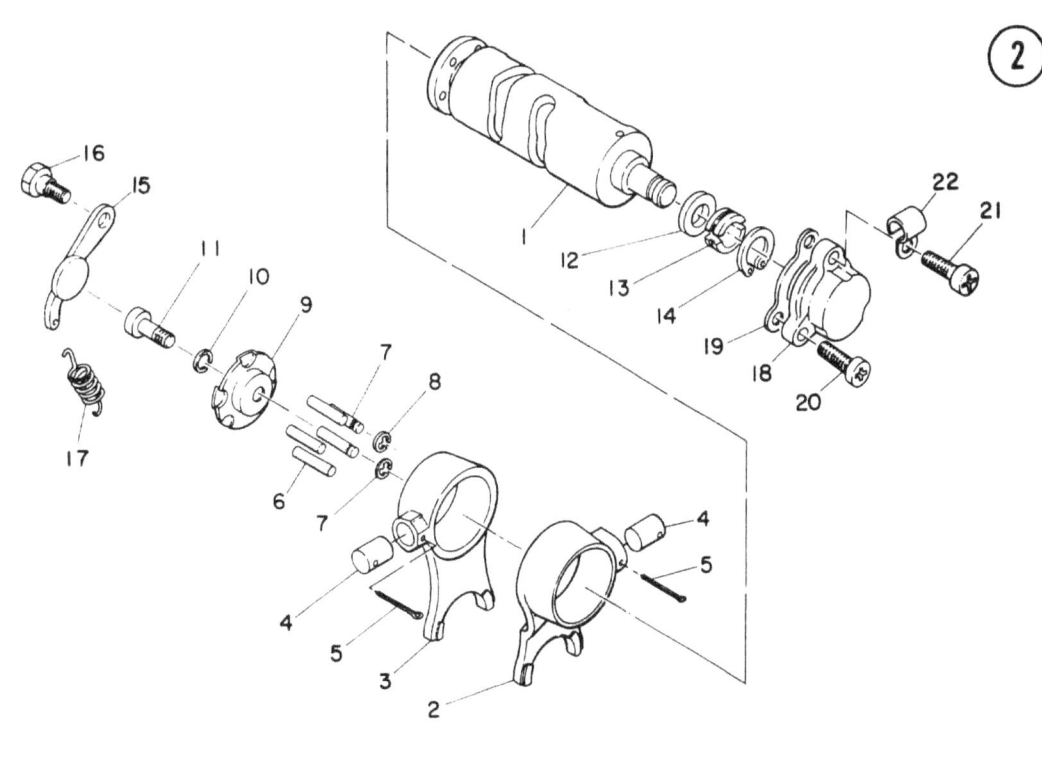
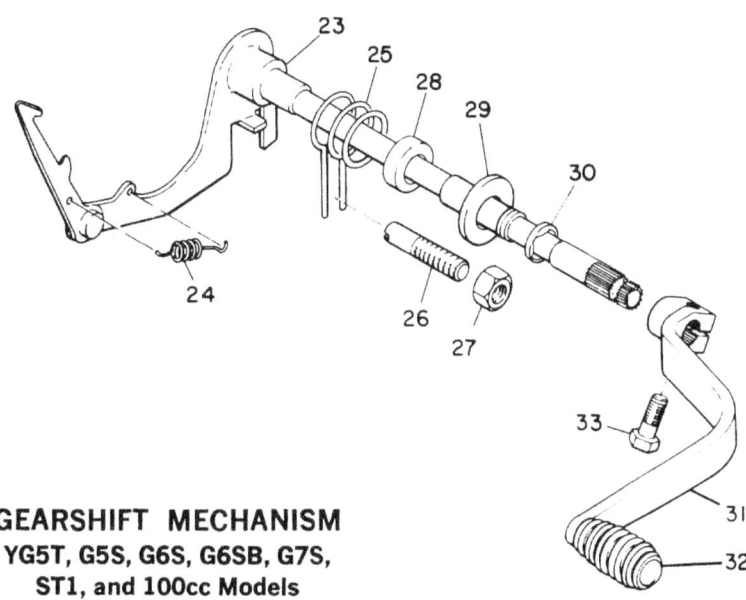

GEARSHIFT MECHANISM
YG5T, G5S, G6S, G6SB, G7S, ST1, and 100cc Models

1. Shift cam
2. Shift fork #2
3. Shift fork #1
4. Cam follower pin
5. Cotter pin
6. Dowel pin
7. Locating pin
8. Circlip
9. Side plate
10. Spring washer
11. Pan head screw
12. Plain washer
13. Shift cam holder
14. Circlip
15. Stopper lever assembly
16. Stopper bolt
17. Stopper spring
18. Cover
19. Gasket
20. Pan head screw
21. Pan head screw
22. Clamp
23. Change shaft assembly
24. Shift arm spring
25. Shaft return spring
26. Adjustment screw
27. Nut
28. Oil seal
29. Change axle washer
30. Circlip
31. Change lever
32. Change lever cover
33. Bolt

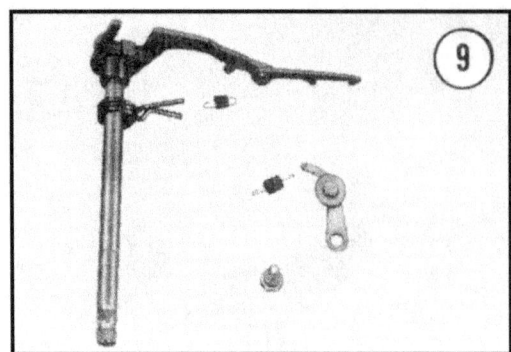

This mechanism requires linkage adjustment whenever the shifter assembly is disassembled, removed, or if the transmission has been jumping out of gear.

Refer to **Figure 10** during this procedure for parts identification and location. With the transmission in either 2nd or 3rd gear, and no pressure on the shift lever, check for equal clearance at points A and A1'. If these distances are not equal, loosen the adjustment screw locknut and turn the adjustment screw. It is eccentrically-shaped and will pivot the linkage. Tighten the locknut and doublecheck the clearances.

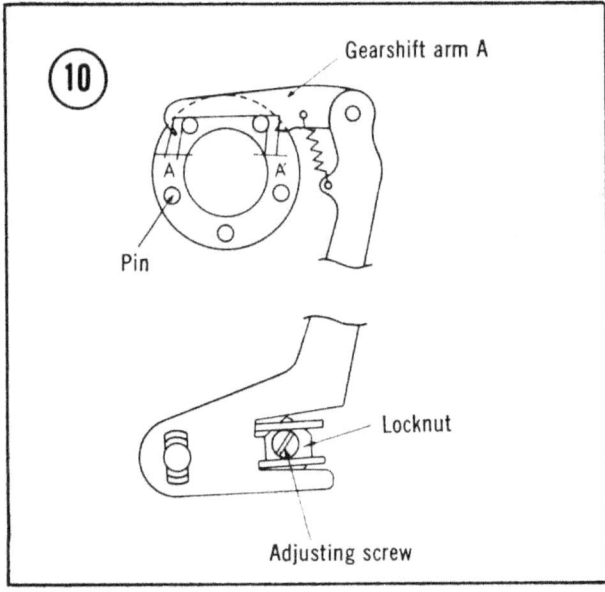

GEARSHIFTER MECHANISM

This procedures applies to the following models:

YJ1 and 2
YG1

These models are equipped with the 4-speed ball-lock transmission. The gear box consists of the main axle, drive axle, 4-driven gear, 16 steel balls, and the shifter rod.

1. The shifter consists of the shifter rod driving mechanism and the shifter cam plate driving mechanism. **Figures 11 and 12** (following 2 pages) are exploded views of the 2 major gearshift assemblies.

2. The transmission operates by a shifter rod pushing steel balls to engage the desired gear on the main axle. **Figure 13** (page 38) illustrates this action.

3. Note that the shifter can be disassembled without removing ball retaining springs from the drive axle.

4. The transmission must be in fourth gear when the shifter rod washer, retainer, spring washer, and nut are installed on the shifter rod. These parts must be installed correctly or the transmission will not work properly. Refer back to Figures 11, 12, and 13 for details.

5. When reassembling the unit, install the drive axle, shifter rod, and then the shifter assembly. Temporarily attach the gear change shaft and pedal. Try shifting gears as noted in **Figure 14**. If the shifter rod and cam plate don't work right, make an adjustment. The stopper pin must be centered in one of the notches in the cam plate. If it is off-center, adjust the cam plate-to-change lever relationship by means of the adjustment bolt (3, Figure 12). Loosen the locknut and turn the screw until it is centered in the slot as shown in Figure 14.

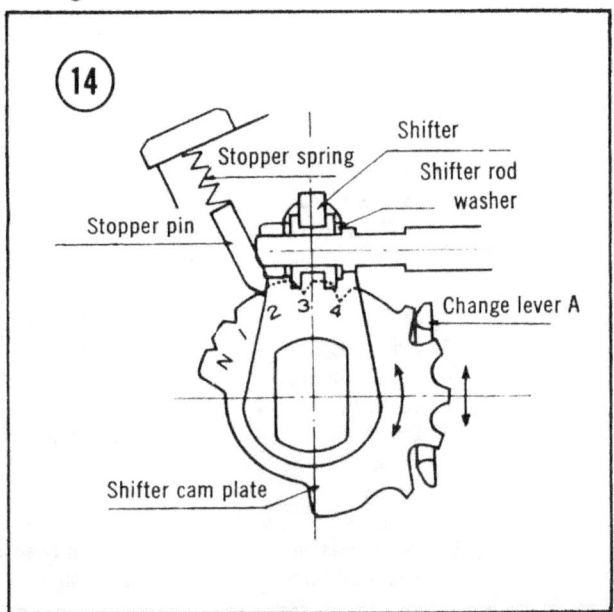

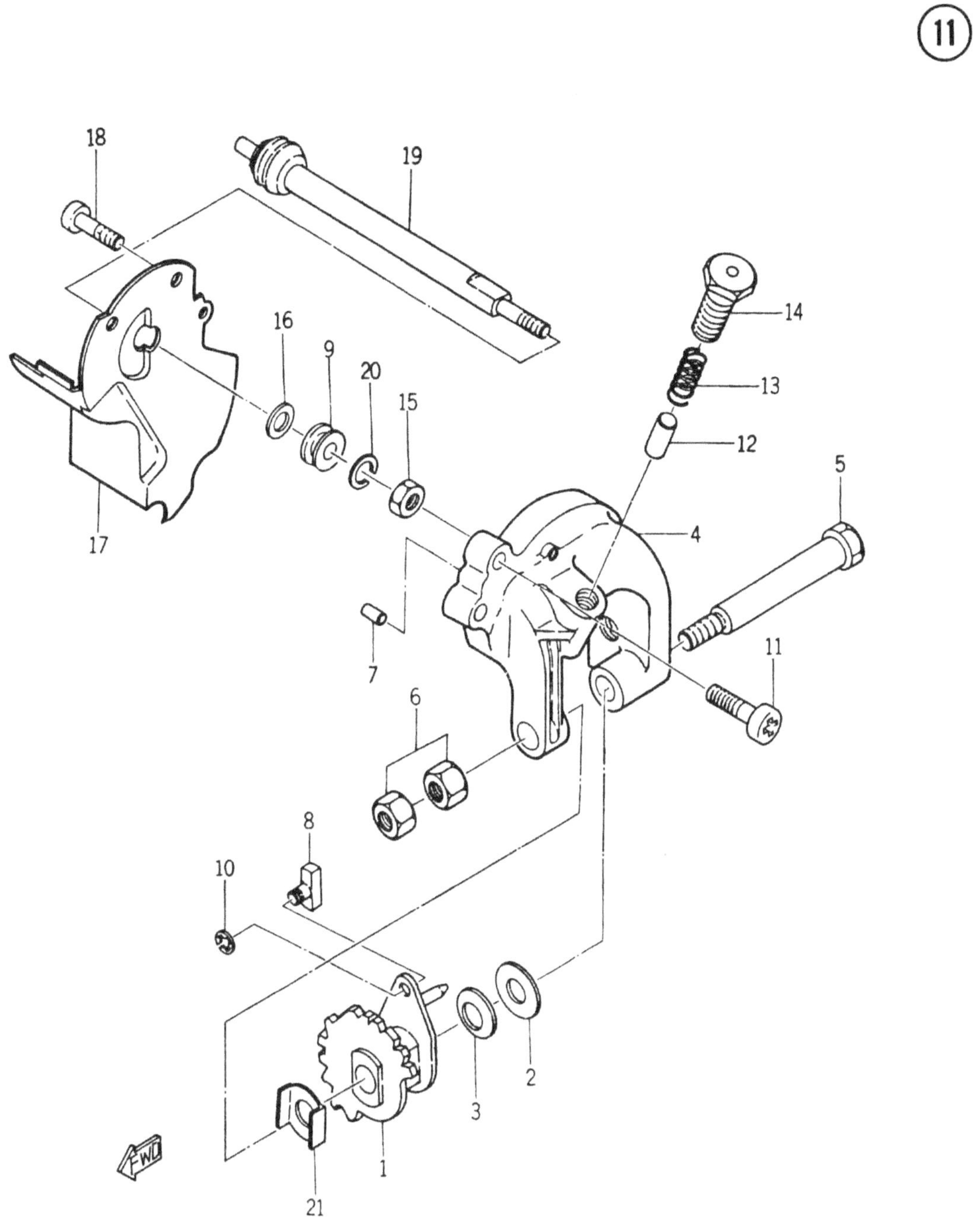

GEARSHIFT MECHANISM — YJ1 AND YJ2

1. Cam plate
2. Thrust plate
3. Wave washer
4. Shifter bracket
5. Cam shaft
6. Nut
7. Dowel pin
8. Shifter
9. Shifter retainer
10. Circlip
11. Pan head screw
12. Cam stopper
13. Cam stopper spring
14. Spring screw
15. Nut
16. Rod shim
17. Dust seal
18. Pan head screw
19. Shifter rod
20. Lockwasher
21. Thrust plate

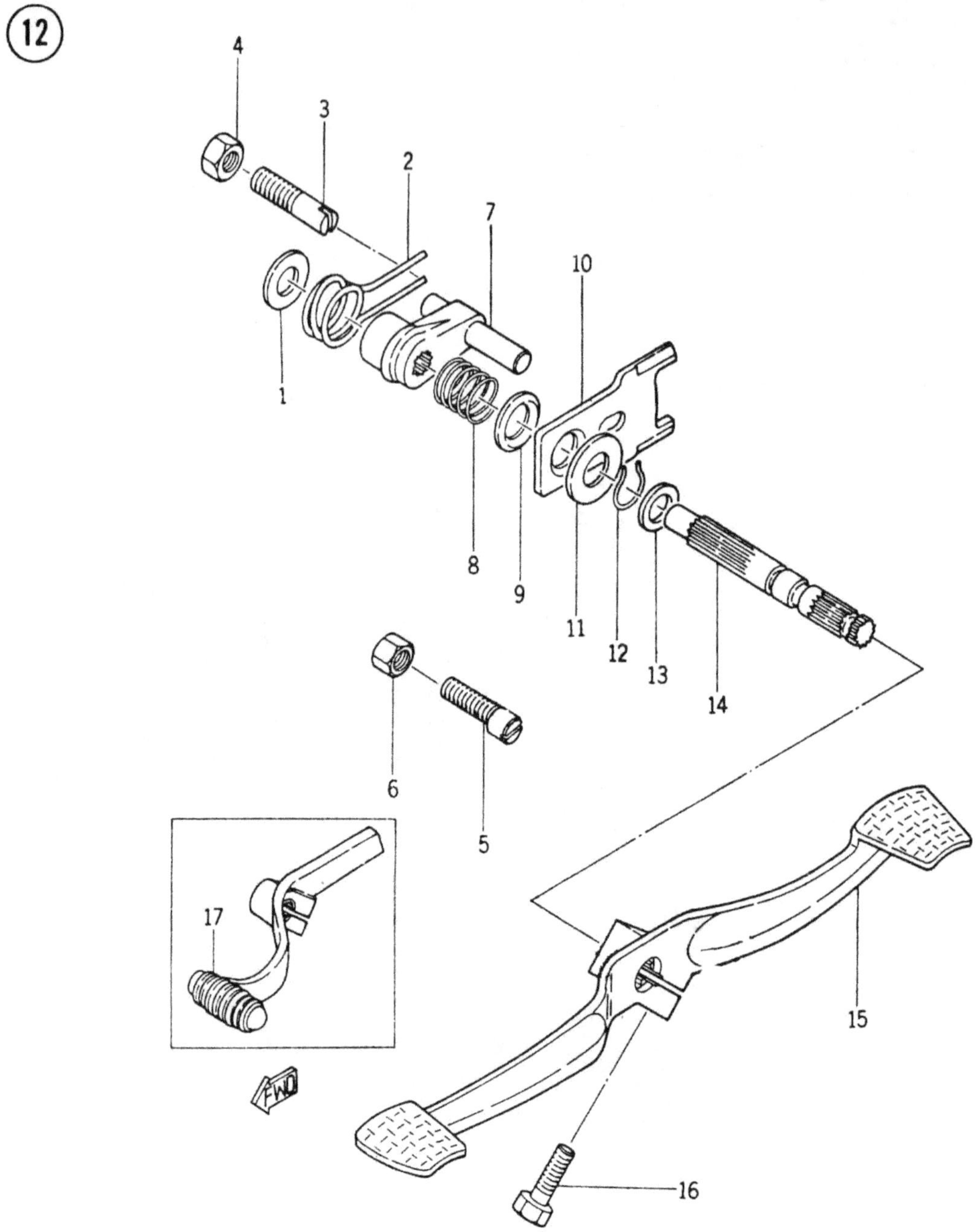

GEARSHIFT MECHANISM — YJ1 AND YJ2

1. Return spring washer
2. Shaft return spring
3. Adjustment screw
4. Locknut
5. Lever stop screw
6. Stop screw nut
7. Change lever
8. Lever spring
9. Spring cover
10. Change lever
11. Stopper plate
12. Change shaft clip
13. Change shaft washer
14. Change shaft
15. Change pedal
16. Bolt
17. Change pedal cover

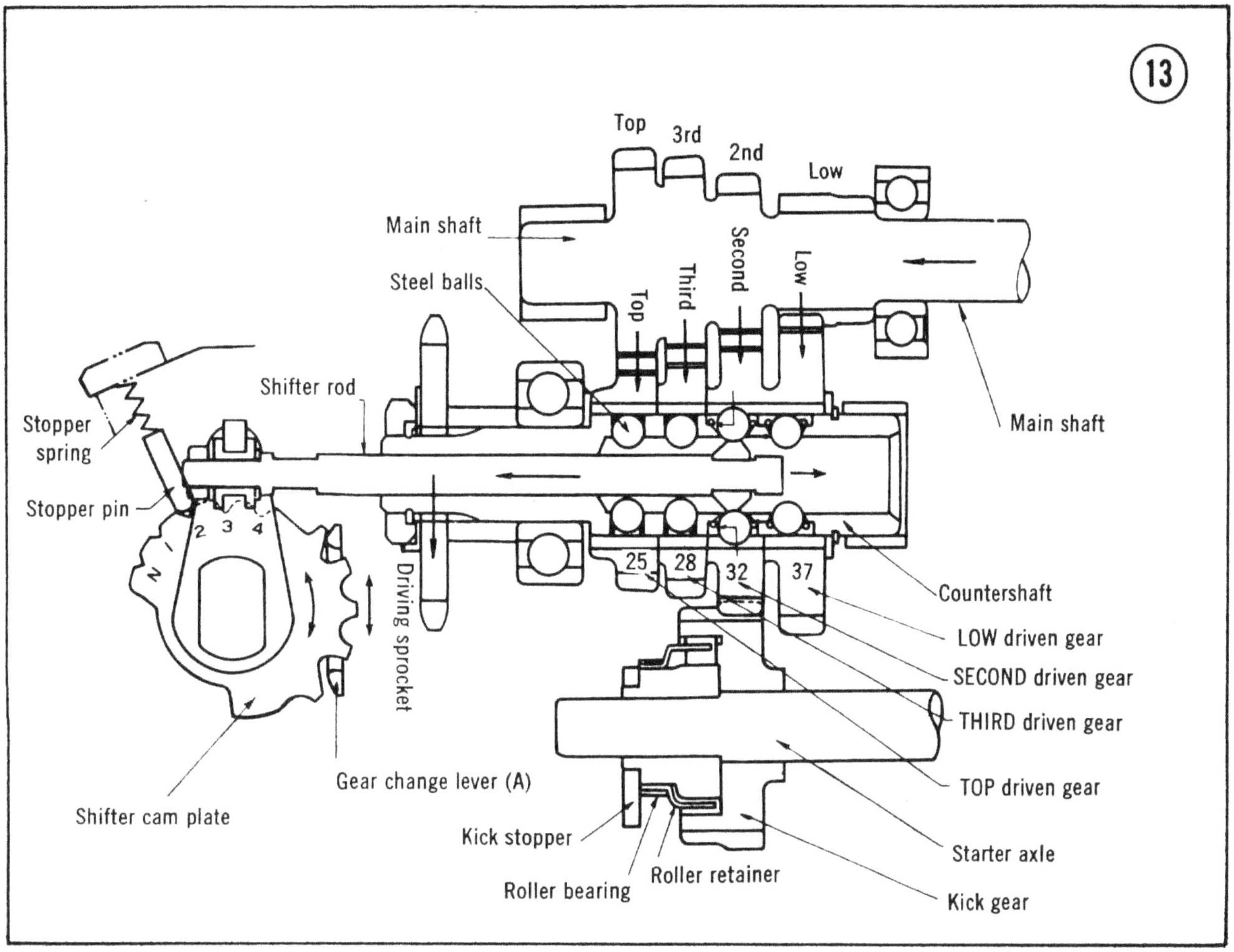

⑬

Top 3rd 2nd Low
Main shaft
Steel balls — Top Third Second Low
Shifter rod
Stopper spring
Stopper pin
1 2 3 4
Driving sprocket
25 28 32 37
Main shaft
Countershaft
LOW driven gear
SECOND driven gear
THIRD driven gear
TOP driven gear
Gear change lever (A)
Shifter cam plate
Kick stopper
Roller bearing
Roller retainer
Starter axle
Kick gear

GEARSHIFTER MECHANISM

This procedure applied to the following models:

U5 series
MJ1 and MJ2

These models are equipped with a 3-speed ball-lock transmission. **Figure 15** (next page) is an exploded view of the 2 main shifter assemblies that control gear selection. **Figure 16** (page 41) is an exploded view of the same assembly for late MJ2's with slightly modified parts; function is the same.

1. The gear change mechanism (Figure 16) can be easily removed by pulling it out as an assembly. When reinstalling, first assemble all the gear change parts into a complete mechanism; then attach the shifter parts and install the unit in the crankcase.

2. **Figure 17** shows how to remove the shifter mechanism, unscrew the 3 Phillips head screws holding the shifter bracket, and take out the entire shifter mechanism. Then remove the shifter which is attached to the shifter rod. Pull out the shifter rod from the side where the kick-starter idler gear is installed (**Figure 18**).

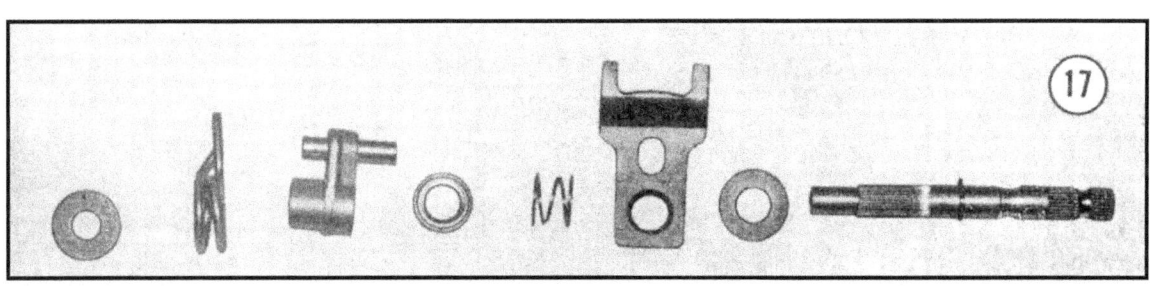

39

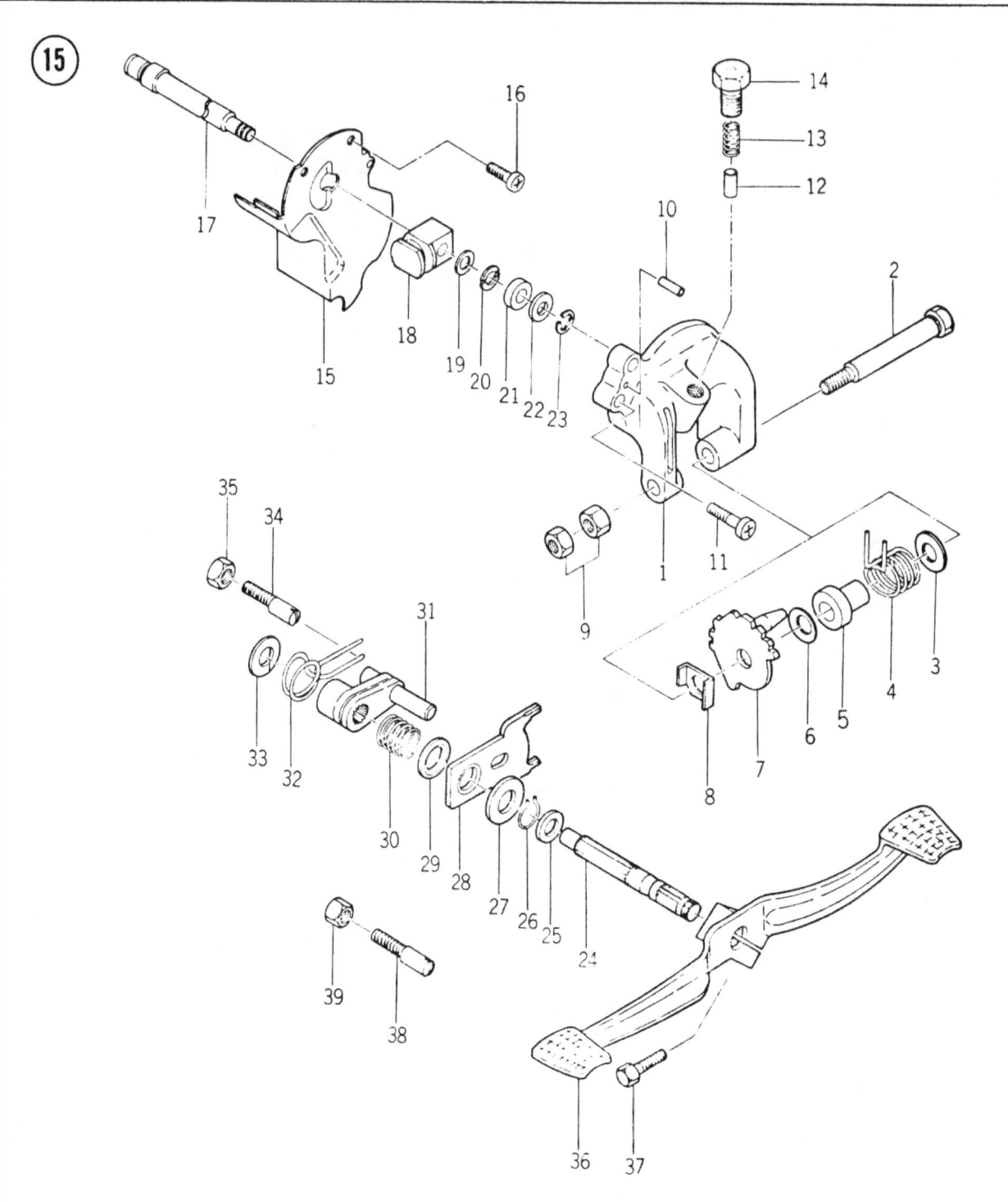

GEARSHIFT MECHANISM — U5, MJ1, EARLY MJ2

1. Shifter bracket
2. Cam shaft
3. Washer
4. Spring
5. Spacer
6. Washer
7. Cam plate
8. Thrust plate
9. Nut
10. Dowel pin
11. Phillips head screw
12. Cam stopper
13. Spring
14. Spring screw
15. Plate
16. Phillips head screw
17. Shifter rod
18. Shifter
19. Shim
20. Ring clip
21. Clip cover
22. Washer
23. Circlip
24. Change shaft
25. Washer
26. Change shaft clip
27. Stopper plate
28. Change lever
29. Spring cover
30. Spring
31. Change lever
32. Return spring
33. Washer
34. Adjustment screw
35. Nut
36. Change pedal
37. Bolt
38. Adjustment screw
39. Nut

GEARSHIFT MECHANISM — LATE MJ2

1. Shifter bracket
2. Pan head screw
3. Cam shaft
4. Washer
5. Shaft spring
6. Spacer
7. Washer
8. Cam plate
9. Thrust plate
10. Nut
11. Spring screw
12. Stopper spring
13. Stopper cam
14. Shifter
15. Shifter rod assembly
16. Rod shim
17. Ring clip
18. Clip cover
19. Washer
20. Circlip
21. Dowel pin
22. Dust seal
23. Pan head screw

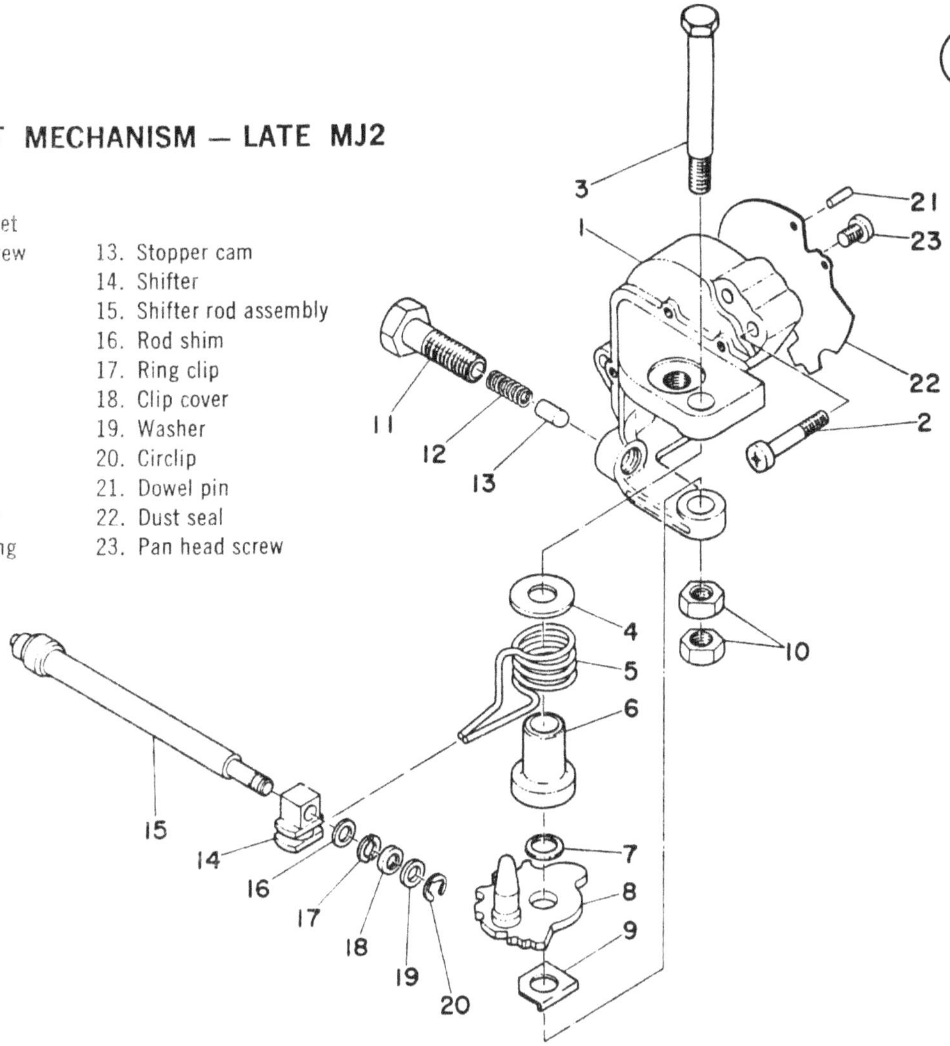

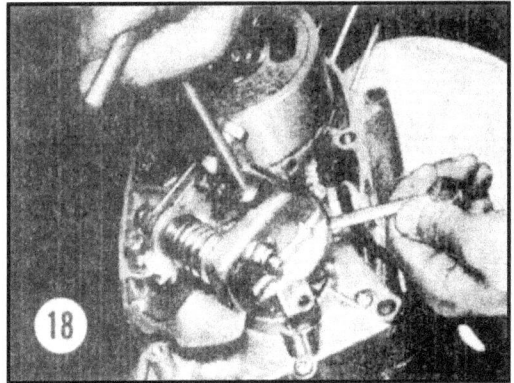

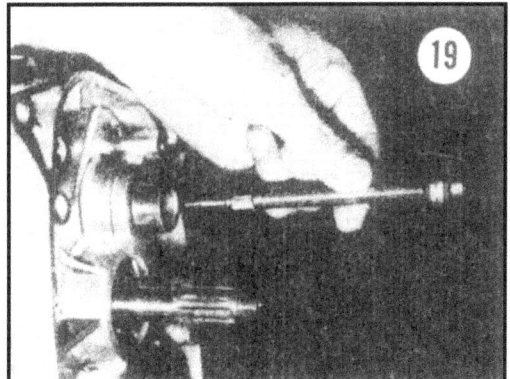

3. When installing the gear change and shifter assemblies, be sure to grease all moving parts.

4. The most common problem with the gear change and shifter assemblies is excessive or insufficient shifter travel. Adjust this by turning the 2 eccentric screws called "lever stop screw" in **Figure 19**.

CLUTCHES

There are 5 different clutches. Disassembly and assembly procedures for each type are explained separately. Service and maintenance procedures applicable to all models appear at the end of this section.

U5 SERIES CLUTCH

The U5 series uses a centrifugal engagement clutch. Internal rollers are forced out as the engine speed increases. These rollers force the 4 clutch plates and 4 friction plates together, causing engagement and movement. **Figure 20** shows a cross-sectional view and **Figure 21** provides an exploded view to aid you during service work.

Disassembly/Assembly

1. Slide stopper ring inward as shown in **Figure 22** and remove it.

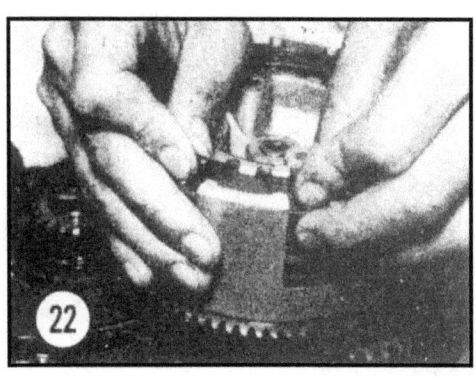

2. Remove clutch and friction plates.

3. Insert the MF2 clutch locking tool in the clutch boss hole. Remove the clutch boss locknut and the boss. See **Figure 23**. The clutch housing will now lift off.

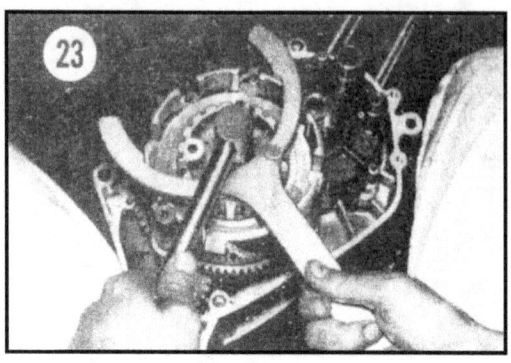

4. Reverse the procedure for assembly. Don't forget to install the washer at the end of the spacer and to assemble the clutch plates in the correct order and position.

5. Measure the clearance between the stopper ring and clutch plate with a feeler gauge. See **Figure 24**. This clearance should be between

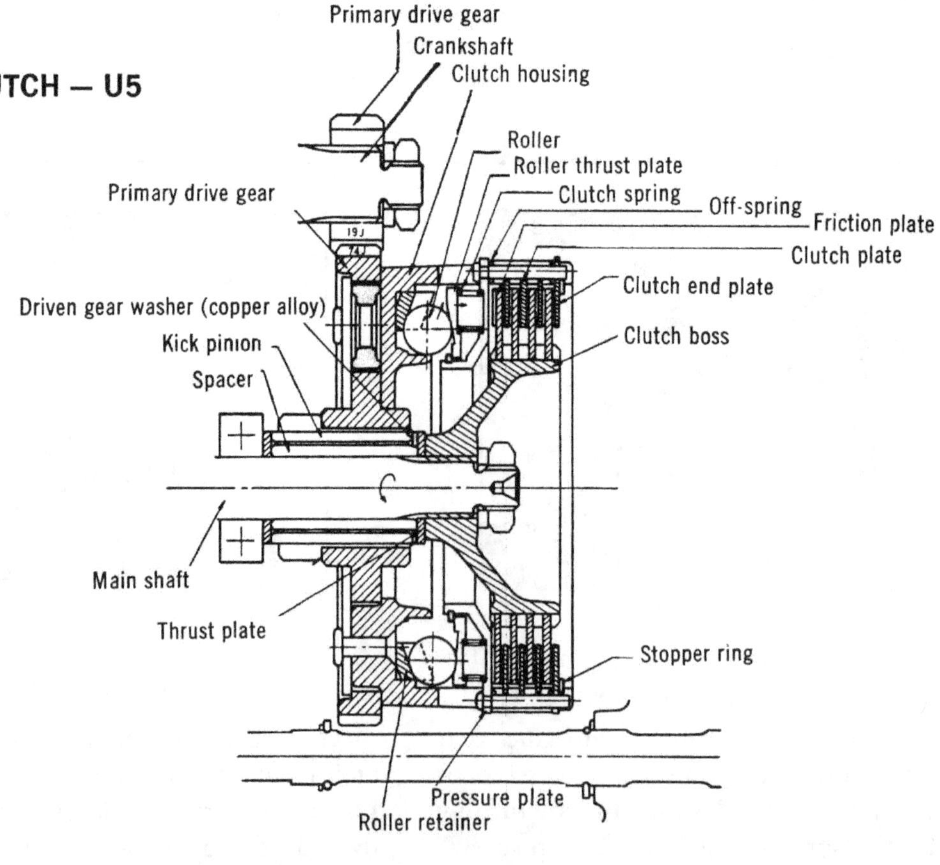

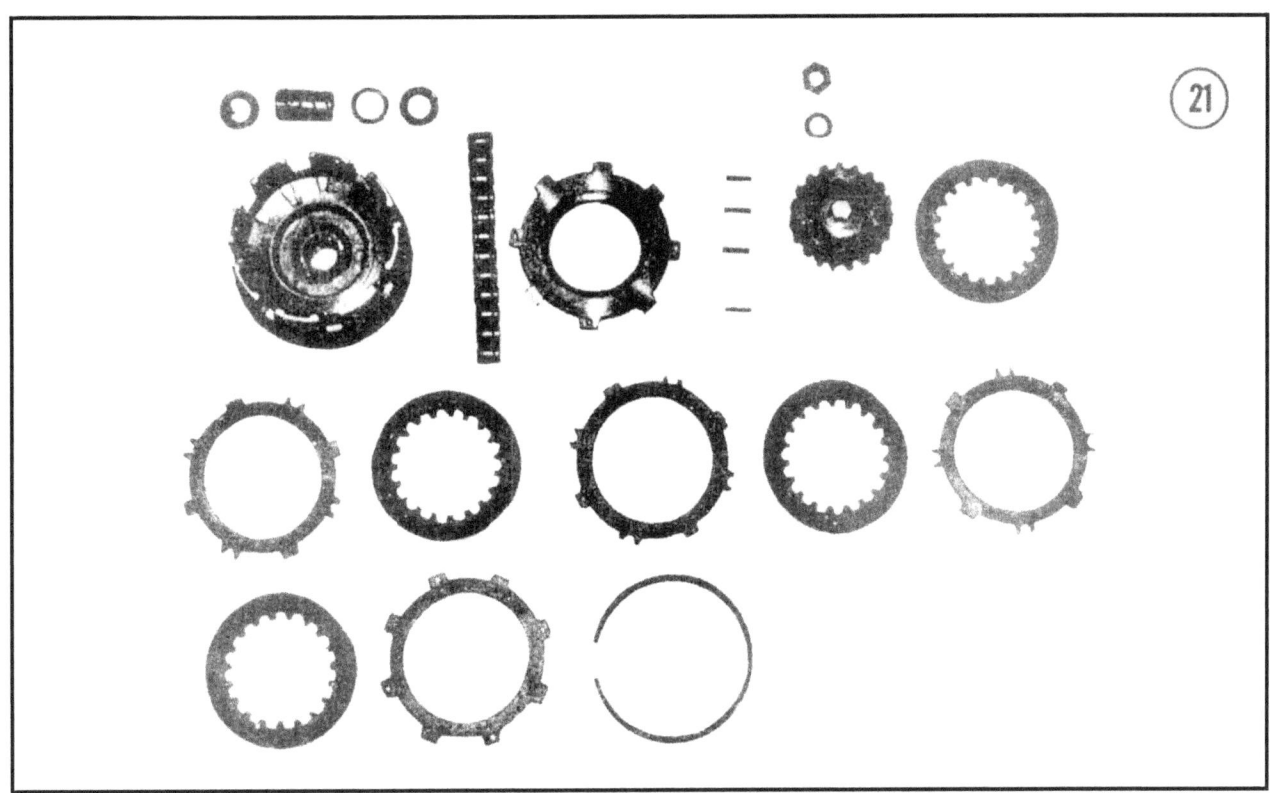

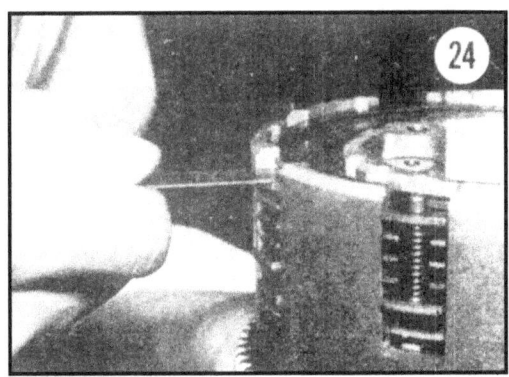

0.040-0.047 in. (1.0-1.2mm). Adjust if necessary by fitting a clutch plate of the proper thickness. They come in 3 thicknesses: 0.047, 0.055, and 0.063 in. (1.2, 1.4, and 1.6mm).

YJ1 AND 2, 80cc, AND 100cc SERIES CLUTCH

Figures 25, 26, and 27 provide different views of the same basic clutch style. Function and all parts are identical for these models except for number of clutch plates and friction plates, plus JT1, JT2, YG1, and MG1 series models do not have a kick pinion gear behind the clutch housing. Clutch plate specifications are listed in **Table 1**.

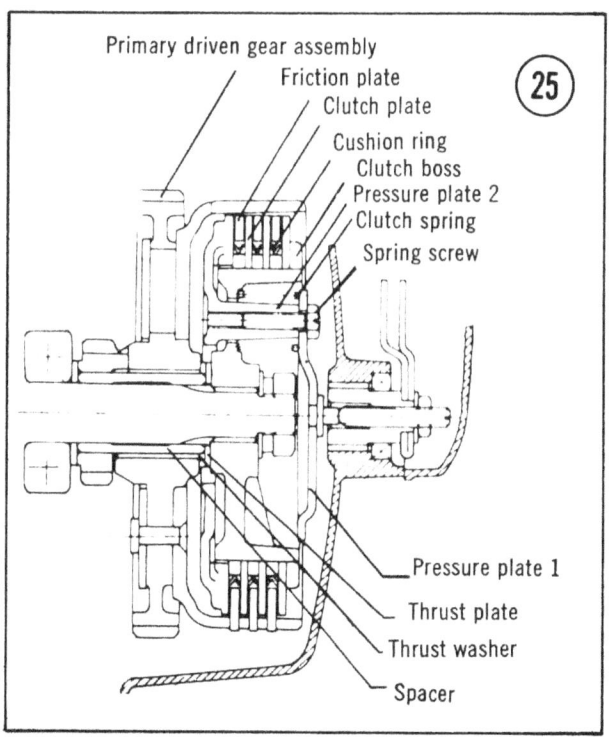

Disassembly/Assembly

1. To remove the pressure plate, remove the 6 clutch spring screws, the springs, and the pressure plate. See **Figures 28 and 29**.

2. Remove the clutch boss as shown in **Figure 30**. Straighten the bent edges of the clutch

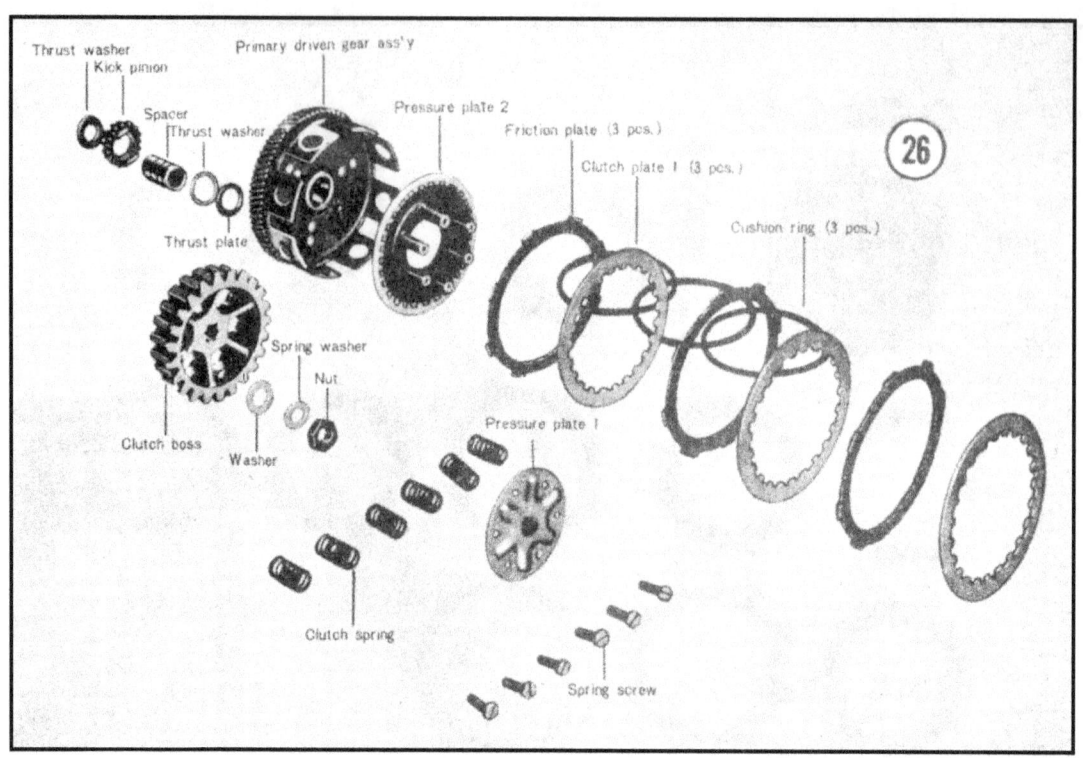

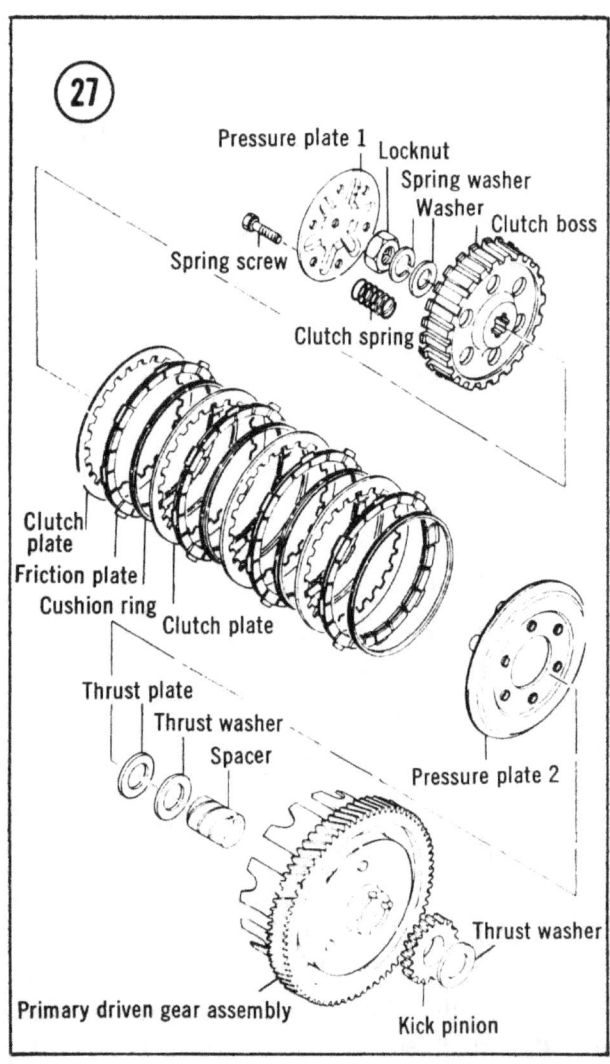

Table 1 CLUTCH PLATE SPECIFICATIONS

Model	Friction Plate	Clutch Plate (Metal)
YJ1 & 2 series	3	3
YG1 series	4	4
YG5T & G5S	3	3
G6S, G6SB & G7S	5	5
YL2 & YL2C	4	5
L5T series	4	4

boss lockwasher. Fit the clutch holding tool over the clutch boss, remove the nut, and then the boss itself.

3. Slide off the clutch boss. Directly behind the clutch boss will be identical thrust washers with

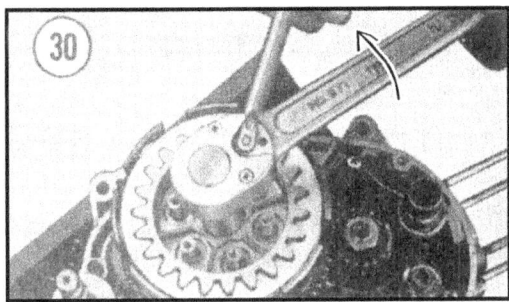

clutch boss after each metal plate as shown in **Figure 31**. The open end faces out. Make sure they are not twisted. These cushions help separate the plates during disengagement. They are helpful, but not required for clutch operation.

8. Add the springs, pressure plate, and spring retaining screws. Tighten the spring retaining screws just slightly until snug. Excessive torque can snap the screw, which will require replacing the primary drive gear assembly.

JT1 AND JT2 CLUTCH

The clutch is of the wet disc type, consisting of 2 cork friction plates and one steel clutch plate. See **Figure 32** (next page) for parts identification and location.

Disassembly

1. Remove all clutch spring holding screws as shown in **Figure 33**, then lift off the pressure plate.

a flat thrust bearing sandwiched between them. Note their position for future installation.

4. Slide off the primary driven gear assembly (outer housing). Behind the outer housing will be a kick gear (except YJ1 and YJ2 and YG1 series). It is a separate gear. Slide it off. Now slide off the spacer and thrust plate next to the transmission bearing.

5. During installation of these parts, be sure that all thrust washers, plates, and bearings are in proper position. If your model has a separate kick gear, make sure its 2 protruding dogs engage the 2 squared off slots in the back of the primary driven gear. Take care; there are also 2 rounded slots that the dogs could accidentally engage.

6. After installing the primary driven gear assembly, slide on the thrust washers, then carefully slide on the clutch boss. Be careful; pulling the clutch boss out after its installation could dislodge the thrust washers and prevent the boss from sliding completely in.

7. After clutch boss installation, slide in alternate metal and fiber plates. If your machine has rubber cushions, these are installed over the

2. Slide out the clutch and friction plates.

3. Slide out the valve-shaped pushrod located in the end of the transmission shaft **(Figure 34)**. In the same hole, behind the pushrod, is a ball

45

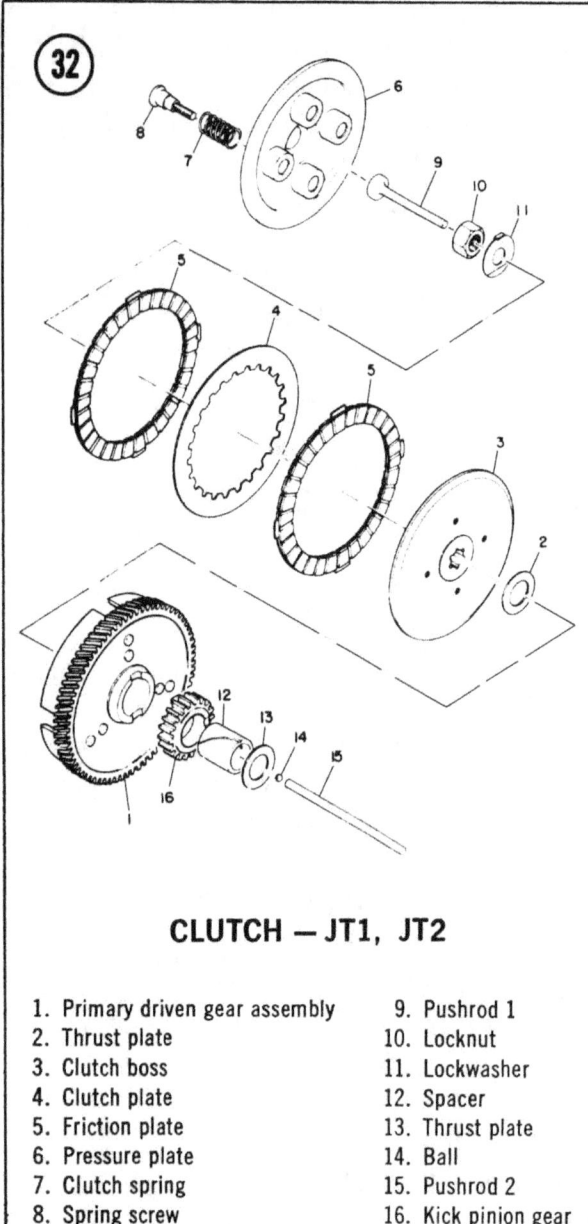

CLUTCH — JT1, JT2

1. Primary driven gear assembly
2. Thrust plate
3. Clutch boss
4. Clutch plate
5. Friction plate
6. Pressure plate
7. Clutch spring
8. Spring screw
9. Pushrod 1
10. Locknut
11. Lockwasher
12. Spacer
13. Thrust plate
14. Ball
15. Pushrod 2
16. Kick pinion gear

bearing. Tip the engine or use a magnet to remove it. A long pushrod will slide out after the ball bearing.

4. **Figure 35** shows how to loosen and remove the clutch locknut by anchoring the clutch with a clutch holding tool. Be sure to first flatten the bend-type lockwasher, if equipped.

5. Slide off the clutch boss. Directly behind the boss is a thrust plate. Remove it, but note its position for future installation.

6. Slide off the primary driven gear assembly (outer housing). Behind the outer housing is a removable kick pinion. Slide it off.

7. Now slide off the spacer and thrust plate next to the transmission bearing. Note their position for future installation.

Assembly

1. Be sure that all thrust washers, plates, and bearings are in proper position.

2. Make sure both kick pinion gear protruding dogs engage the 2 squared off slots in the back of the primary driven gear. Take care; there are also 2 rounded slots that the dogs could accidentally engage.

3. After installing the primary driven gear assembly, slide on the trust washer, then carefully slide on the clutch boss.

4. Install and tighten clutch boss retaining nut.

5. Slide in alternate metal and fiber plates.

6. Install the long pushrod, ball bearing, and short pushrod into the transmission shaft hole. If any are left out, there will be no tension at the clutch lever after assembly and the clutch will not disengage.

7. Add the pressure plate, springs, and spring retaining screws. Tighten the spring retaining screws just until slightly snug. Excessive torque can snap the screw, which will require clutch boss replacement.

MJ1 AND MJ2 CLUTCH

Disassembly/Assembly

Refer to **Figure 36** for an illustration of the clutch used on these models. This illustration can serve as a step-by-step disassembly and assembly procedure for you to follow. Note the position and order of each part.

When installing the clutch housing, note that the retaining nut has a left-hand thread.

During installation, push the pressure plate evenly around its edges to seat the roller bracket ring.

There are 3 clutch plates (metal), one of which is thicker than the others. Install the thicker plate last.

> NOTE: *MJ2 late type clutch:* **Figure 37** *identifies this type of clutch. Parts and function are similar to the MJ2, but part shapes differ slightly. All procedures remain the same.*

MJ2T CLUTCH

Disassembly/Assembly

Figure 38 identifies all parts and their order of assembly of the MJ2T manually operated clutch. It is actuated by a handlebar-mounted clutch lever, then to the clutch via a clutch cable. This differs from the MJ2 which is an automatic, centrifugally-operated clutch. During disassembly and assembly procedures, refer to Figure 38 as needed for visual help on order of parts.

CLUTCH INSPECTION (ALL MODELS)

Clutch Plate Inspection

Measure each clutch spring free length as shown in **Figure 39**. Replace any spring more than 0.04 in. (1.0mm) shorter than the standard free length listed in **Table 2**.

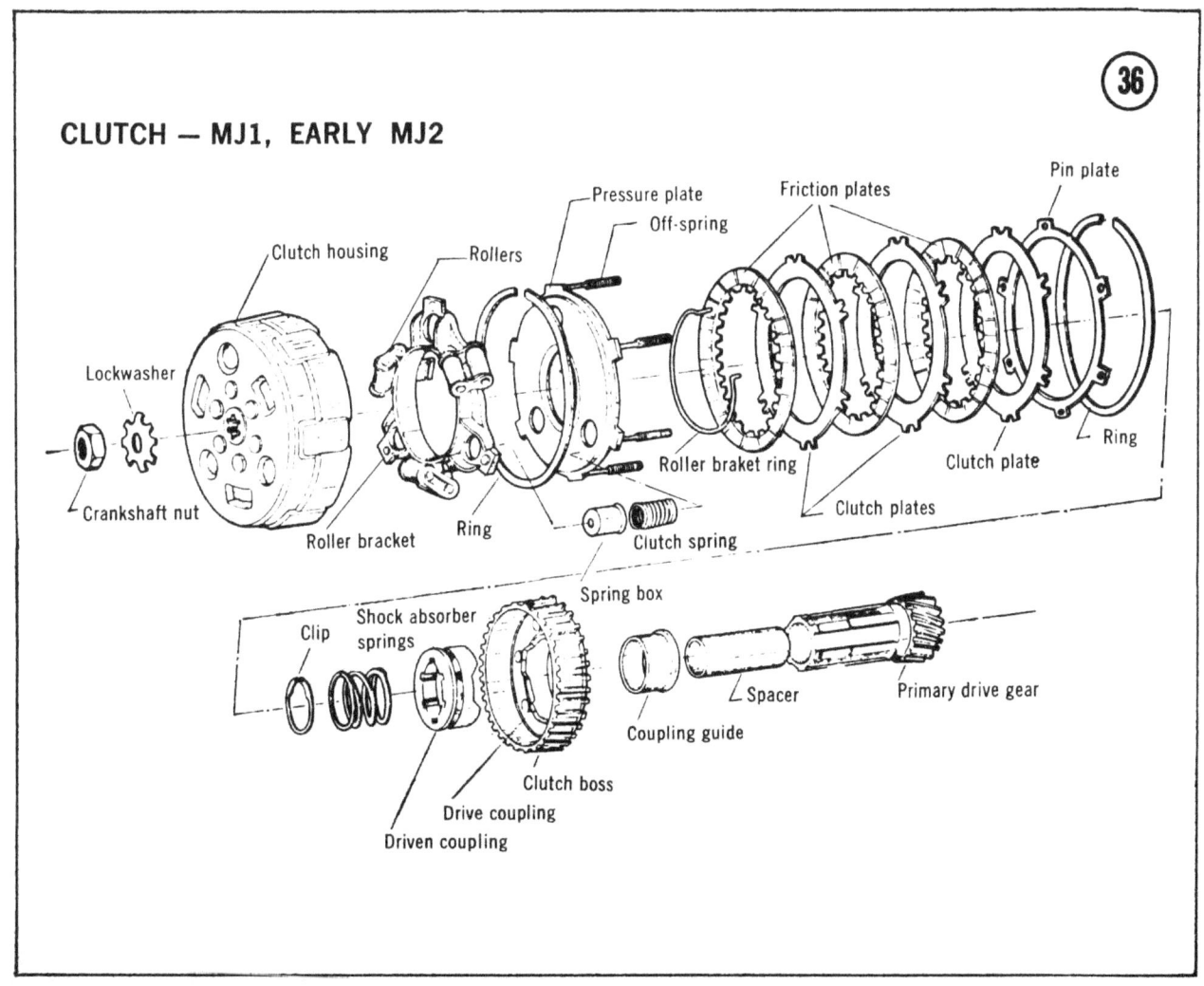

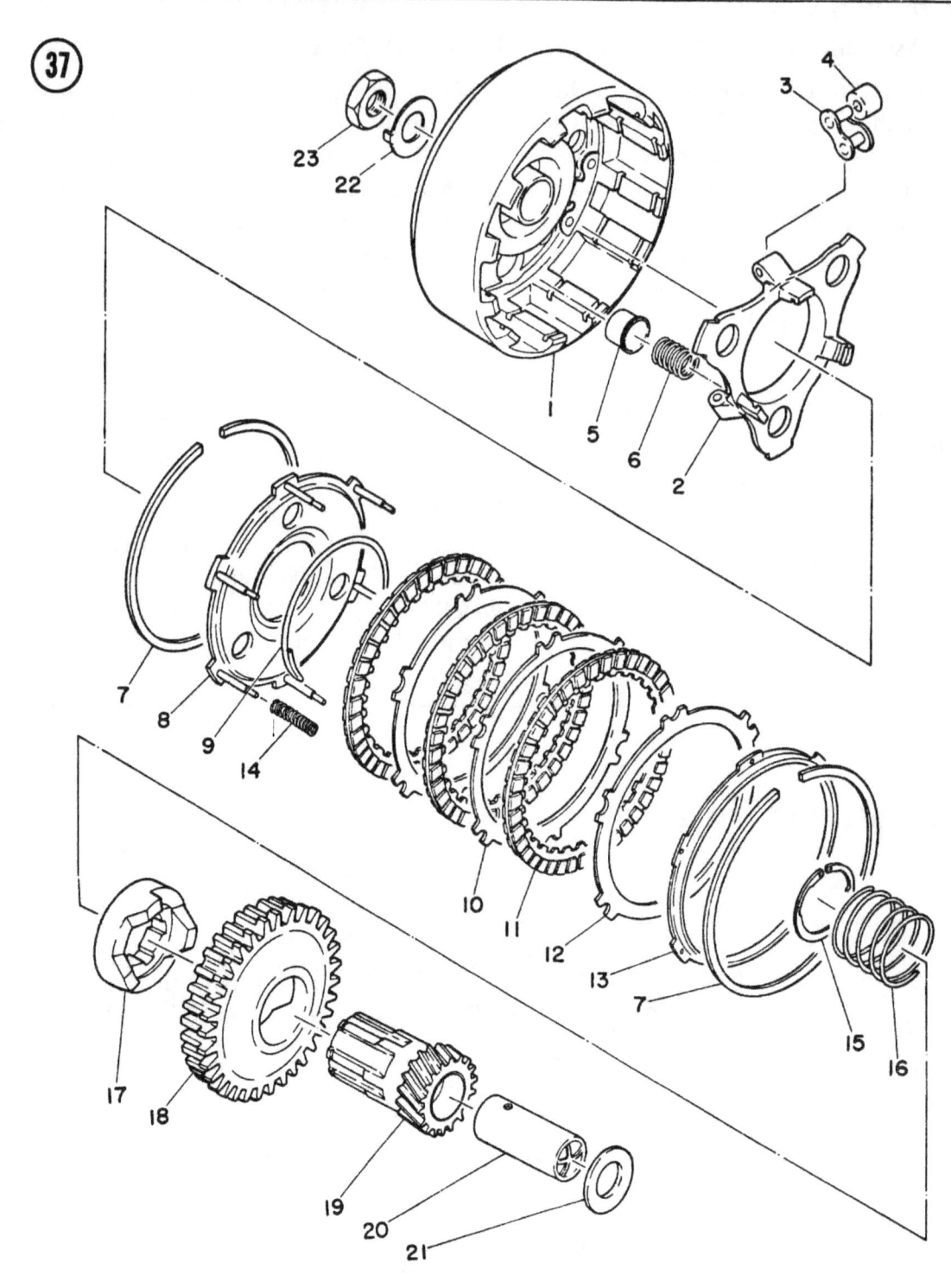

CLUTCH — LATE MJ2

1. Clutch housing
2. Bracket
3. Joint clip
4. Roller
5. Spring container
6. Spring
7. Clip
8. Pressure plate
9. Roller link
10. Clutch plate
11. Friction plate
12. Clutch plate
13. Pin plate
14. Spring
15. Shock absorber clip
16. Shock absorber spring
17. Coupling
18. Clutch boss
19. Primary driven gear
20. Spacer
21. Thrust plate
22. Lockwasher
23. Locknut

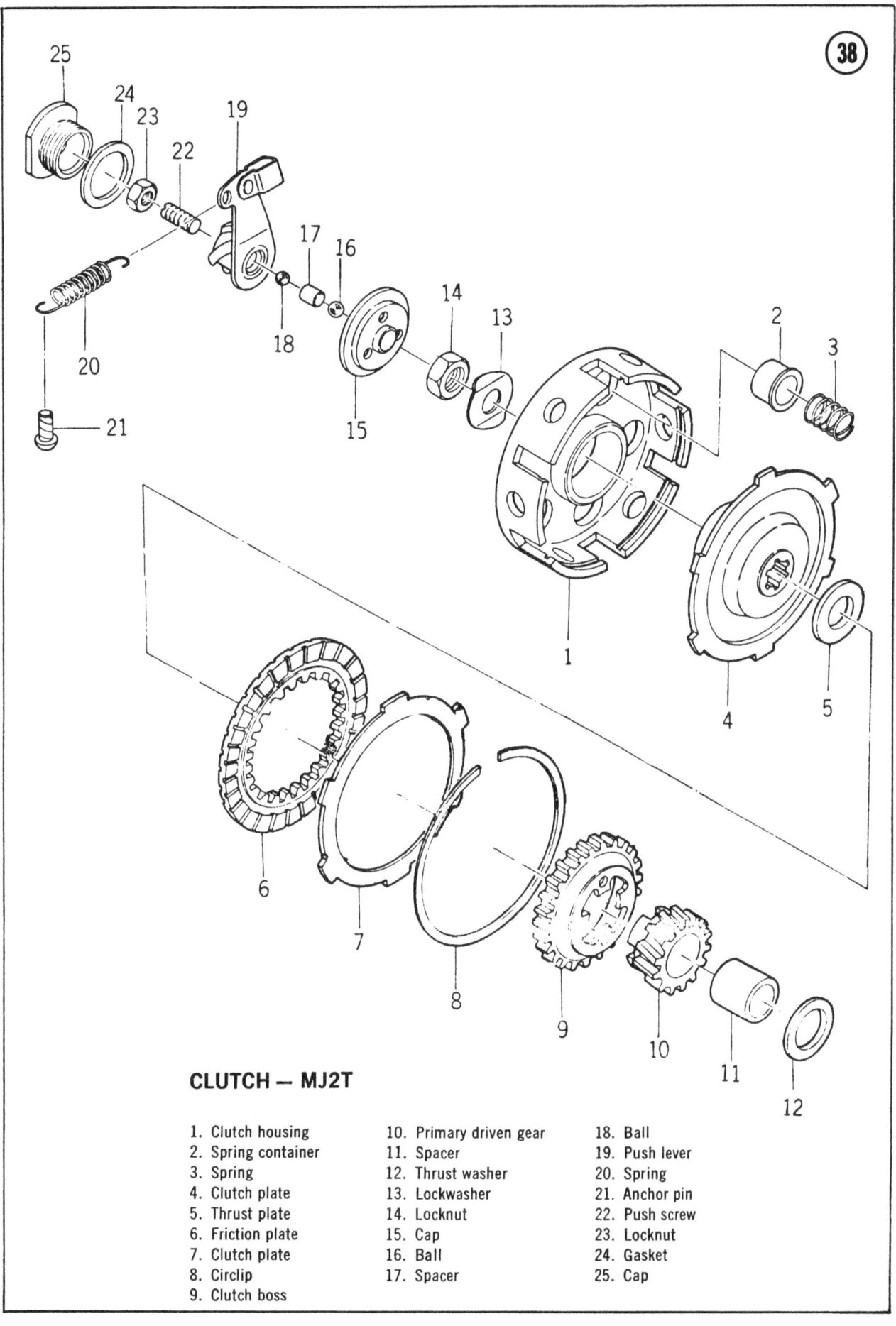

CLUTCH — MJ2T

1. Clutch housing
2. Spring container
3. Spring
4. Clutch plate
5. Thrust plate
6. Friction plate
7. Clutch plate
8. Circlip
9. Clutch boss
10. Primary driven gear
11. Spacer
12. Thrust washer
13. Lockwasher
14. Locknut
15. Cap
16. Ball
17. Spacer
18. Ball
19. Push lever
20. Spring
21. Anchor pin
22. Push screw
23. Locknut
24. Gasket
25. Cap

Table 2   CLUTCH SPRING LENGTH

Model	Length
JT1	1.34 in. (34mm)
YG5-T, G5S, G6S, G6SB	1.06 in. (27mm)

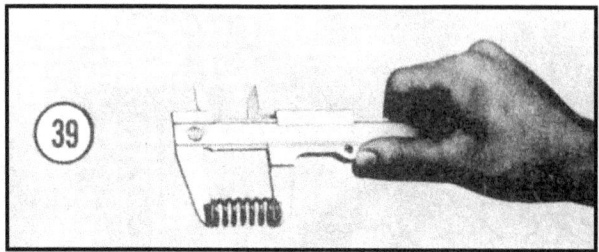

Friction Plate Inspection

Friction plates must be checked for wear as shown in **Figures 40 and 41**. Plates worn more than 0.02 in. (0.3mm) under standard thickness, or showing uneven wear, should be replaced.

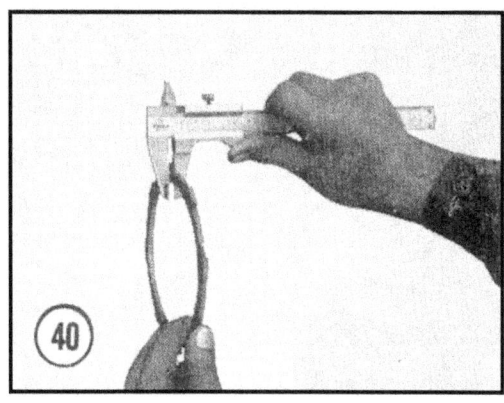

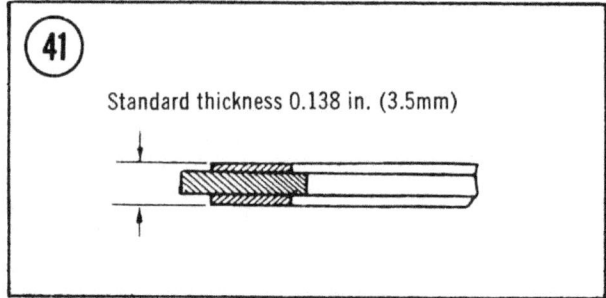

Standard thickness 0.138 in. (3.5mm)

Metal Plate Inspection

These plates normally are not subject to wear, but heat can distort them. They must be flat. Lay each one on a flat surface, such as a piece of glass. If they appear to be cupped at all and the clutch does not want to disengage totally, replace the defective plates. Try to insert a 0.004 in. (0.1mm) feeler gauge around the outer and inner edges. If it slips past, the edge is cupped.

Clutch Housing Inspection

To inspect this assembly, insert the primary gear retaining collar (spacer) in the primary driven gear boss and check for radial play as shown in **Figure 42**. If the play is excessive, replace the collar. Allowable clearance is 0.00035-0.0019 in. (0.009-0.048mm). If any scratches are evident, replace the spacer to avoid impaired clutch action.

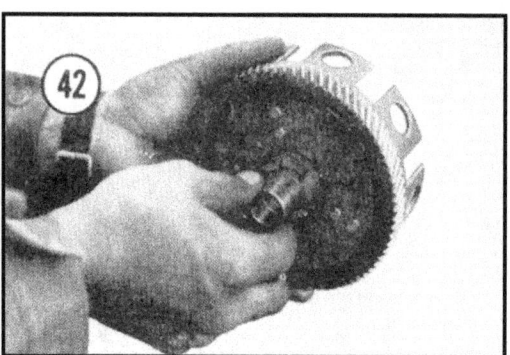

Primary Gear Retaining Collar Inspection

Place the primary gear retaining collar around the main shaft as shown in **Figure 43** and check for radial play. If the radial play does not fall within the limits of 0.0008-0.0024 in. (0.020-0.062mm), replace the collar. If the collar shows step wear on its outer surface, replace it.

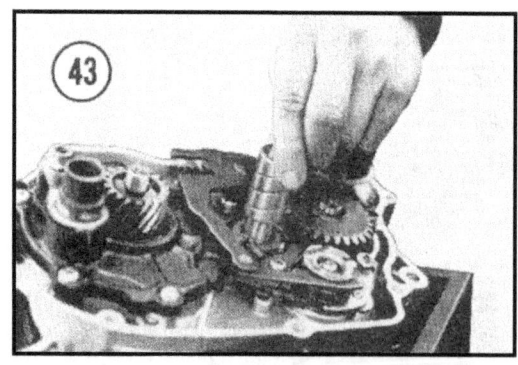

CLUTCH ADJUSTMENT

To adjust the clutch, remove the carburetor cover on the right side crankcase cover. Loosen the adjusting screw locknut as shown in **Figure 44**. Slowly tighten the adjusting screw until resistance is felt. This indicates free-play is removed. Back off the screw ¼ turn and tighten the locknut. This should be the proper adjustment unless clutch or friction plates are excessively worn.

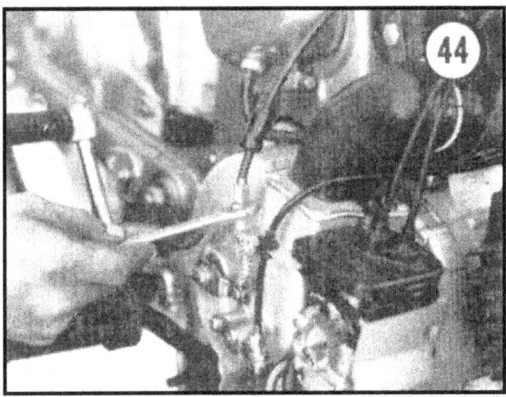

To adjust the clutch cable, loosen the locknut fitted on the crankcase cover where the clutch cable enters the crankcase cover (**Figure 45**). To reduce the play of the cable, loosen the adjusting screw. Adjust until clutch lever play is 0.08 to 0.12 in. (2-3mm) as shown in **Figure 46**. Fully tighten locknut.

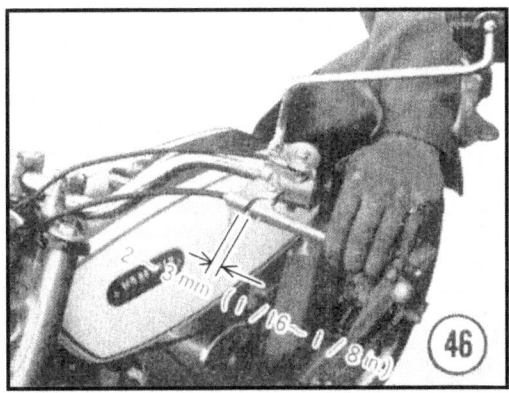

PRIMARY DRIVE GEAR

Feed a rolled-up rag between the teeth of the primary drive gear and primary driven gear to lock them, then loosen the primary drive gear locknut. See **Figure 47**.

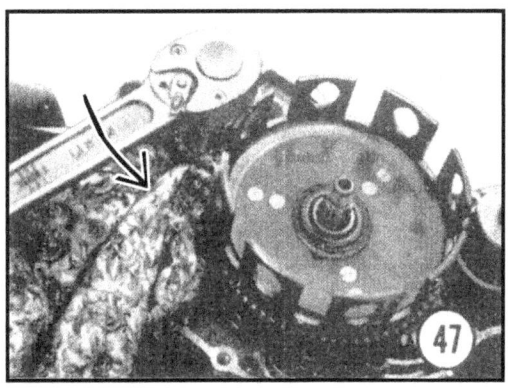

TRANSMISSION

These procedures apply to the following models:

U5	MJ1 and 2
YJ1 and 2	YG1

These models are similar in design and function. The U5 series, and the MJ1 and 2 series are equipped with 3-speed ball-lock transmissions. The remaining models have 4-speed ball-lock transmissions.

Figures 48 through 51 provide details of parts and their locations for individual models. During disassembly and assembly procedures, refer to these illustrations for details as needed.

The following procedure is specifically for this type transmission—the ball-lock type. You may find that your model will have an extra shim or slightly different part design. Use this procedure as a guide, but lay out your pieces in order and position of their removal to aid later assembly.

1. Remove the drive axle circlip (**Figure 52**).
2. Remove the drive axle washer (**Figure 53**).
3. Remove the 1st gear wheel (**Figure 54**).
4. Remove the nylon oil pump gear (U5 series, **Figure 55**).
5. Remove 2nd and 3rd gear wheels.
6. Remove the main axle, complete with gears (**Figure 56**).
7. Remove the drive axle (**Figure 57**).

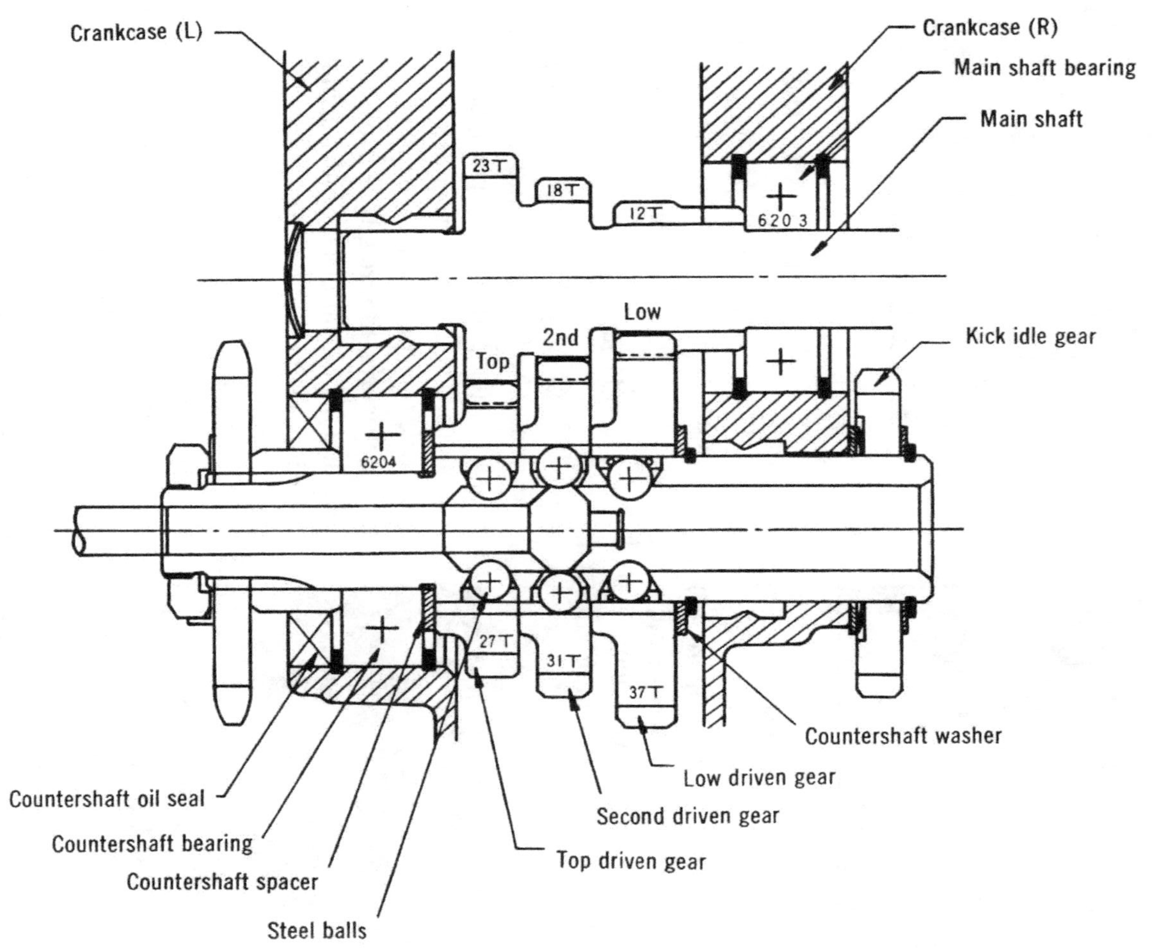

TRANSMISSION (See Text)

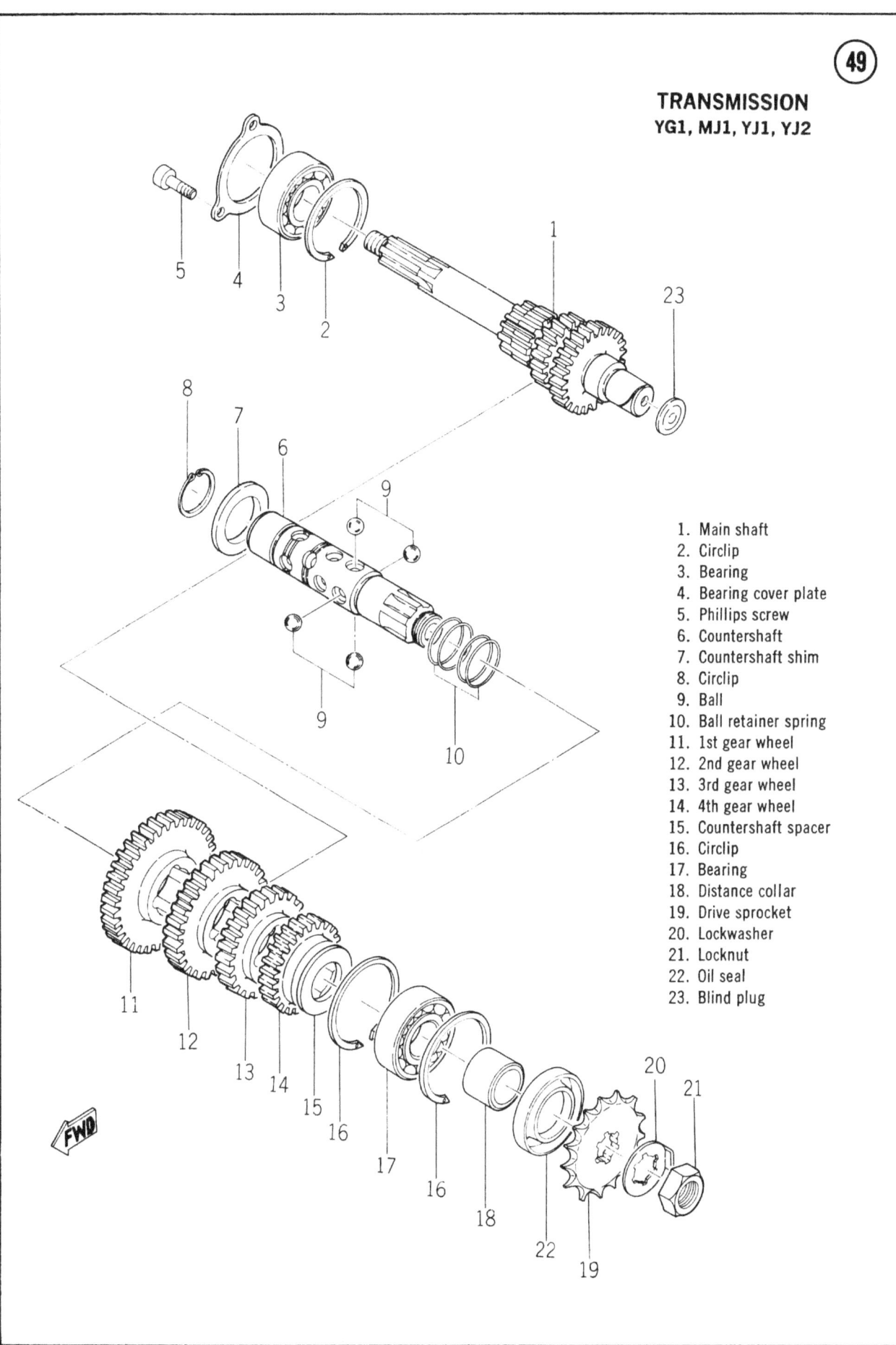

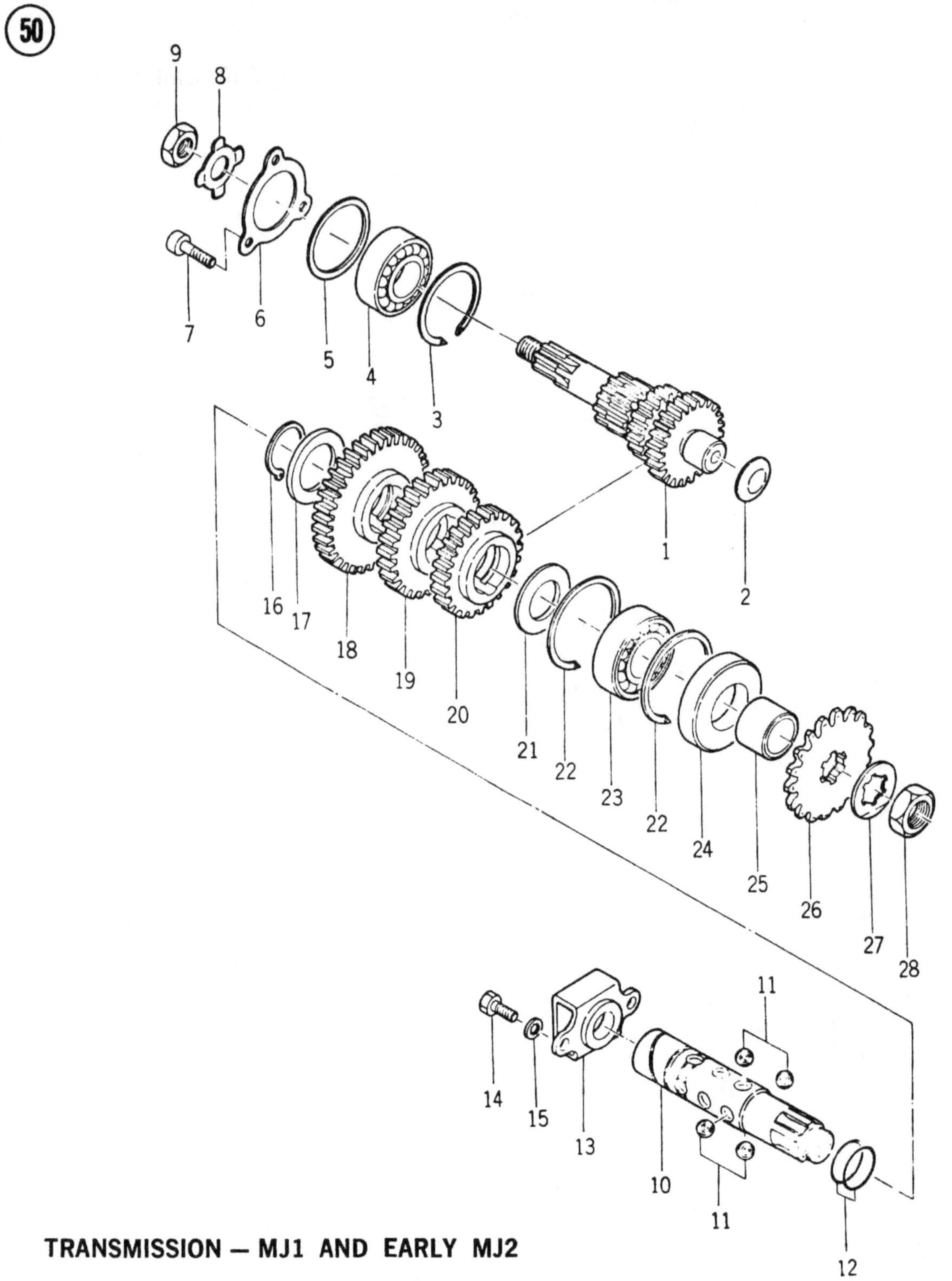

TRANSMISSION — MJ1 AND EARLY MJ2

1. Main shaft
2. Blind plug
3. Circlip
4. Bearing
5. Shim
6. Bearing cover plate
7. Phillips screw
8. Lockwasher
9. Locknut
10. Countershaft
11. Ball
12. Ball retainer spring
13. Countershaft oil bucket
14. Phillips screw
15. Washer
16. Circlip
17. Washer
18. Low driven gear (1st)
19. Second driven gear (2nd)
20. Top driven gear (3rd)
21. Thrust washer
22. Circlip
23. Bearing
24. Seal
25. Spacer
26. Drive sprocket
27. Lockwasher
28. Locknut

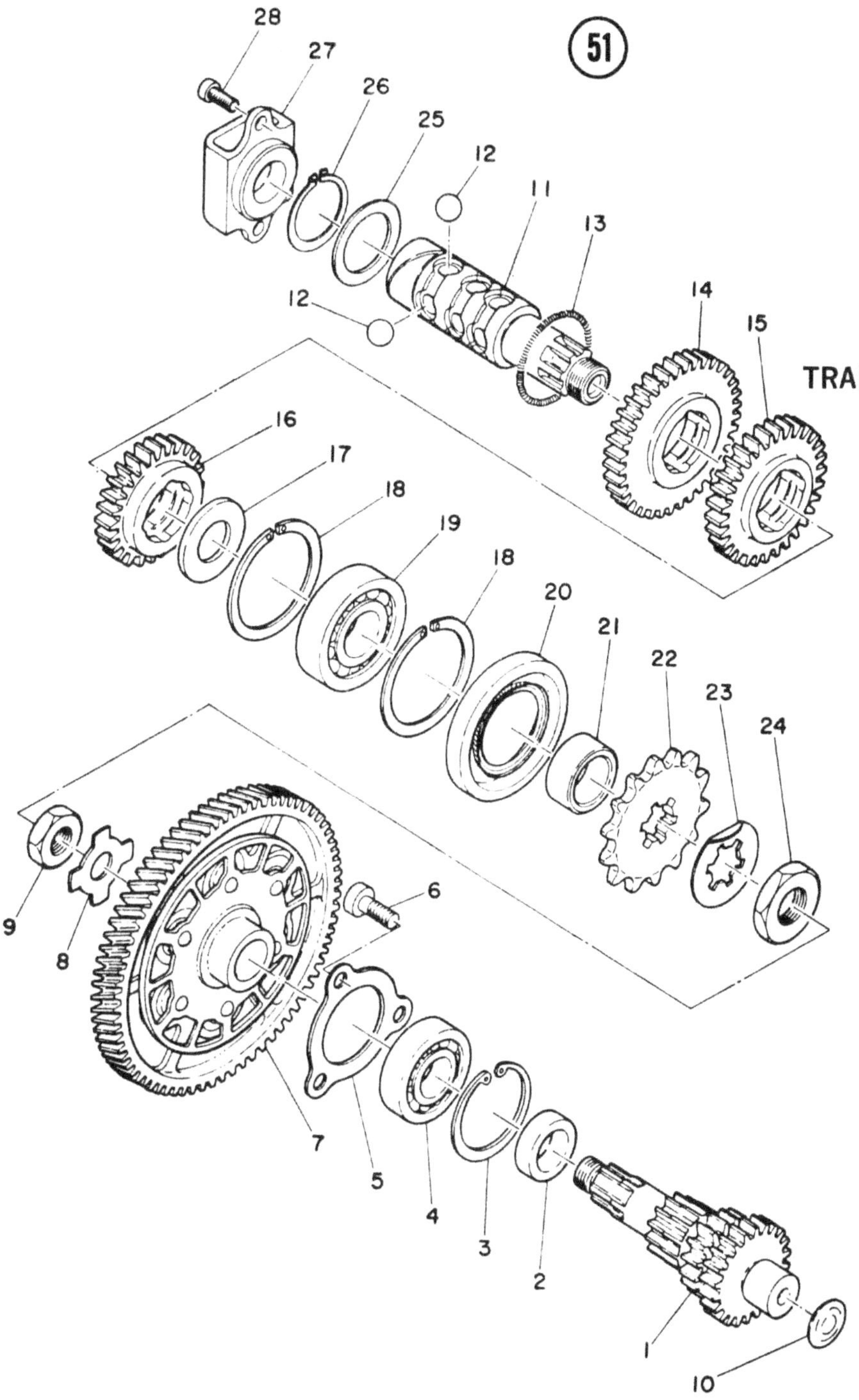

51. TRANSMISSION – LATE MJ2

1. Main shaft
2. Spacer
3. Circlip
4. Bearing
5. Bearing cover plate
6. Phillips screw
7. Primary driven gear
8. Lockwasher
9. Locknut
10. Blind plug
11. Countershaft
12. Ball
13. Ball retainer spring
14. 1st gear wheel
15. 2nd gear wheel
16. 3rd gear wheel
17. Thrust washer
18. Circlip
19. Bearing
20. Oil seal
21. Spacer
22. Drive sprocket
23. Lockwasher
24. Locknut
25. Shim
26. Circlip
27. Oil bucket
28. Phillips screw

52.

53.

55

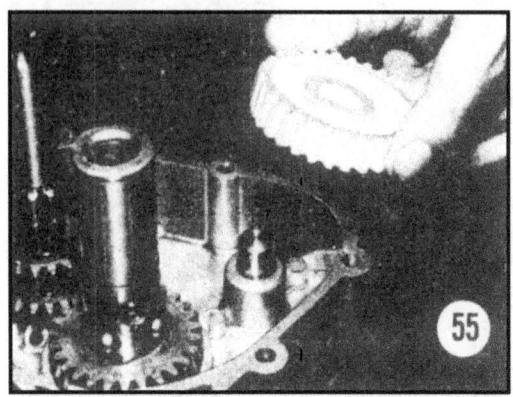

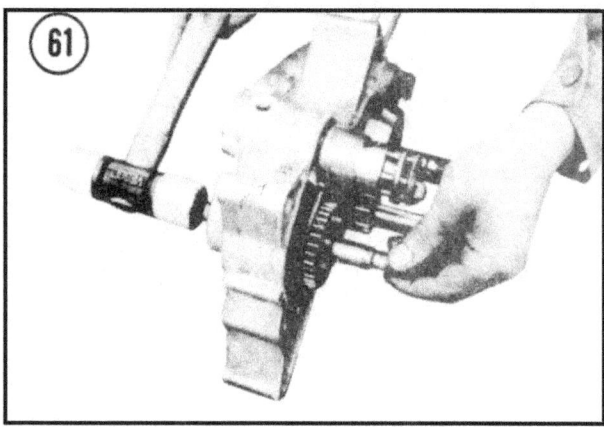

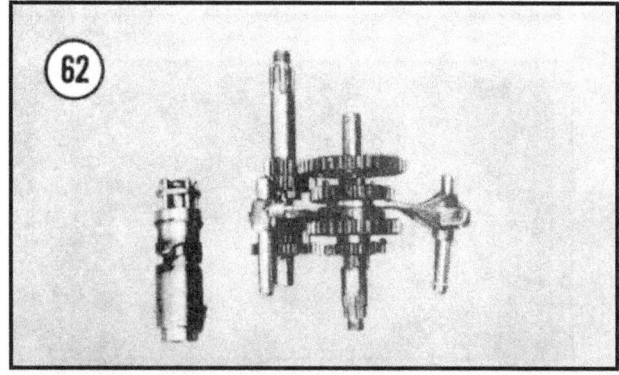

the ground throughout the entire speed range. **Figures 58 and 59** provide an exploded view and cross-sectional view to explain parts location and function.

1. To remove the transmission, pull out the 2 shift fork guide bars (**Figure 60**).

2. Remove both the transmission and shifting assemblies by tapping the drive shaft end with a soft hammer (**Figure 61**).

3. When reassembling, install the transmission and shifter as a unit in the left crankcase half. The transmission must be in neutral during installation. See **Figure 62**.

TRANSMISSION

These procedures apply to the JT1/2 series. The constant mesh wide ratio, 4-speed transmission is design to provide maximum power to

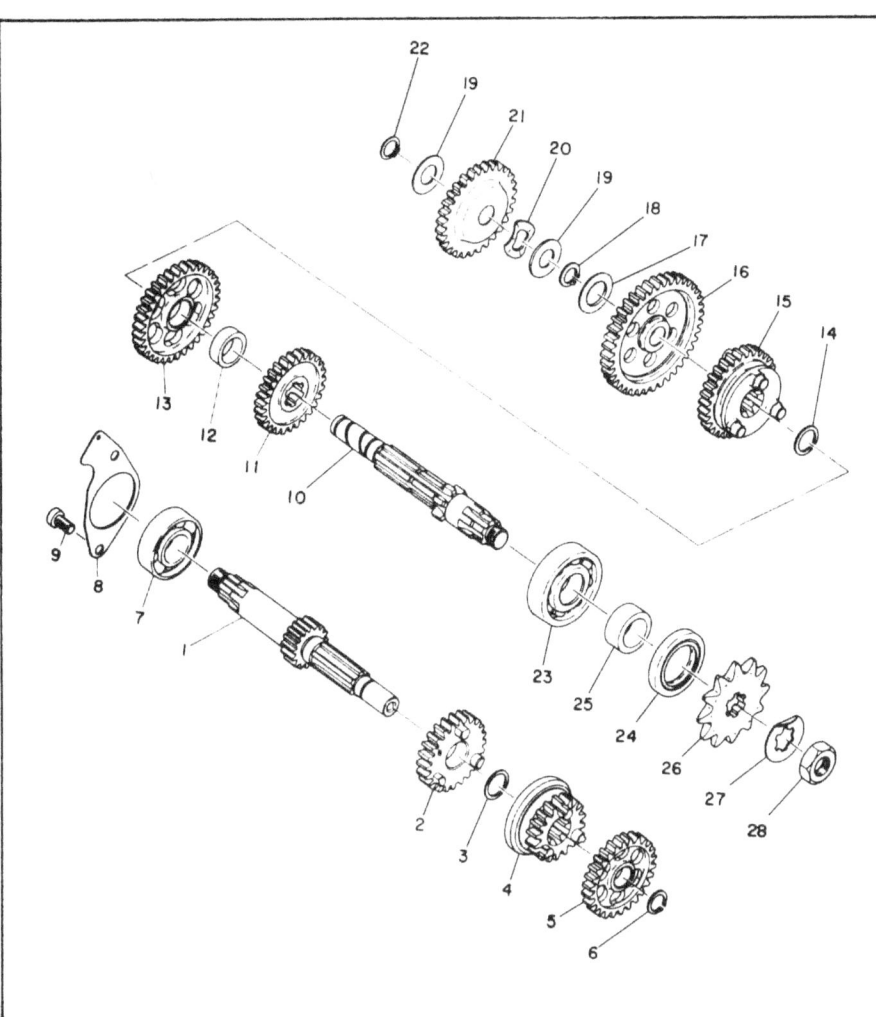

TRANSMISSION (JT1 AND JT2)

1. Main shaft
2. 3rd pinion gear
3. Circlip
4. 2nd pinion gear
5. 1st pinion gear
6. Circlip
7. Bearing
8. Bearing cover plate
9. Bolt
10. Countershaft
11. 4th wheel gear
12. Distance collar
13. 2nd wheel gear
14. Circlip
15. 3rd wheel gear
16. 1st wheel gear
17. Shim
18. Circlip
19. Thrust washer
20. Wave washer
21. Kick idle gear
22. Circlip
23. Bearing
24. Oil seal
25. Distance collar
26. Drive sprocket
27. Lockwasher
28. Nut

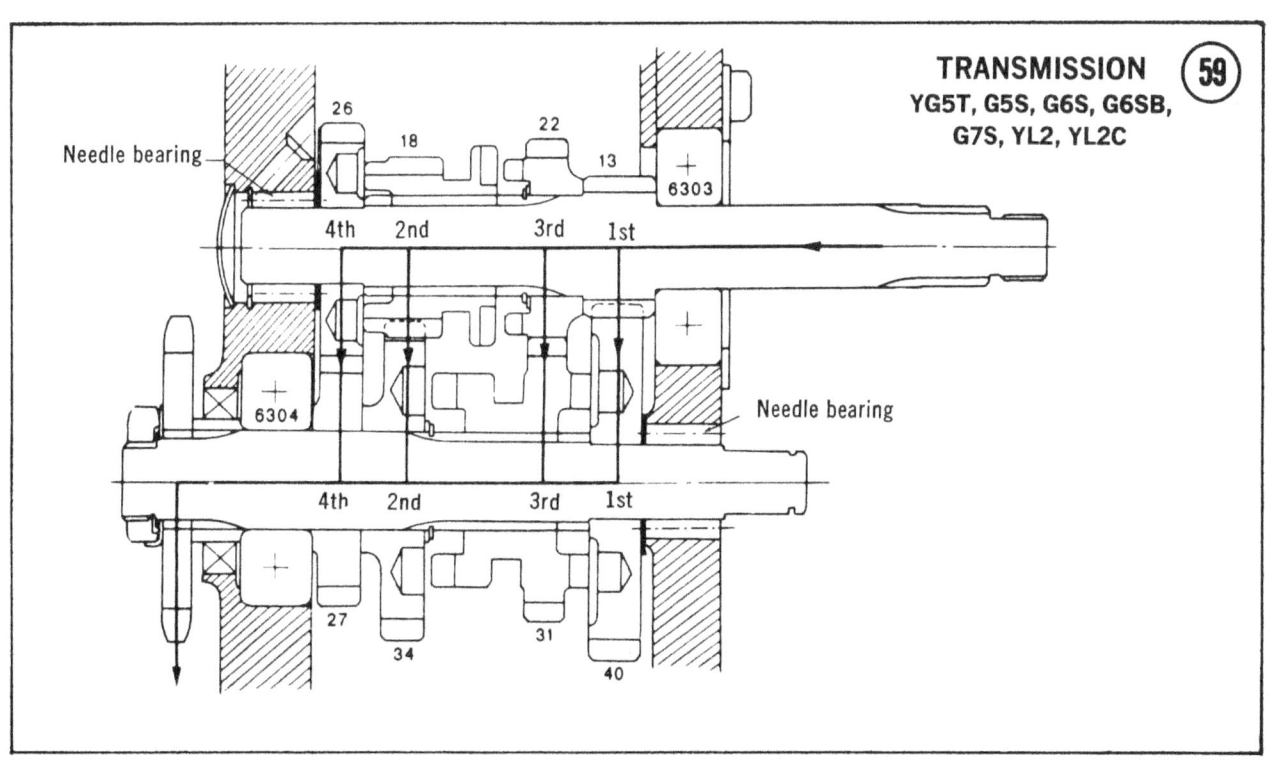

TRANSMISSION YG5T, G5S, G6S, G6SB, G7S, YL2, YL2C

TRANSMISSION ASSEMBLY
YG5T, G5S, G6S, G6SB, G7S, YL2, and YL2C

1. To remove the transmission, take off the shift drum seal cover, circlip, holder, and washer from the gearshift drum on the left side of the engine, shown in **Figures 63 and 64**.

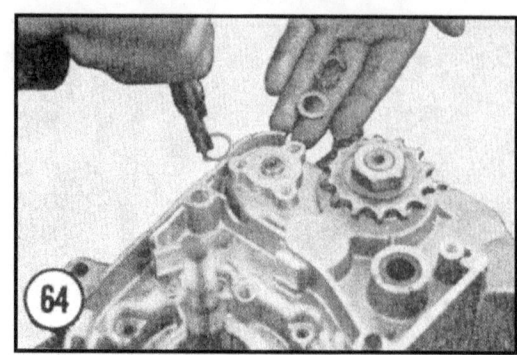

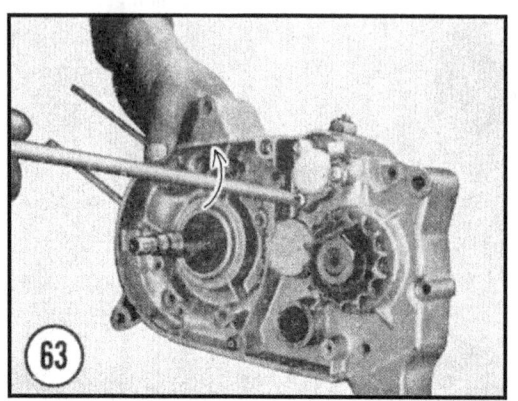

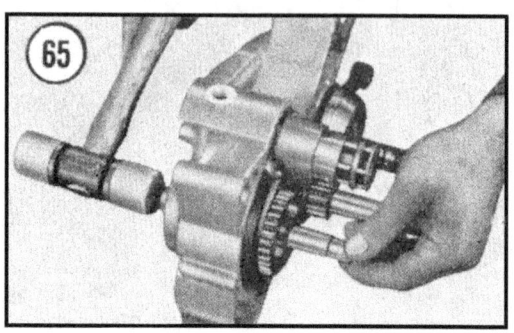

2. Remove the neutral stopper mechanism.

3. Remove the transmission and shifter as a unit (**Figure 65**).

4. Refer to **Figures 66 and 67** for cross-sectional and exploded views of the transmission for details of assembly, arrangement, and parts.

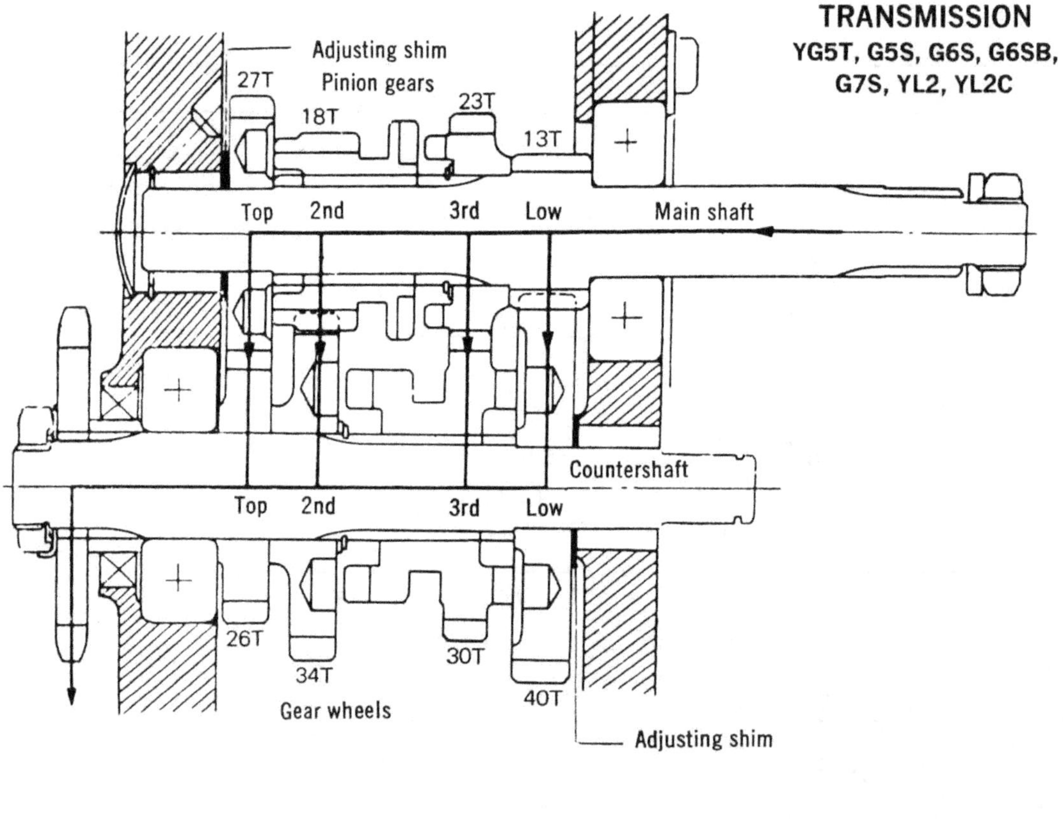

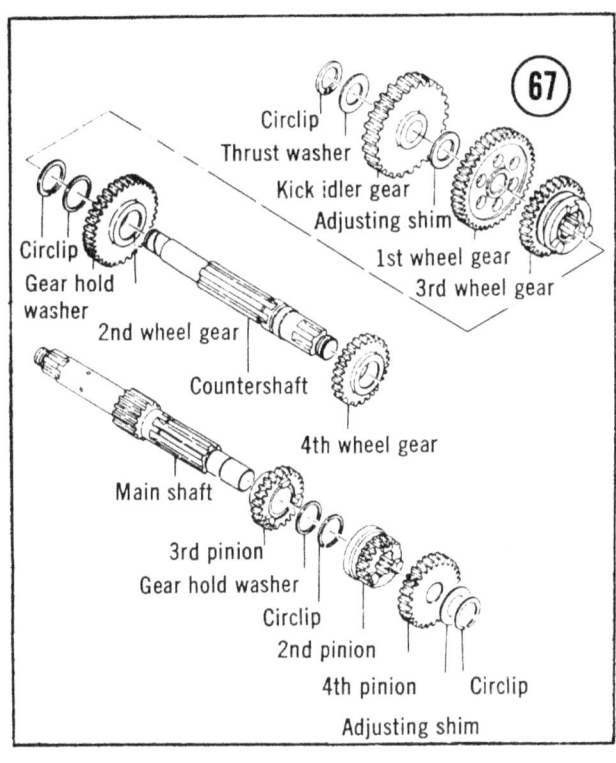

5. **Figure 68** shows how to reinstall the transmission and shifter as a unit in the left crankcase half after they are assembled. The gear assembly and shifter drum cannot be installed separately.

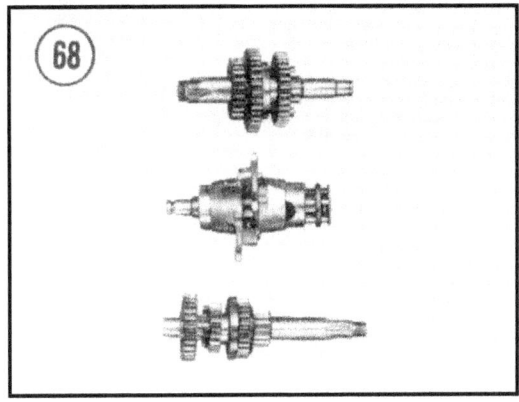

6. Never reassemble the crankcase halves with the transmission in 1st gear; bending of the shift forks will result.

CHAPTER FIVE

FUEL SYSTEM

There are 2 basically different carburetor designs used on the models covered in this manual. The JT series models use a Teikei Y16P carburetor. All others use a Mikuni VM carburetor with different venturi sizes. See Chapter Eight for specifications.

BASIC PRINCIPLES

Mixture Control Components

The carburetor fuel and air supply can be broken down into systems that most affect carburetor performance at a particular throttle setting. Learning which system is operating at a throttle setting is useful in diagnosing malfunctions and when changing jetting. If there is a carburetor malfunction, and if it could be isolated to a particular throttle setting, then you would be able to pinpoint the problem circuit and parts. Examining these parts could turn up the problem.

Proper jetting could be checked by operating your machine at a set throttle opening for several miles, then stopping to examine spark plug color. If you held half-throttle and the color was too dark or too light, you would know to change the needle clip position. It has the most effect from ¼-¾ throttle opening.

The carburetor components are divided up by throttle opening positions. The parts and jets most affecting throttle response at each point are discussed.

0-⅛ Throttle Opening—The pilot jet controls fuel supply. The pilot air screw controls air supply. Normally there is no reason to differ from factory-recommended settings in this circuit.

⅛-¼ Throttle Opening—The throttle slide *cutaway* (**Figure 1**) controls air supply. Fuel is still supplied by pilot jet system. The higher the cutaway section is, the leaner the mixture will be. Less cutaway richens the mixture. This part, and related fuel/air mixture, rarely need changing on standard machines.

¼-¾ Throttle Opening—Fuel supply is mainly controlled by jet needle position and needle jet. A clip fits into 1 of 5 grooves in the top of the needle. Where this clip is placed determines jet needle position. The top groove is called the #1 clip position. To make mid-range fuel mixture richer, place the clip in a lower groove. This raises the needle and allows more fuel to pass. Raise the clip for a leaner mixture. Clip positions are listed in Chapter Eleven under your model. The last number of its total number indicates the clip position. For example, if the jet

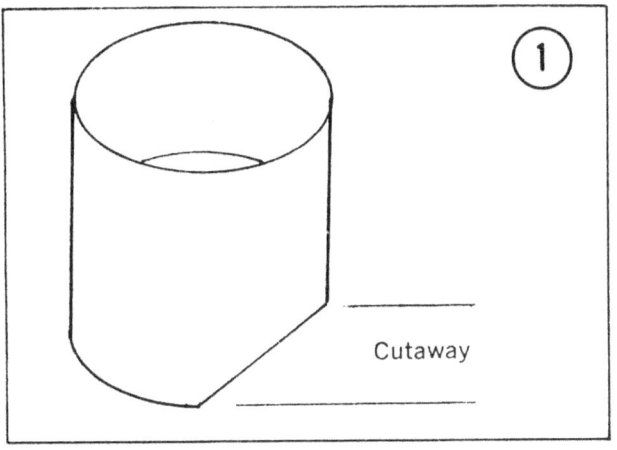
Cutaway

needle number is 5F4-3, then 3 is the clip position. Put the clip in the #3 groove, counting from the top.

Sometimes a clip position change is needed to adapt to climate, elevation, or riding conditions. However, if you must change clip position more than 1 groove away from factory specifications to get proper engine performance, check for a mechanical malfunction.

¾-full throttle opening—The main jet controls fuel supply. The slide and venturi size control air supply. Main jet size number is stamped on the side or end of the jet. Larger numbers provide more fuel and a richer mixture. Main jet numbers are in increments of 5 when below #100, and in steps of 10 above #100. For example, #95, #100, and #110 cover 3 main jet sizes, 1 step each.

A main jet size change of 1 to obtain more correct spark plug color is okay. If a main jet 2 or more sizes larger or smaller is needed, consider troubleshooting.

> NOTE: *Always change main jets 1 size at a time. Always make a performance and spark plug check after each main jet size change.*

For access to the main jet, you must remove the float bowl. This requires carburetor removal.

Starter Jet System

To provide a rich starting mixture, the carburetor is equipped with a special starter jet circuit. Pulling the starter plunger up opens a separate carburetor fuel and air system that richens the total carburetor mixture.

Throttle Operation

The throttle cable is actually in 2 pieces. One piece extends from the throttle grip to plastic junction box under the gas tank. The other cable runs from carburetor up to the same junction box. Both cables require free-play. This permits the cable to flex but does not cause accidental acceleration.

PERIODIC MAINTENANCE

There is no set rule regarding carburetor overhaul frequency. A machine used primarily for street riding may go 5,000 miles without attention, provided it does not show signs of carburetor malfunction. If the bike is used in dirt, it may require an overhaul in less than 1,000 miles. If you ride competition, much more frequent cleaning is advised.

Throttle response will be a good guide to determine frequency of overhaul. Poor engine performance, hesitation, and little or no response to idle mixture adjustment are all symptoms of possible carburetor malfunction. As a general rule for non-competition models, overhaul the carburetor each time you perform a full engine decarbonization.

Whenever the carburetor is disassembled and overhauled, install a carburetor repair kit. It usually includes all paper gaskets and a fuel needle assembly.

Remove the float and shake it to check if gasoline is inside. If fuel leaks into the float, the float chamber fuel level will rise, resulting in an overrich mixture. Replace the float if it is deformed or leaking.

Replace the float valve if its seating end is scratched or worn with a step. Check the float valve spring for fatigue. Depress the float valve gently with your finger and make certain the valve seats properly. If the float valve spring is weak, fuel will overflow, flooding the float chamber whenever the fuel petcock is open.

If fuel overflows, make the checks described in the foregoing paragraphs. Also check for dirt or dust in the fuel, which could prevent the float valve from seating. If any dirt is found, clean the fuel tank, petcock, fuel line, and carburetor.

To clean the carburetor, disassemble it completely and wash all parts in carburetor cleaning solvent. Dry the parts with compressed air. All jets and other delicate parts should be cleaned by blowing compressed air through them after the float bowl has been removed. Use new gaskets upon reassembly of the carburetor. Never attempt to clean jets with wires or pins.

TEIKEI Y16P

Disassembly/Assembly

Figure 2 shows an exploded view of this carburetor.

1. Remove the mixing chamber top shown in **Figure 3**. The starter jet plunger and slide come off at the same time.

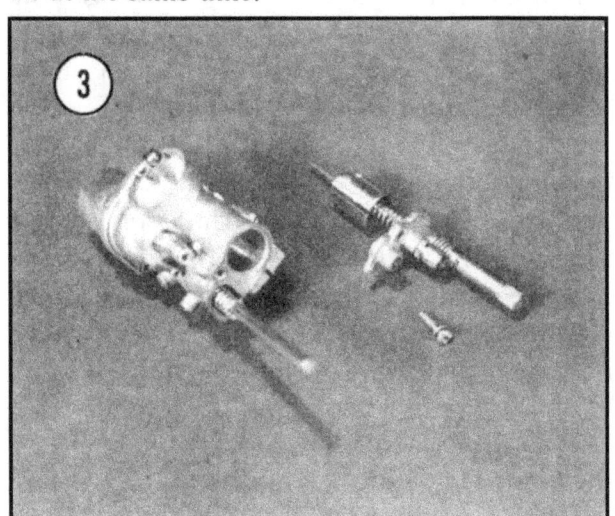

2. If disassembling the slide assembly, see Figure 3. First remove the idle speed rod (throttle bar) retainer cotter pin, then slide out the rod. Pull the return spring out of the slide, then push the needle and spring seat out of the slide.

3. Remove the float bowl. See **Figure 4**.

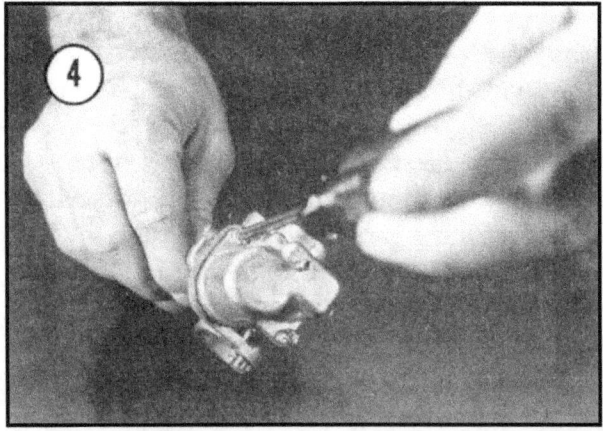

4. Tip the float bowl upside down to allow the float to slide out (**Figure 5**).

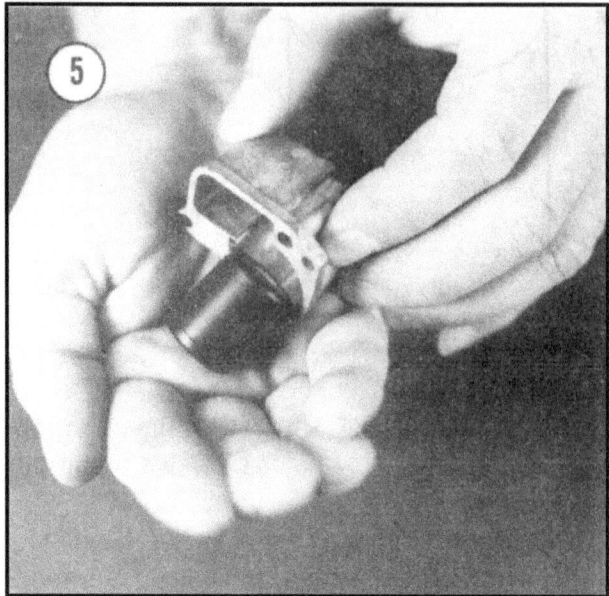

5. On early carburetors, remove and inspect the rubber O-ring inside the float bowl (5, Figure 2). Later models do not have an O-ring.

6. Remove the main jet (**Figure 6**).

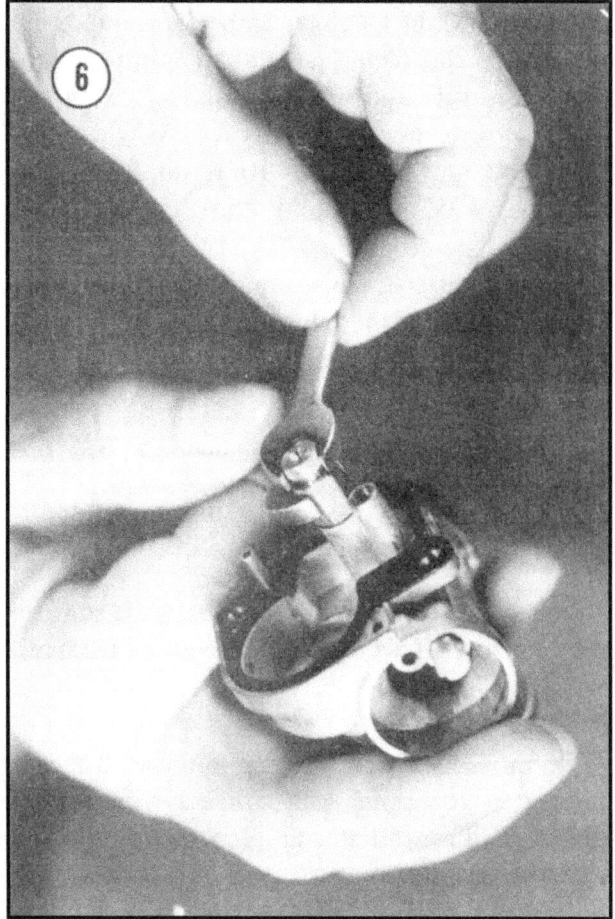

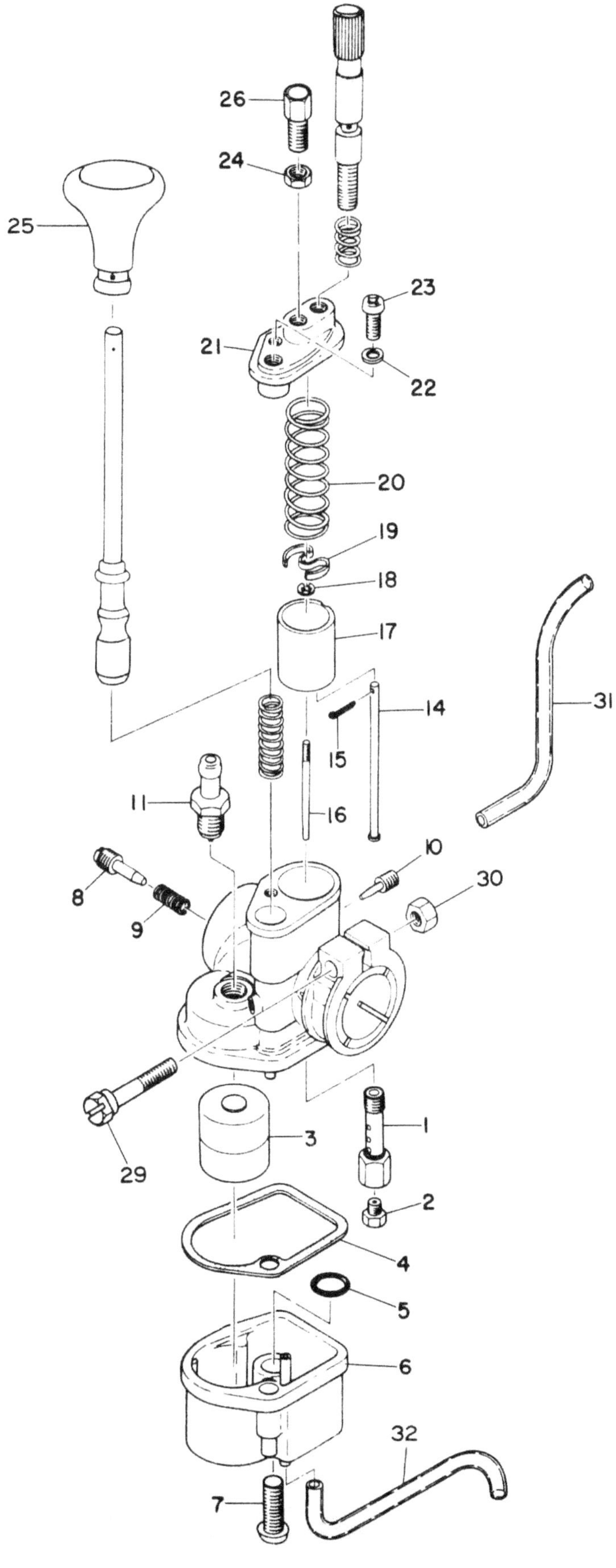

TEIKEI Y16P CARBURETOR

1. Main nozzle
2. Main jet
3. Float
4. Float chamber gasket
5. O-ring
6. Float chamber body
7. Pan head screw
8. Air adjusting screw
9. Air adjusting spring
10. Pilot jet
11. Valve seat assembly
12. Starter flange assembly
13. Plunger spring
14. Throttle bar
15. Cotter pin
16. Needle
17. Throttle valve
18. Clip
19. Spring seat
20. Throttle valve spring
21. Mixing chamber top
22. Spring washer
23. Pan head screw
24. Wire adjusting nut
25. Starter knob
26. Wire adjusting screw
27. Throttle stop spring
28. Throttle screw
29. Body fitting screw
30. Nut
31. Air bend pipe
32. Overflow pipe

7. Screw out the main nozzle/needle jet (**Figure 7**).

8. Screw out the pilot jet (**Figure 8**).

9. Screw out the valve seat (needle and seat) as shown in **Figure 9**.

10. Screw out the idle air screw (**Figure 10**).

11. Assembly is the reverse of these steps.

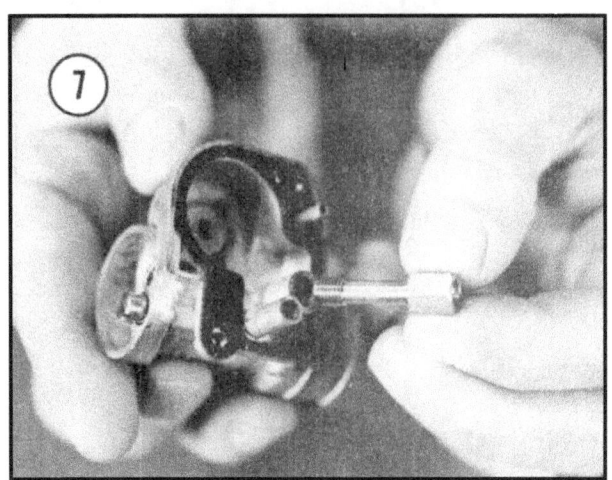

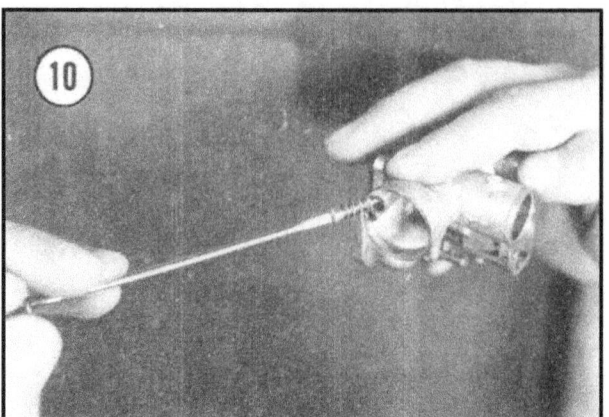

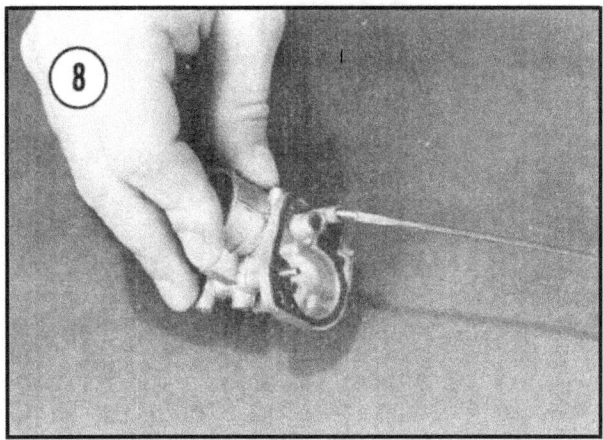

MIKUNI VM

Disassembly/Assembly

Figure 11 shows an exploded view of this carburetor.

1. Remove all 4 float bowl retaining screws. Pull off the float bowl (**Figure 12**).

2. Turn the carburetor upside down as shown in **Figure 13**, then pull out the float pivot pin. This frees the float assembly.

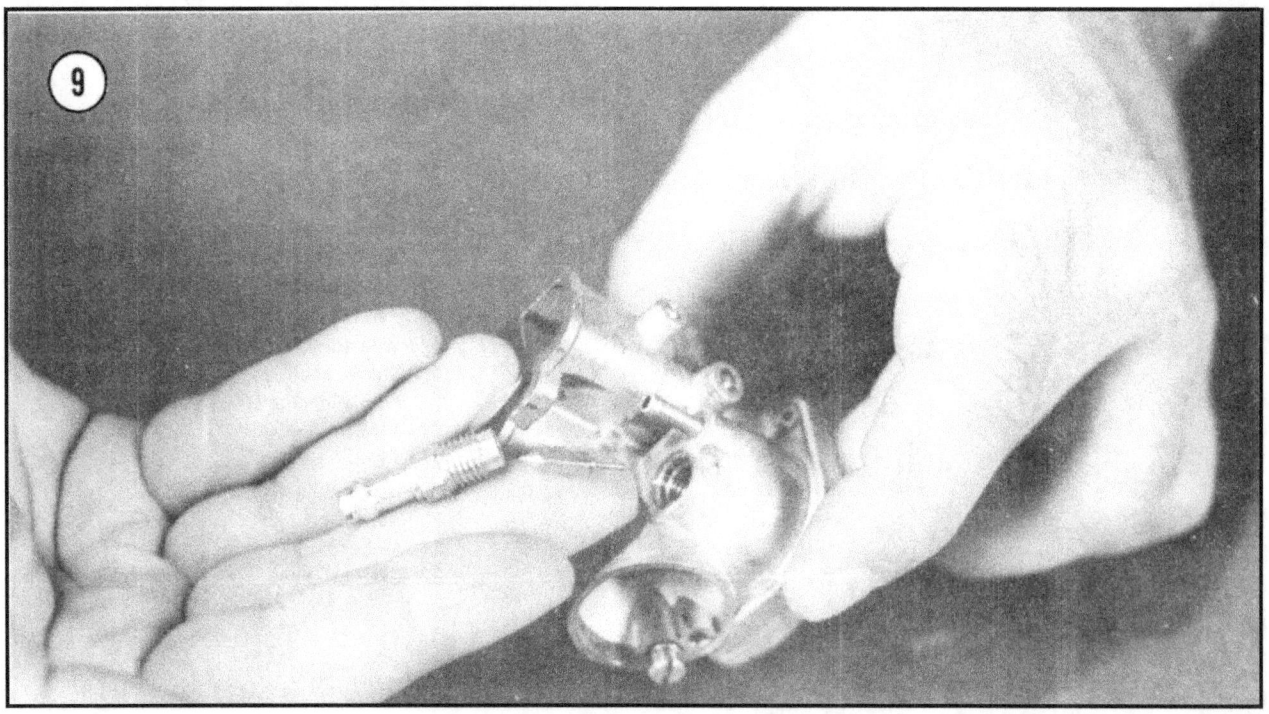

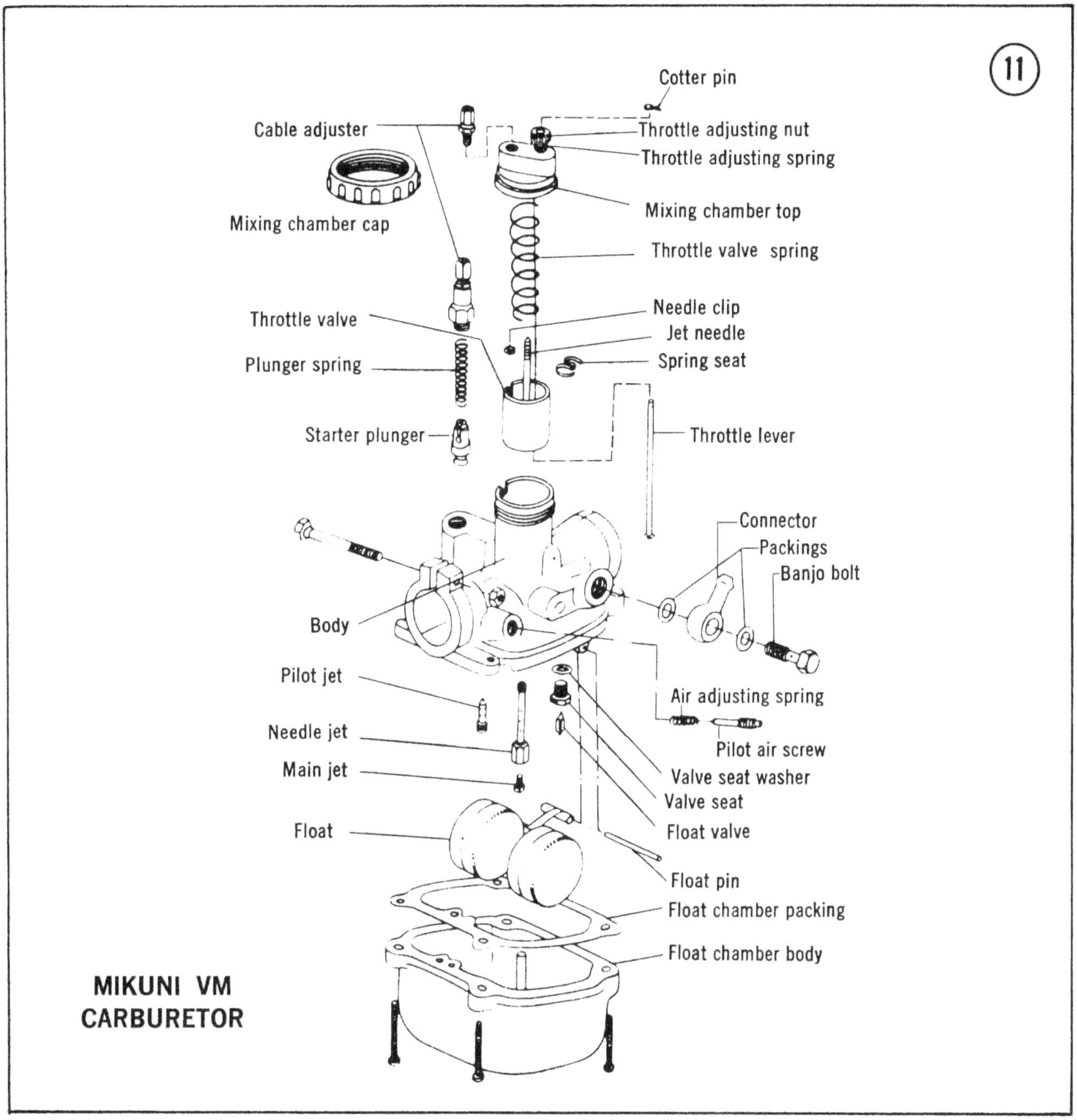

⑪

MIKUNI VM CARBURETOR

Labeled parts: Cotter pin, Cable adjuster, Throttle adjusting nut, Throttle adjusting spring, Mixing chamber cap, Mixing chamber top, Throttle valve spring, Throttle valve, Needle clip, Jet needle, Plunger spring, Spring seat, Starter plunger, Throttle lever, Connector, Packings, Banjo bolt, Body, Pilot jet, Air adjusting spring, Needle jet, Pilot air screw, Main jet, Valve seat washer, Valve seat, Float, Float valve, Float pin, Float chamber packing, Float chamber body

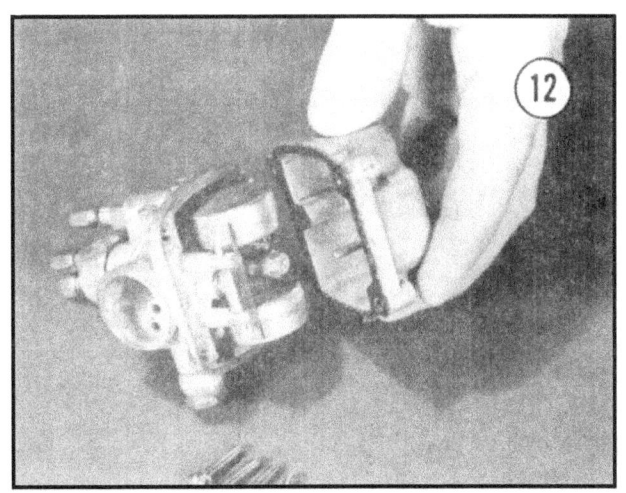

⑫

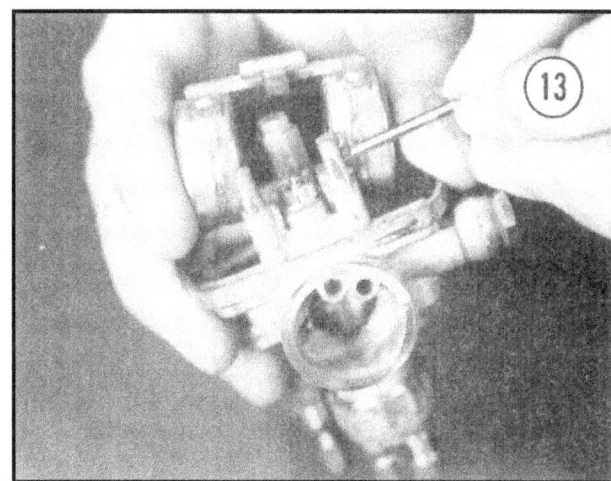

⑬

3. Loosen and remove the float valve (also called fuel valve, fuel needle, or needle valve) identified in **Figure 14**. Immediately remove the fuel needle that fits loosely in the valve.

4. Remove the pilot jet as shown in **Figure 15**,

5. Remove the main jet from the needle jet (**Figure 16**).

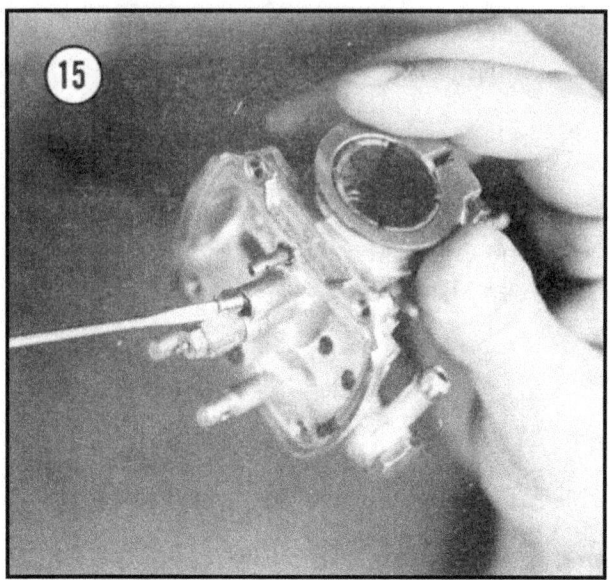

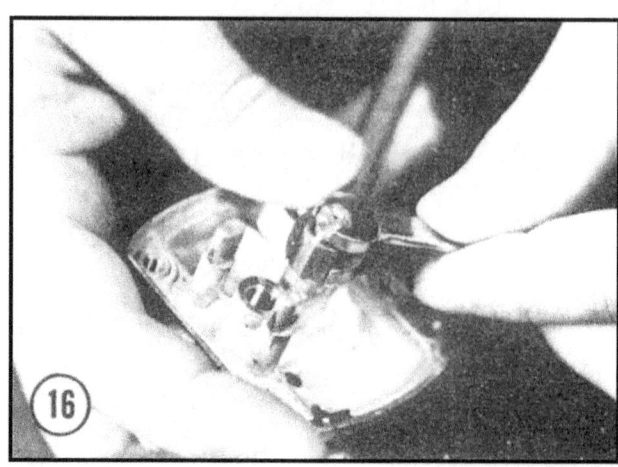

6. Remove the main nozzle/needle jet as shown in **Figure 17**.

7. Remove the idle mixture screw (**Figure 18**).

8. Remove the starter jet system.

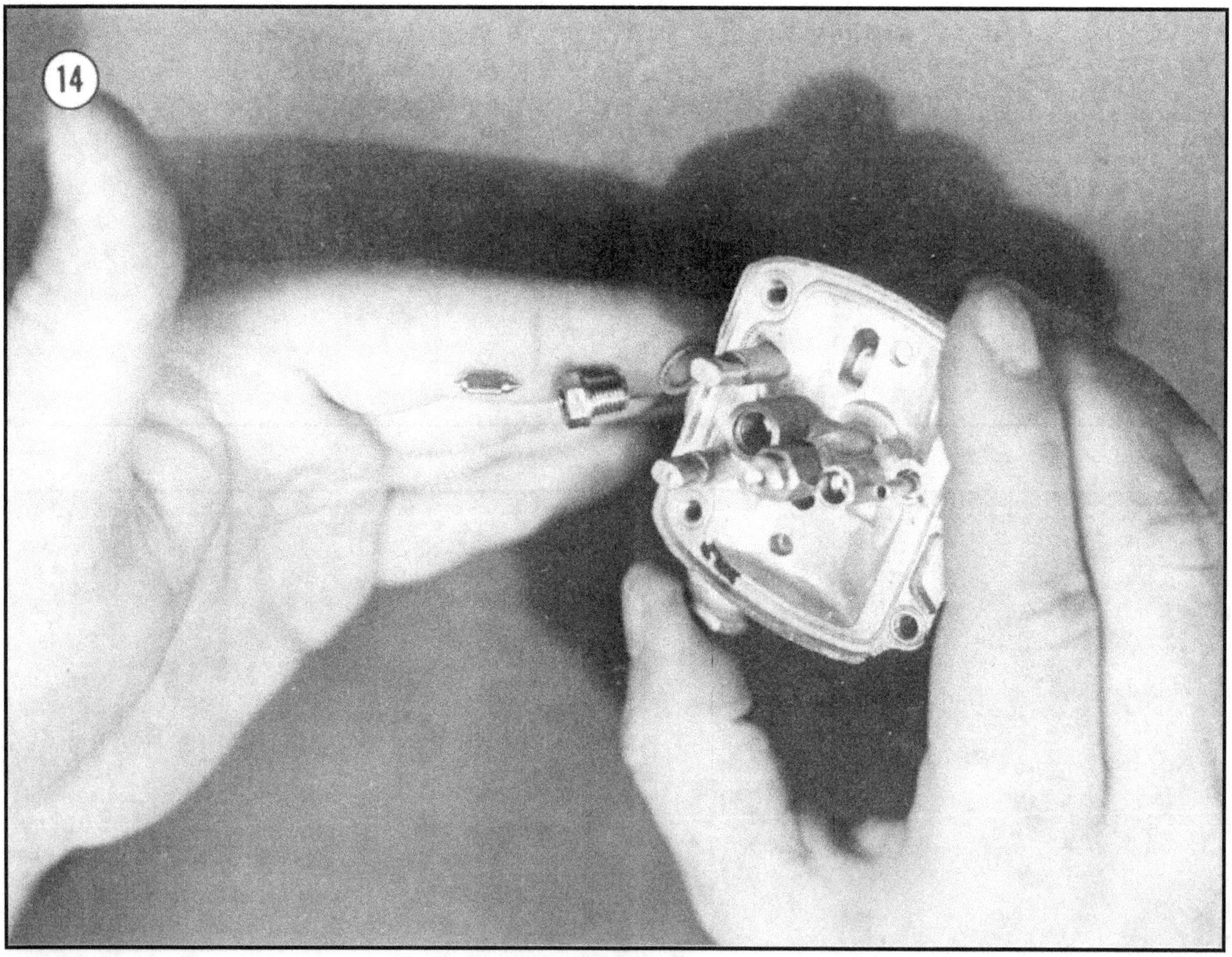

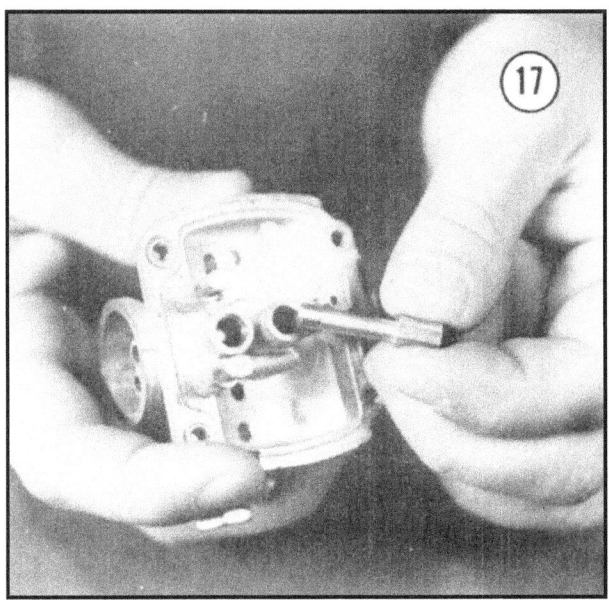

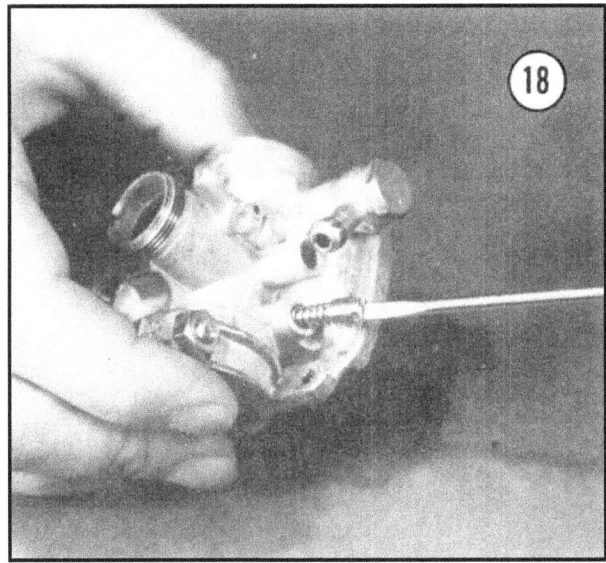

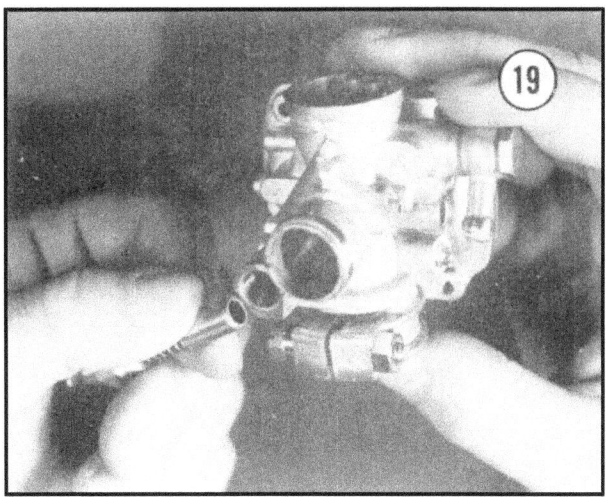

Remove the float chamber body and turn over the mixing body. Let the float arm rest on the needle valve without compressing the spring. Measure the distance from the top of the float to the float bowl gasket surface. If it is not within 0.04 in. (1.0mm) of the amount listed in **Table 1**, bend the float tang up to increase or down to decrease the measurement (**Figures 20 and 21**).

Table 1   FLOAT LEVEL SETTINGS

Model	Float Level (mm)
50cc	23.0
JT series	None
60cc (except JT)	23.0
80cc	20.5
100cc	22.0

CAUTION
Solvent will ruin the rubber-tipped plunger. Pull the plunger out as shown in **Figure 19.**

9. Assembly is the reverse of these steps.

CARBURETOR ADJUSTMENTS

Float Level Adjustment

The carburetor float level was set at the factory, but rough riding, a worn needle valve, or a bent float arm can cause the float level to change. If float level rises, a rich mixture will result, leading to poor performance and spark plug fouling. If the float level is too low, the resulting lean mixture can cause engine damage.

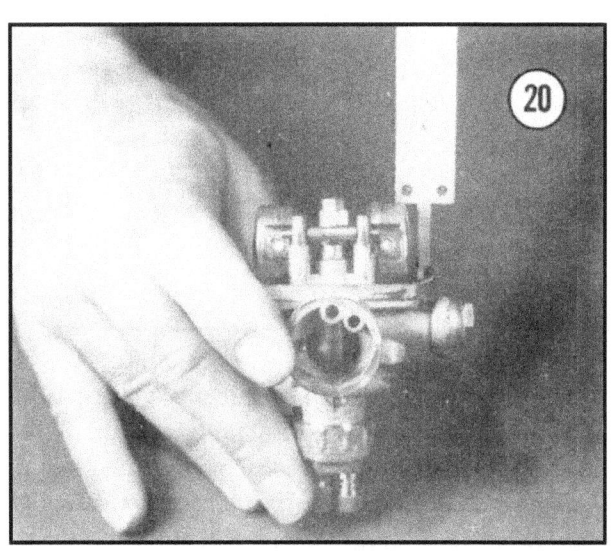

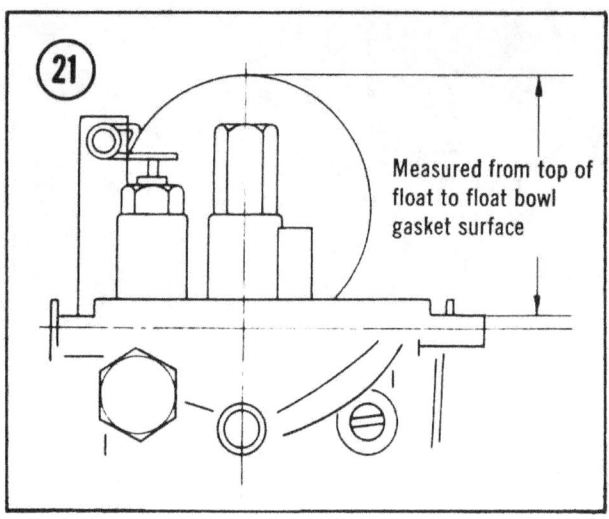

Idle Mixture and Idle Speed Adjustment

To adjust the idle mixture (idle air), turn the idle air screw in until it lightly seats, then back it out the amount listed for your model in **Table 2**. See **Figure 22** for idle air location.

Table 2   IDLE AIR SCREW SPECIFICATIONS

Model	Turns Out
50cc	1¼
60cc	1½
YG1 series	1½
YG5S, G6S, G6SB, G7S	1¾
YL2 series	1½
L5T series	1¾

Setting idle speed requires a fully warmed up engine. With the engine running, turn the knurled rod on top of the carburetor as shown in **Figure 23** until the engine idles at about 1,400 rpm, or at the rpm of your preference.

Throttle Cable Free-play

1. First, check free-play at the throttle grip. With the grip at a fully closed position, slide the outer cable housing away from the grip to determine existing cable free-play. **Figure 24** shows that you need .04 inch (1mm) free-play. To make an adjustment, loosen the locknut as shown and twist the adjuster. Tighten locknut.

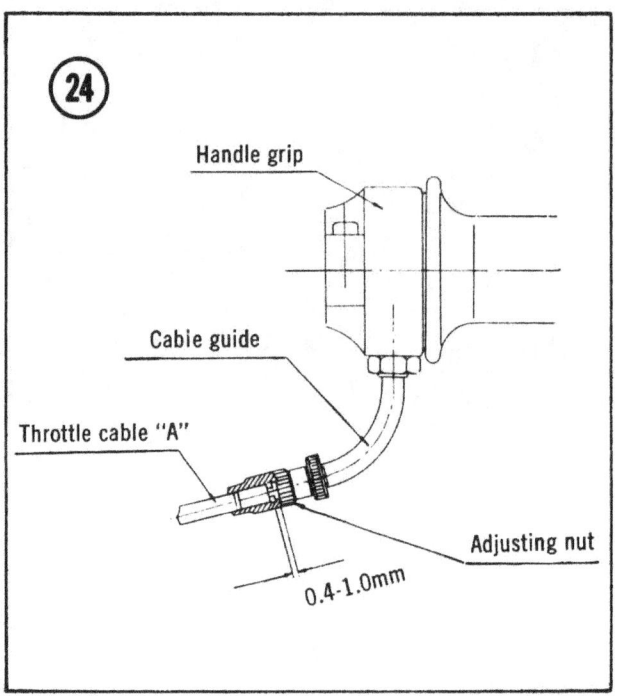

2. Check for 1mm of throttle cable free-play where it enters the carburetor cap. **Figure 25** shows where to check. To determine existing free-play, gently lift the outer cable housing until you feel resistance. Let the cable housing drop until seated. This dropped distance is the free-play. To change it, loosen the locknut and screw the adjuster in or out to obtain correct free-play.

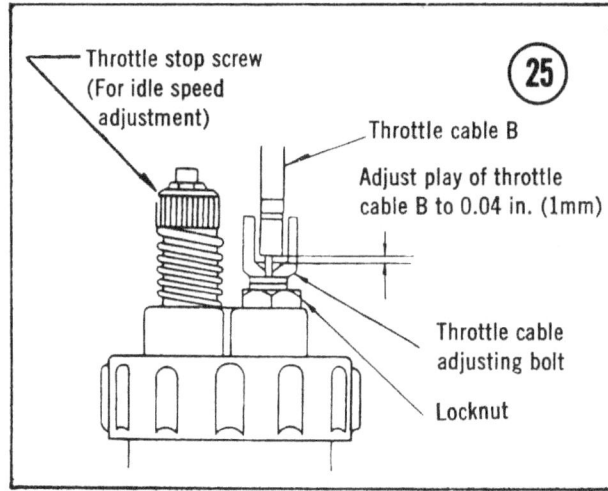

Throttle Cable Replacement

Figure 26 shows the entire cable assembly. To replace any cable requires disconnecting the entire assembly at points 1, 2, 3, and 4 as described in the following steps.

> NOTE: *If you have a non-Autolube machine, disregard any mention of the Autolube system.*

1a. *Mikuni*—Screw off the carburetor cap and lift out the slide.

1b. *Teikei*—Remove the mixing chamber top and lift out the slide.

2. Unhook the throttle cable from slide. On the Mikuni you must lift the spring out of the slide, then remove the butterfly-shaped needle retainer plate. On the Teikei, it slides out a slot in the side of the slide.

3. Remove both screws that hold the throttle grip retaining caps together, then pull the caps apart for access to the cable end.

4. Slide the end of the wire from its anchor hole in the actuator.

> NOTE: *For proper installation, notice which direction the wire is wound around the actuator channel.*

5. At the Autolube pump, unhook the Autolube wire. You must rotate the pulley by hand to provide slack in the wire, then slip the end out of its anchor hole in the pulley.

> NOTE: *Notice the direction this wire is wound around the pulley to ensure correct installation later.*

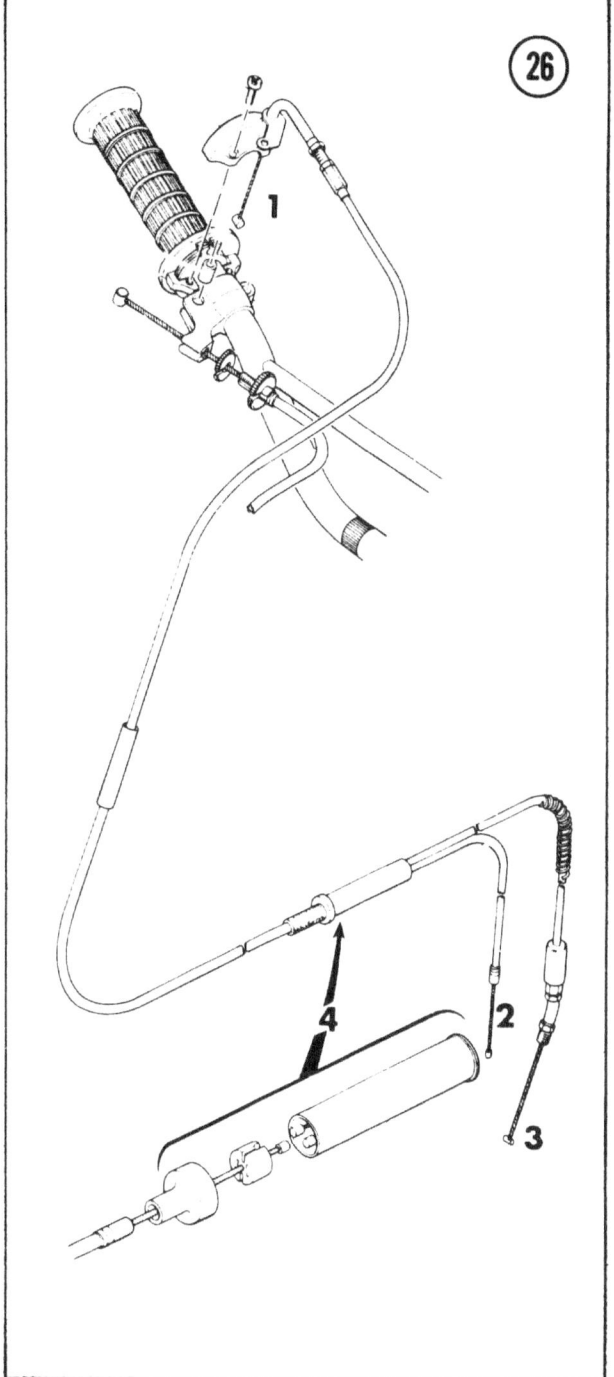

6. Grasp both ends of the cable junction and pull apart (4, Figure 26).

7. To replace any cable, unhook its end from the white plastic junction piece, pull the cable out of the junction box, slide the new cable in, and hook it onto the white piece.

Reassembly

1. Hook up the Autolube cable first, then the cable to the carburetor, and lastly, the cable to the throttle grip.

2. You must adjust throttle cable free-play, idle speed, and Autolube cable (pump mark alignment).

AIR FILTER

Paper Filters

All models except the JT series have paper filament filters. This filter is located in the metal can directly above the engine and below the gas tank (**Figure 27**).

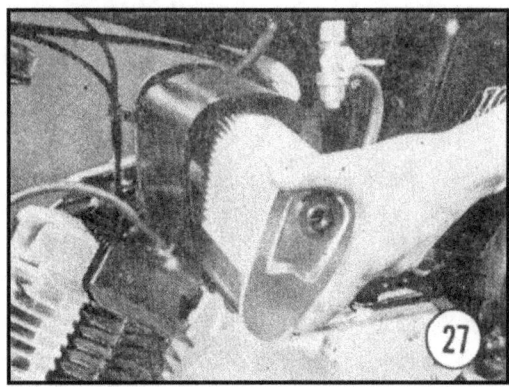

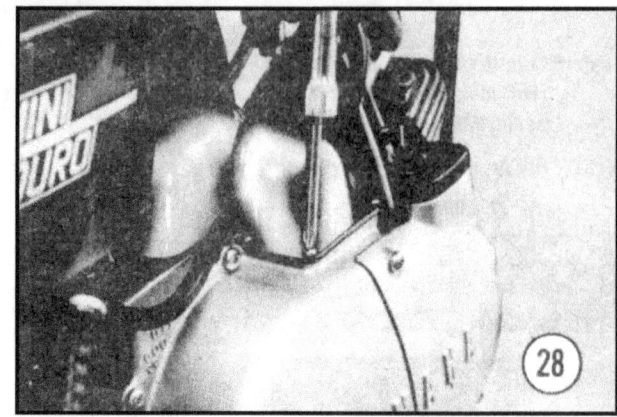

To clean this type filter, carefully tap against a hard surface to dislodge the dirt. If possible, blow it off with air. If the entire outer filter surface remains brown from dirt, replace it.

The filter should never be exposed to water, oil, or solvents. Water swells the fibers and restricts air flow. Take special care when washing the machine.

> NOTE: *Do not run your machine without an air filter. Dirt would quickly enter the engine and cause expensive damage. Also, less air restriction would lean out the fuel/air mixture.*

JT1 and JT1L Foam Filter

Your models were originally equipped with a foam filter shaped as shown in **Figures 28 and 29**. You are strongly advised to replace this filter with the type now installed on JT2 models. Service procedure for the old style filter is not given due to the frequency of failure and lack of efficiency of the filter.

JT2 and JT2M Foam Filter

Your air filter is a porous foam filter that must be clean and oil impregnated to work properly. Although there is no set time or mileage maintenance interval, filter condition will be the best

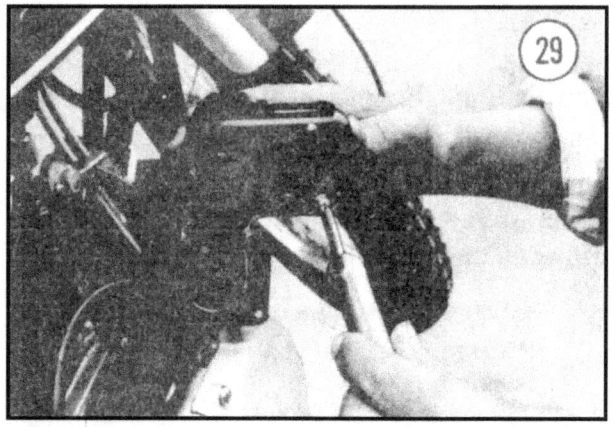

judge. If the entire outer filter surface is brown with dirt, or there are large patches of caked dirt, clean it. Try to clean the filter after every full day in the dirt. You cannot clean the filter too often.

> NOTE: *Do not run your machine without an air filter. Dirt would quickly enter the engine and cause damage. Also, less air restriction would lean out the fuel/air mixture.*

1. Remove the air filter case. As shown in **Figure 30**, it is held by 1 bolt.

2. Remove the air filter case cap and pull out the filter (**Figures 31 and 32**).

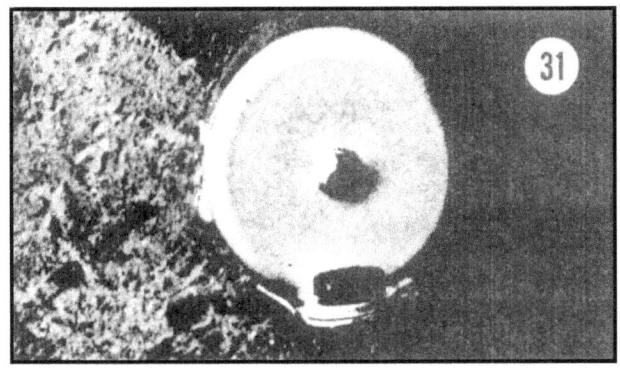

3. Rinse the filter in solvent until all dirt is gone. Squeeze dry. If you want to be thorough, wash in soap and water to remove remaining dirt particles. Rinse, squeeze out, and let dry.

4. Pour SAE 20 or 30 oil onto the filter and work it into the foam. Squeeze out the surplus. It should be impregnated, but not dripping. Use special filter oil or the same brand oil used in your Autolube (or pre-mix) to maintain oil compatibility.

5. Grease the mating end of the filter cap, then install the filter. This will prevent dirt from seeping past the end.

FUEL TANK

Figures 33, next page (MJ1/MJ2) **and 34**, below (YJ1/YJ2) provide details for fuel tank removal and installation.

For the U5 series, remove and install fuel tank as follows.

1. Remove seat bracket bolts and seat. See **Figure 35**.

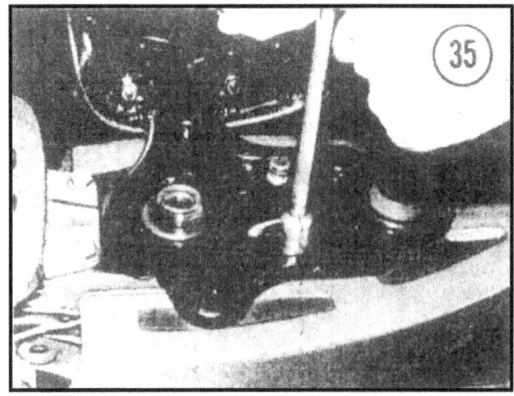

2. Remove luggage rack bolts. **See Figure 36**.
3. Remove bolts at top of rear shocks.
4. Remove fuel tank. See **Figure 37**.
5. Installation is the reverse of these steps.

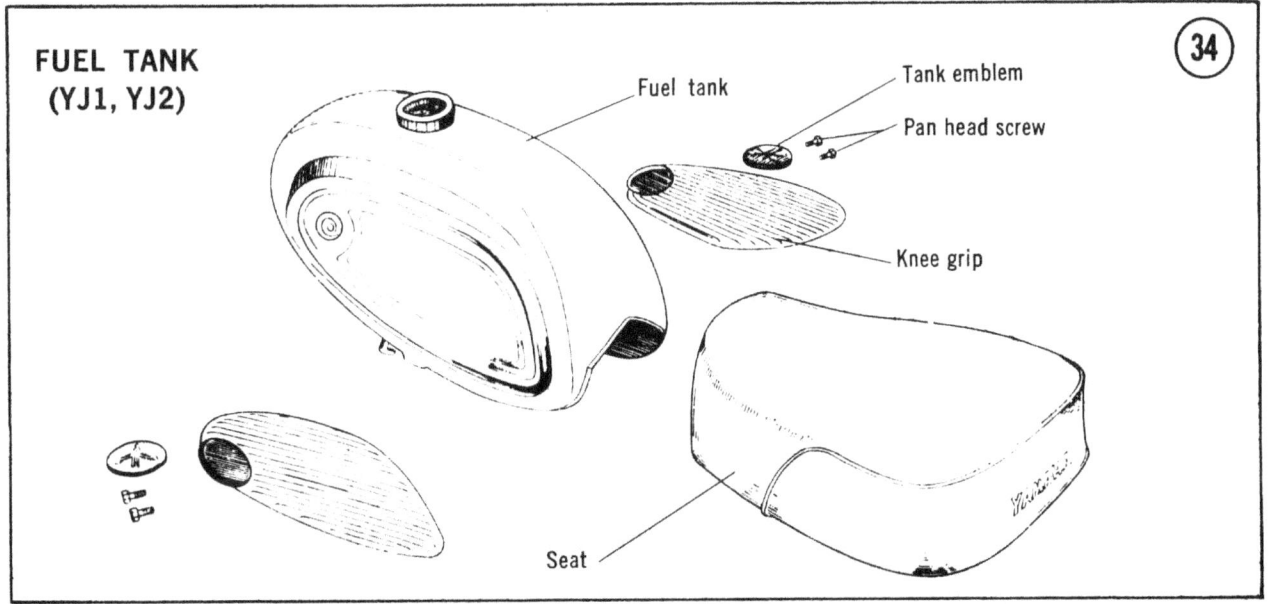

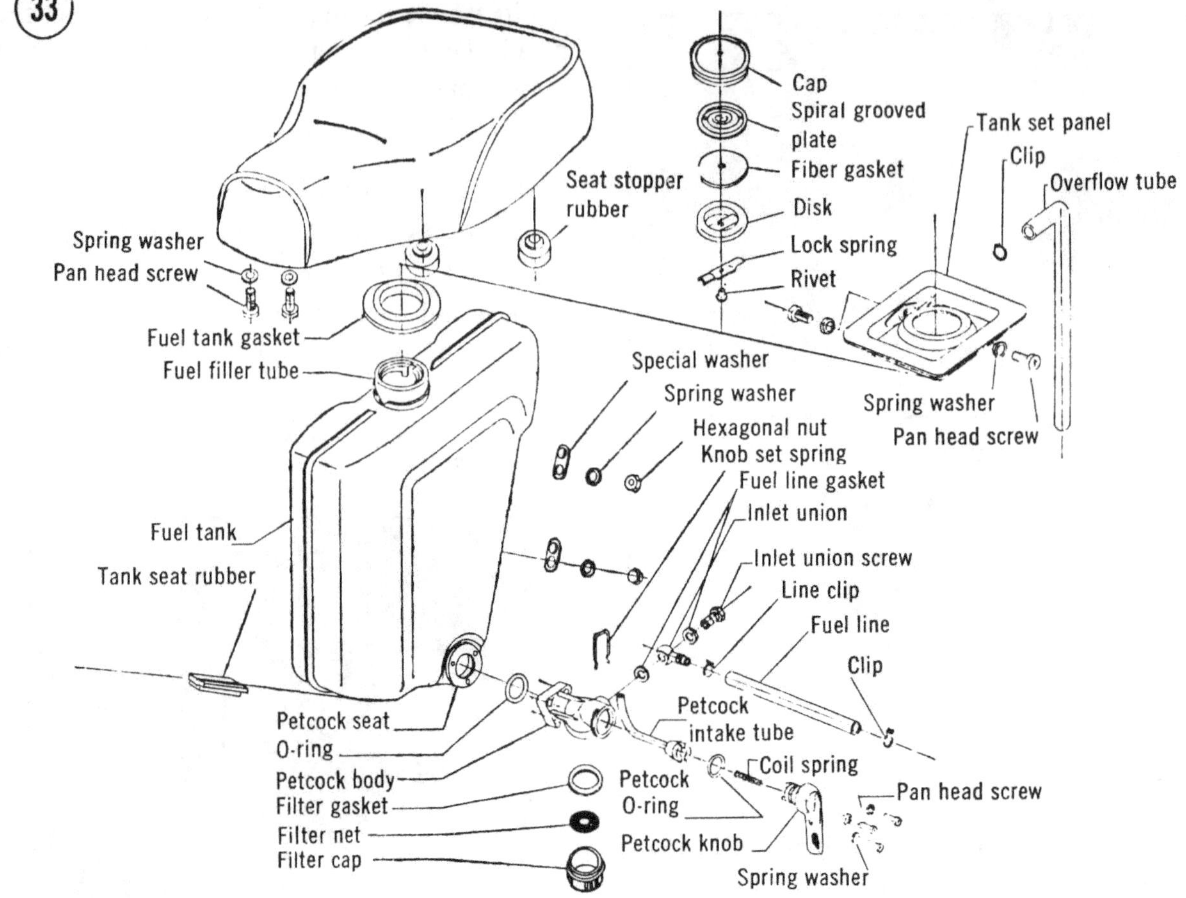

FUEL TANK—MJ1, MJ2

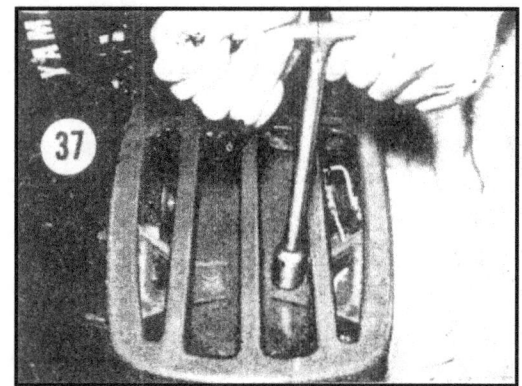

CHAPTER SIX

ELECTRICAL SYSTEM

This chapter includes repair and replacement procedures for the ignition, lighting, and charging systems.

MAGNETO IGNITION SYSTEM

Models using this system are:

U5	G5S
YJ1/2	G6S
JT1/2 series	G6SB
YG1 series	G7S

Figures 1 (next page) **and 2** illustrate a typical point-type magneto system. As the flywheel rotates, a voltage is developed in the magneto ignition source coil. When the breaker points open, this energy (150-300 volts) is discharged into the ignition coil, where it is stepped up to the 12,000-14,000 volts required to jump the gap at the spark plug.

> NOTE: *Early YG1 series combined the primary source coil and ignition coil, and mounted this unit on the magneto backing plate.*

Breaker Point Maintenance

Ignition point contact surfaces become oxidated from electrical arcing, oil film, and condensation. This film is non-conductive, which prevents point contact.

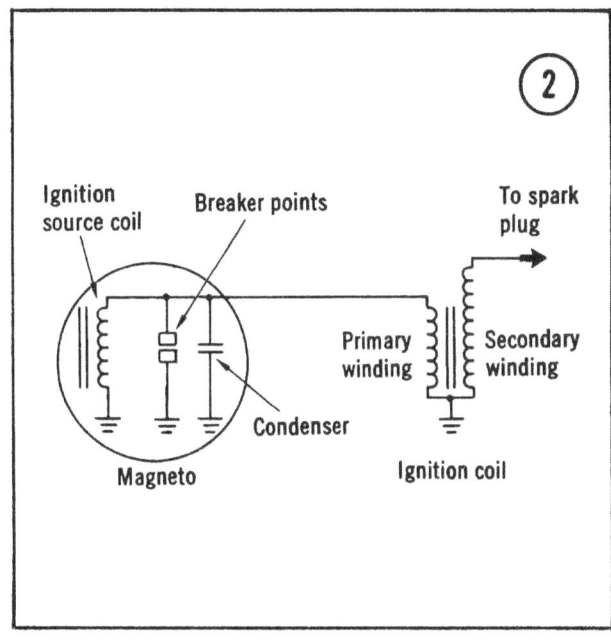

1. If the point surfaces are not heavily pitted, file with a point file (flexstone) to loosen oxidation.

2. Hold points open and spray with an electrical contact cleaner.

3. Let the points snap closed on a piece of hard, uncoated paper, such as a business card, cut into strips. Pull the paper from between the points. Repeat until the paper comes out clean.

> NOTE: *Do not attempt to file away heavy point pitting. Replace instead.*

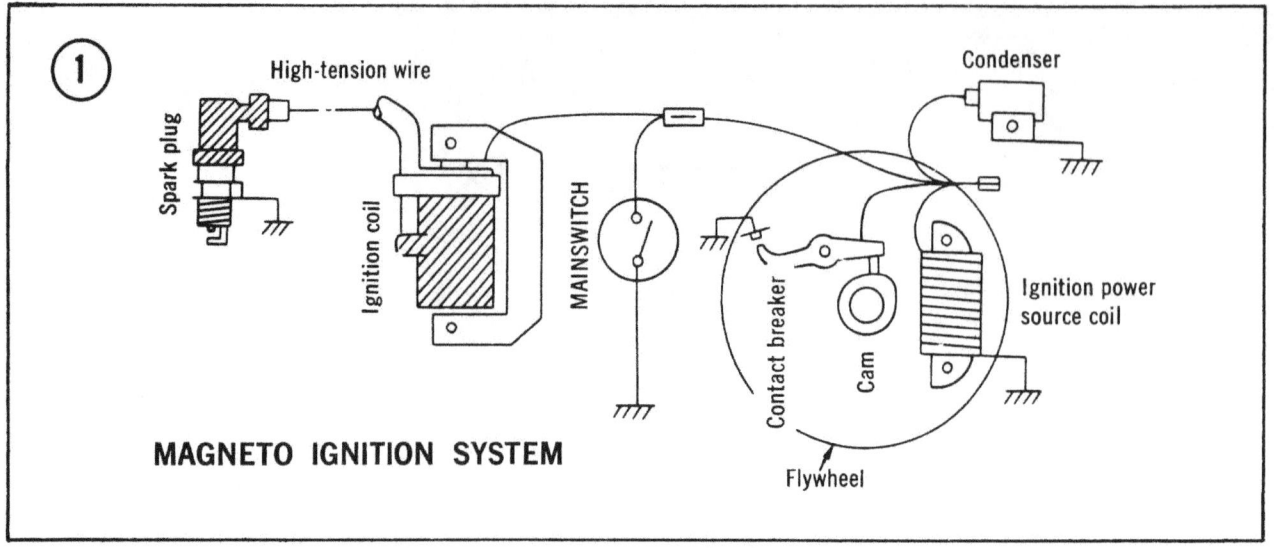

MAGNETO IGNITION SYSTEM

Breaker Point Replacement

The breaker points are attached to a single one complete unit.

1. Remove the rotor (flywheel).
2. Disconnect the condenser-to-breaker points wire at the points. Remove the small locknut and lockwasher, then slip the wire off.
3. Remove screw (8, **Figure 3**) and remove point assembly.
4. To install the points, note the pivot pin protruding out the bottom of the point plate. Insert this pin into its hole in the backing plate, then install and lightly tighten the setscrew.
5. Attach the lead wire from condenser-to-breaker point. Place the wire between flat washer and lockwasher, then tighten the locknut.
6. Apply a couple of drops of light oil to the felt lubricator (12, Figure 3) to decrease rubbing block wear.
7. Spread a light coat of grease on the tapered crankshaft end, install the flywheel locating key, then slide the flywheel on, add flat washer, lockwasher, and tighten the locknut.
8. Replacing the point changes ignition timing. Reset it.

Ignition Timing

Any change in point gap, including normal point wear, point maintenance, or point replacement, changes ignition timing. It is essential to adjust ignition timing whenever the points are serviced.

NOTE: *If you are checking ignition timing, always clean points first.*

Timing is critical and requires correct tools. If you do not have these tools, let a Yamaha dealer set the timing. Tools needed are:

a. Dial gauge—Yamaha part No. 908-90030-02-00, **Figure 4**

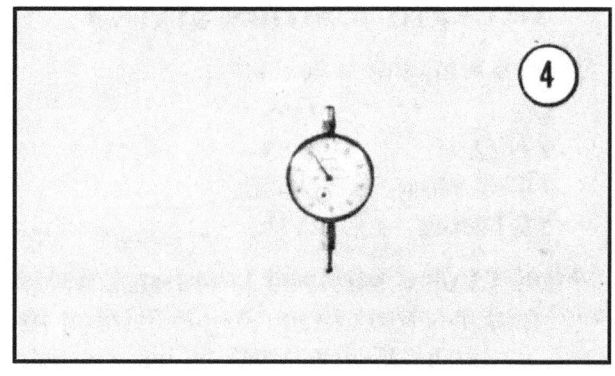

b. Dial gauge adapter Yamaha part No. 908-90010-39-00, **Figure 5**

NOTE: *This tool is used on machines that can be timed without removing the head.*

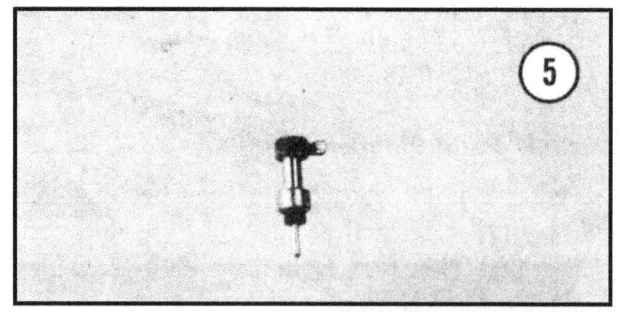

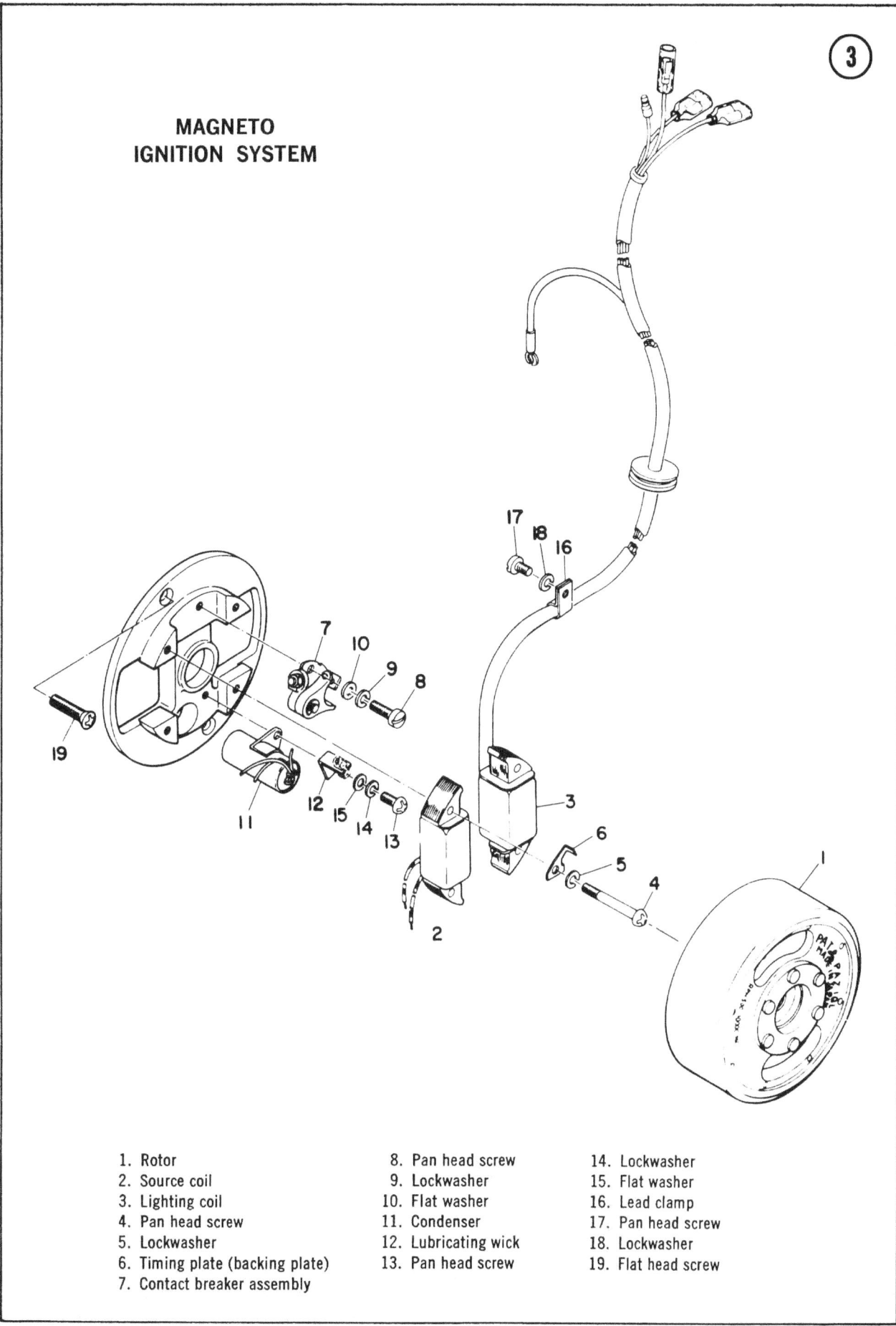

c. Dial gauge stand—Yamaha part No. 908-90010-37-00, **Figure 6**

NOTE: *Used to hold dial gauge if head must be removed.*

d. Dial gauge stand bolt—Yamaha part No. 908-90010-38-00, **Figure 7**

NOTE: *Attaches to stud. Mounting adaptor for tool in Figure 6.*

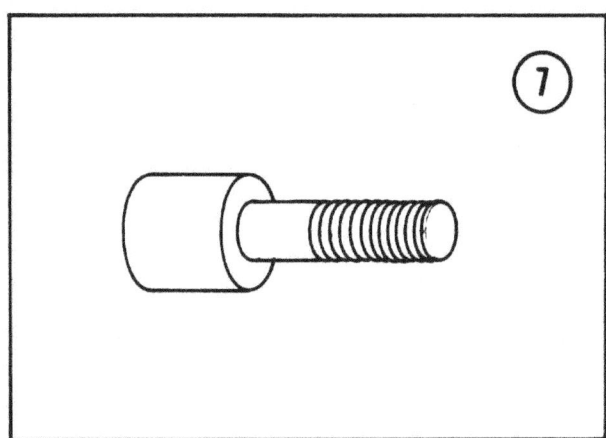

e. Point checker—Yamaha part No. 908-90030-31-00, **Figure 8**

NOTE: *Remove the head for timing if your model's spark plug is tipped more than 7° from straight up.*

1a. On engines that do not require head removal, remove the spark plug. Screw the long gauge needle into the dial gauge. Loosen the gauge stand setscrew and insert the dial gauge into the stand. Tighten the setscrew (**Figure 9**).

1b. On models requiring head removal, remove it as stated in Chapter Three. Mount the dial gauge as shown in **Figure 10**.

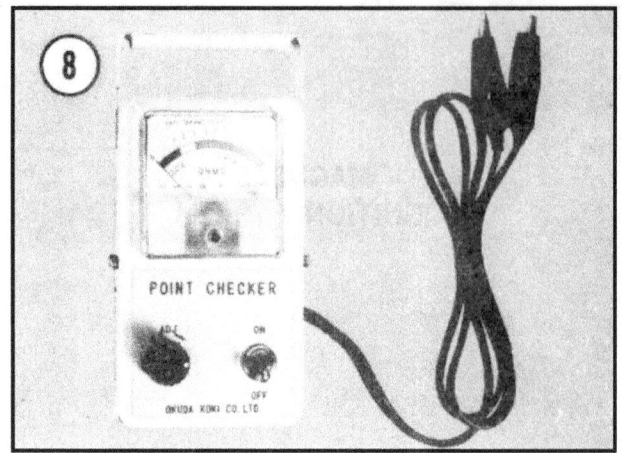

2. Use the dial gauge to find piston top dead center. Starting with the piston low in the cylinder, rotate the crankshaft in either direction until the piston pushes on the dial gauge and the dial needle rotates. The needle will continue sweeping in a counterclockwise direction as long as the piston travels upward. When the needle stops, then reverses its direction of sweep, that stopping point is piston top dead center. Find

top dead center, then rotate the dial gauge face until the *zero* lines up with the needle.

3. Turn the crankshaft backwards in a clockwise direction until tht needle has made 4 complete sweeps of the dial face. This puts the piston 0.0mm before TDC (each sweep of the face equals 1.0mm).

4. Rotate the crankshaft forward (counterclockwise) until you have moved from 4.0mm BTDC to whatever distance is stated in the specifications. If timing must be set at 1.8mm BTDC, you must rotate the crankshaft counterclockwise from the original 4.0mm position until you are only 1.8mm BTDC. From 4.0 to 1.8 millimeter equals 2.2mm, or 2 complete sweeps of the dial, plus 20 of the smallest marks on the dial face.

5. Hook a point checker across the points. To do this, disconnect the magneto wires and isolate the black ignition wire. Connect one point checker lead to the black wire that goes back to the points, then connect the other meter lead to a ground (cylinder fin, engine case).

6. Refer to Figure 3 and loosen the point plate securing screw (part 8) just enough to permit plate movement.

7. Place a screwdriver in the outer plate edge, then rotate the plate until the meter shows the points just opening (**Figure 11**). On the Yamaha meter, the points are closed when the needle is completely to the left side of the scale. The points open just as the needle swings to the right side of the scale. Now tighten the point plate securing screw.

> NOTE: *When the points open, the meter needle will swing only to about 2 ohms, halfway into the green scale.*

8. The point plate tends to move as the setting screw is tightened. It may be necessary to repeat the adjustment and tightening sequence several times.

> NOTE: *Timing tolerance is plus or minus 0.1mm BTDC. If you set timing to occur at 1.8mm BTDC, the points must just open between 1.7 and 1.9mm.*

Condenser Inspection

The condenser acts as a mechanical sponge to soak up electricity when the points start to open.

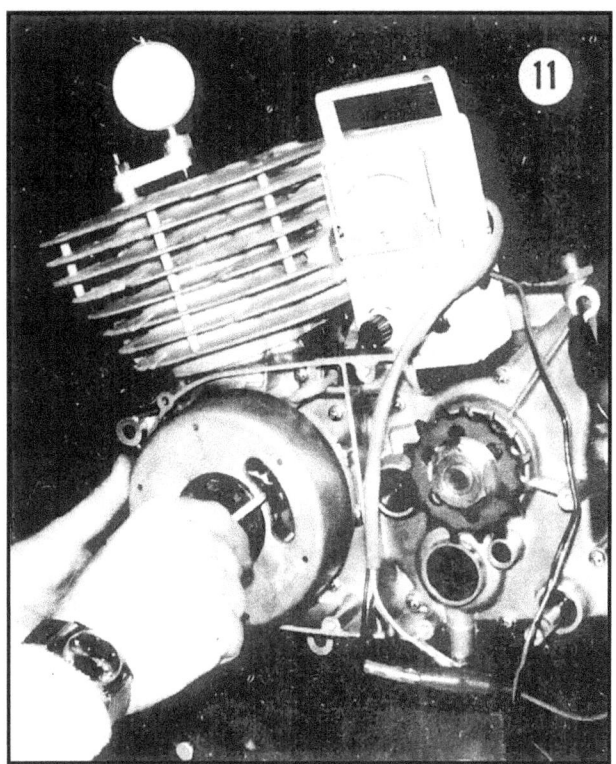

This minimizes arcing and point burning.

Examine both breaker point surfaces to determine if the condenser needs replacement. **Figure 12** illustrates excessive metal transfer from one point to another, which means the condenser is not performing properly. Replace it.

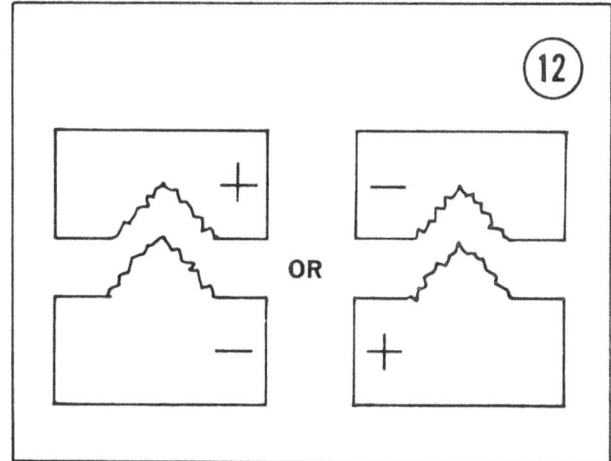

Condenser Replacement

1. Refer to **Figure 13**. Unsolder all wire connections on top of the condenser.

2. Remove the single retaining screw, then lift it out of its hole in the backing plate.

3. Place the new condenser into position, install and tighten the retaining screw.

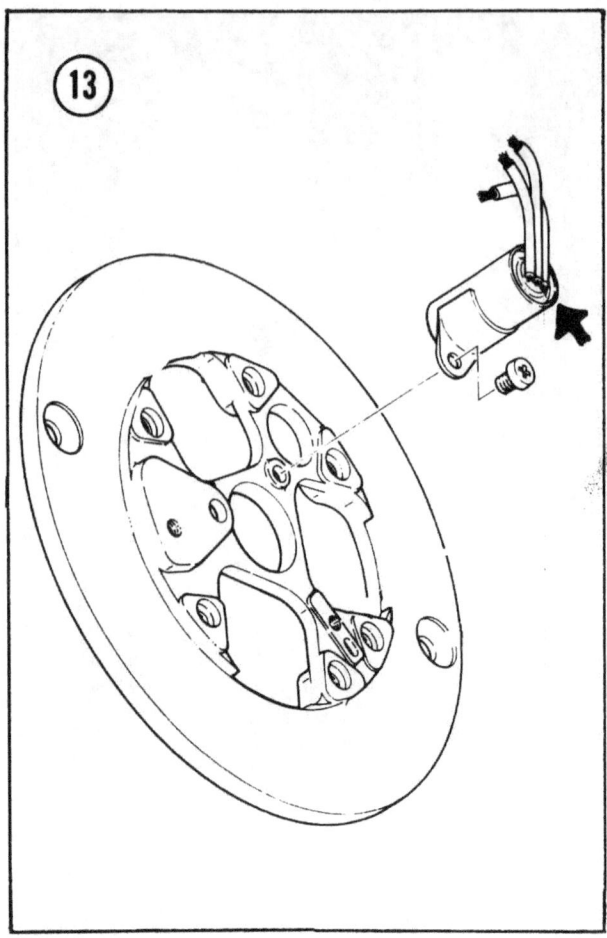

4. Solder all wire connections back on top of the condenser. Do this quickly, and with as little heat as possible, to protect wire insulation and condenser.

BATTERY/COIL IGNITION SYSTEM

This system is used in the following models:

U5E	YL2
U5L	YL2C
MJ1/2	5T
YG5T	

Figure 14 illustrates the ignition system used on these models. When the points are closed, current flows from the battery through the primary winding of the ignition coil, thereby building a magnetic field around the coil.

When the points open, the current is interrupted, causing the magnetic field to collapse. As the field collapses, a very high voltage is induced in the coil secondary winding, which causes the spark plug to fire.

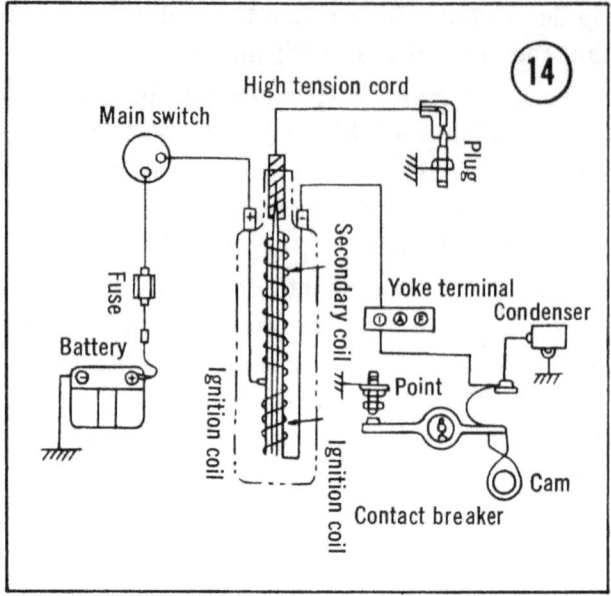

Breaker Point Adjustment

Figure 15 illustrates the type of ignition points used on these motorcycles. Before adjusting the points, examine them for any pitting or burning. Pitted or burned points will impair ignition system performance and should be replaced.

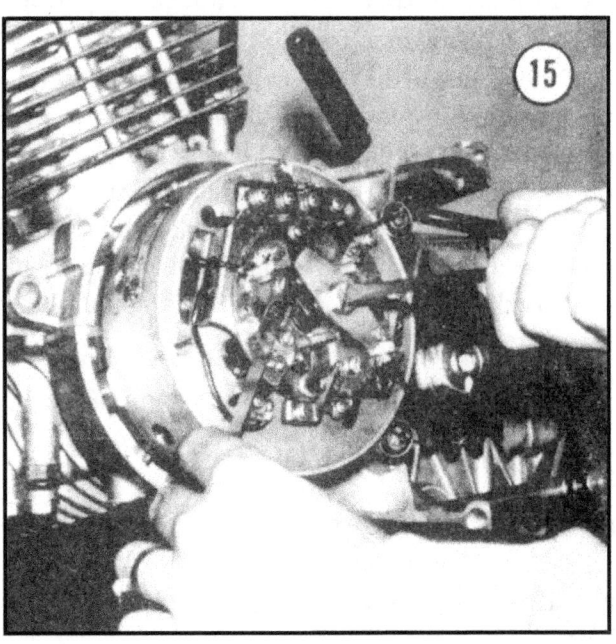

To check point gap, rotate the armature slowly until the points are open to their widest position, then measure the gap with a feeler gauge. The gap should be 0.012-0.015 in. (0.3-0.4mm) for all models. Note that any pitting of the points will make accurate measurement of the gap impossible.

To change the point gap, you will have to move the point mounting plate. Once the 2 mounting plate screws have been loosened, you can put a screwdriver into the slot in the back of this point (**Figure 16**) and rotate the stationary point closer or farther away from the movable point until correct point gap is achieved. Retighten the point lock screws and check both point gap surface parallelism.

The points must be parallel to each other. One must not be tipped away from the other.

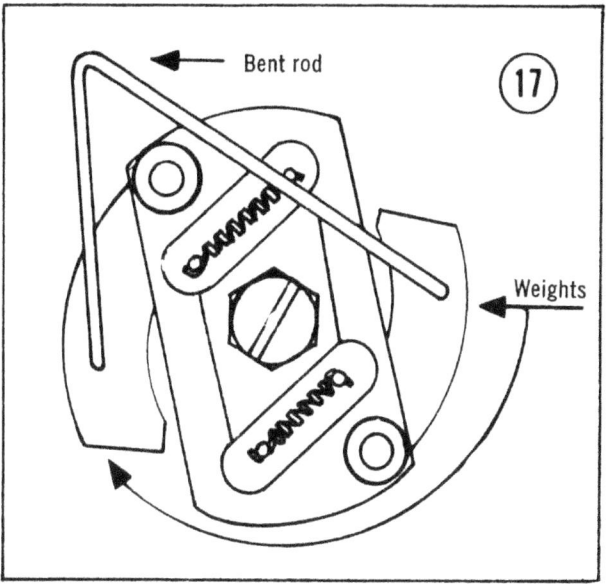

Breaker Point Maintenance and Replacement

Point maintenance and replacement on the generator unit is basically identical to the steps listed previously in the *Magneto* section. Refer to those instructions for details.

Condenser Inspection and Replacement

Inspection and replacement is basically identical to the procedure listed previously in the *Magneto Ignition* section. Refer to those instructions for details.

Ignition Timing

This procedure is basically identical to the timing procedure listed in the *Magneto Ignition* section. Refer to that procedure, except for the following special instructions.

1. Gap the ignition points prior to setting ignition timing.
2. Leave the head attached. Use the dial gauge stand that screws into the spark plug hole to mount the dial gauge.
3. Wedge the ignition advance unit into the full advance position and hold until timing is completed. See **Figure 17**. Bend a piece of coat hanger or welding rod in half, then place the ends into the holes of the advance weight arms as shown. The arms must be forced out to their maximum travel.
4. Battery/coil models do not have a black ignition wire like the magneto models. Instead, trace the breaker point wire back to the orange color-coded terminal on the face of the yoke. Clip your meter lead to this terminal.

CAUTION
The ignition key must be turned OFF. If left on, battery voltage to that terminal will burn out your meter.

Ignition Coil

All secondary ignition coils are basically identical in function. Design differs slightly. The following checks apply to any model you may have.

As a quick check on coil condition, disconnect the high voltage lead from the spark plug and hold it close to the cylinder head in a position so that you can observe the spark as you crank the kickstarter. The ignition coil can be considered in good condition if the spark jumps approximately ¼ inch (7 millimeters) and has a blue-white color.

If an ohmmeter is available, you may wish to measure the resistance of the coil windings. **Figure 18** shows where to touch your ohmmeter leads to measure primary and secondary winding resistances. They both share a common grounding point. See **Table 1** for specifications.

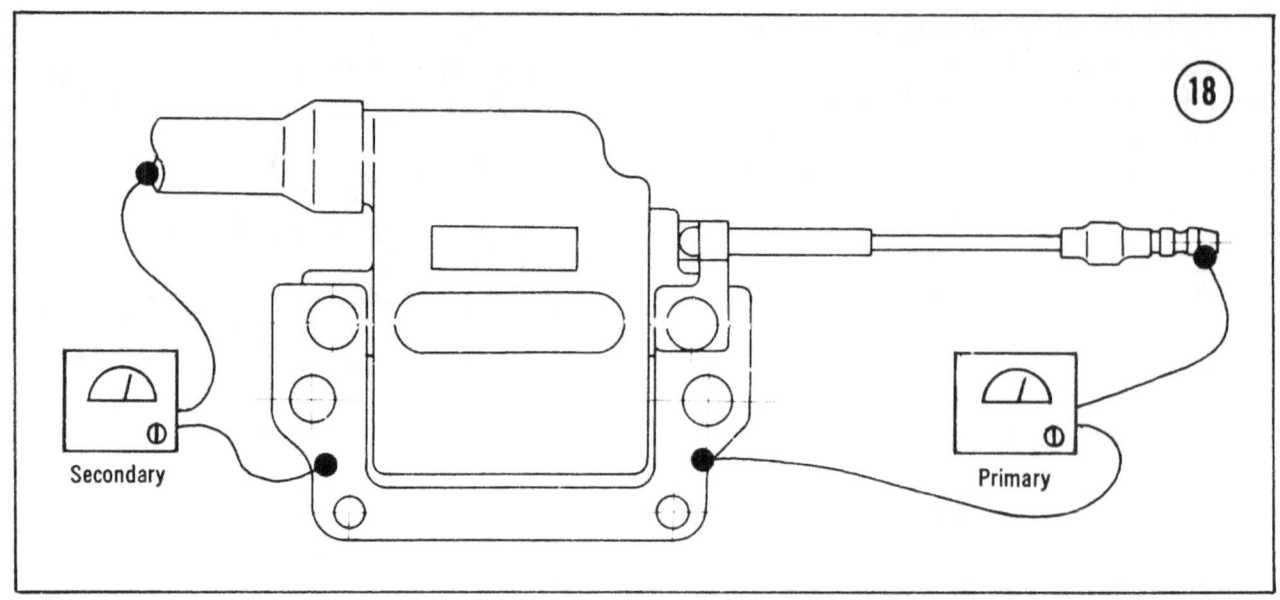

Table 1 IGNITION COIL RESISTANCE SPECIFICATIONS

Model	Primary Resistance (ohms)	Secondary Resistance (ohms x 1,000)
U5 series	4.5	8-9
YJ1/2 series	4.9	8-9
MJ1/2 series	4.9	8-9
JT1/2 series	4.9	11
YG1 series	4.9	4
YG5T	.6	5
G5S, G6S, G6SB, G7S	.6	5
100cc models	4.9	7-8

LIGHTING/CHARGING SYSTEM (MAGNETO)

Lighting and charging voltage is generated in the magneto. Flywheel magnets passing around a lighting/charging coil (2 coils on some machines) induce voltage in this coil. AC voltage comes out the yellow magneto wire, through the switches, then to the headlight and meter lights. Battery charging voltage comes out the magneto, is changed from AC voltage to DC voltage at the rectifier, then to battery and remaining battery-operated parts.

There are 2 slightly different lighting/charging systems used; the early and the late type. The main differences are changes in the battery charging circuit and amount of lighting parts operating on DC voltage.

NOTE: *The JT1 is not equipped with a lighting system.*

Early Type

Models with this lighting/charging wiring circuit are the U5, YJ1, YJ2, and YG1 series. **Figures 19 and 20** provide typical wiring diagrams.

The stoplight and horn operate off DC voltage from the battery. All other lighting parts operate off AC voltage from the yellow magneto wire. The yellow wire also supplies nighttime battery charging voltage at the same time it lights the headlight. The green magneto wire supplies daytime battery charging voltage.

With the engine running, measure AC voltage from the yellow magneto wire to ground. Do not disconnect the yellow wire, just clip onto the yellow wire connector about 6 inches above the magneto. With headlight on, and battery fully charged, you should be within ½ volt of the readings listed in **Table 2**.

If low voltage is present, examine the headlight circuit and battery charging circuit for high resistance such as disconnected wires, corroded junctions, and the like.

Table 2 LIGHTING VOLTAGE SPECIFICATIONS

Voltage/RPM	Remarks
5.5 or more at 2,500	Lights on
8.0 or less at 8,000	Lights on

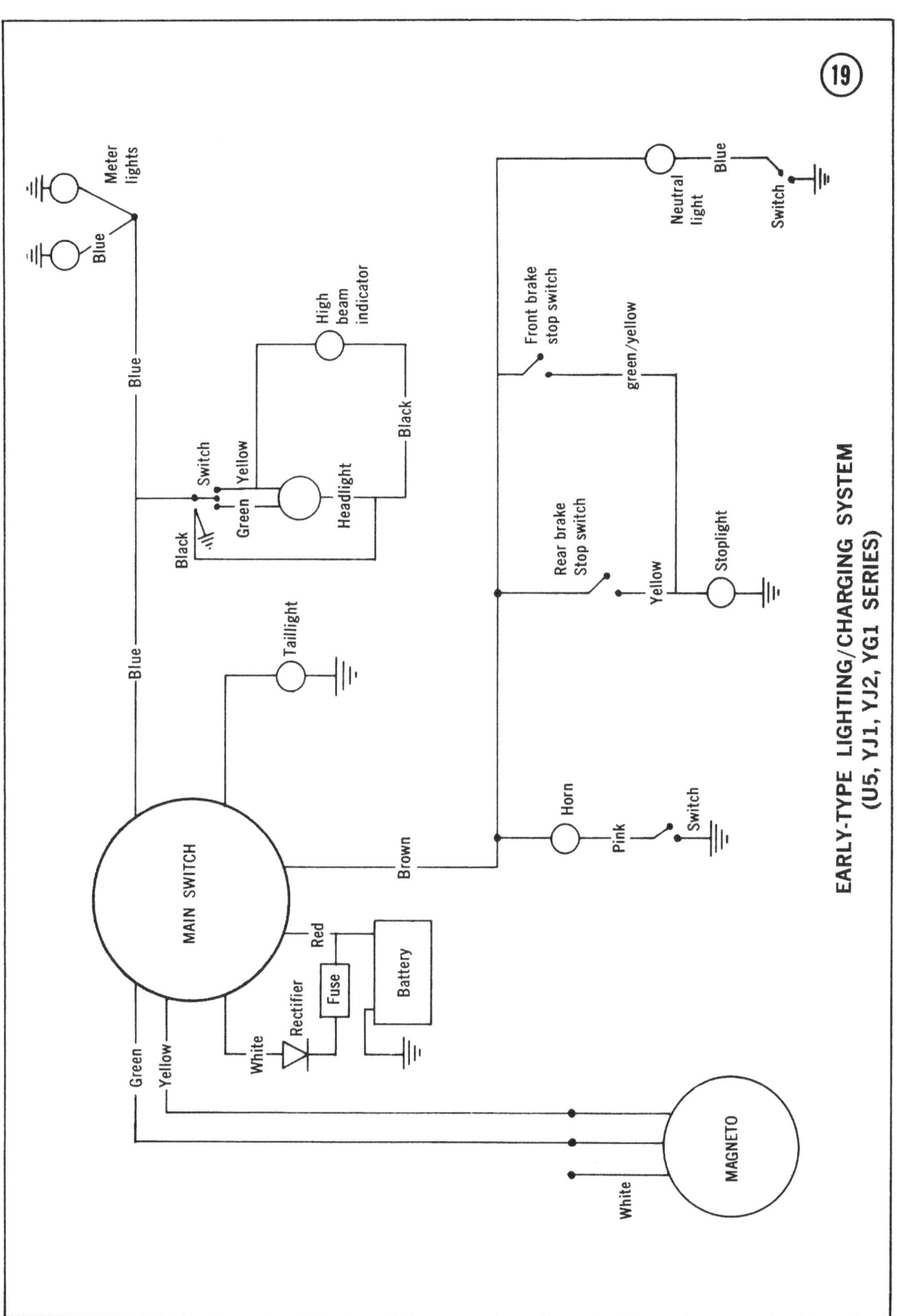

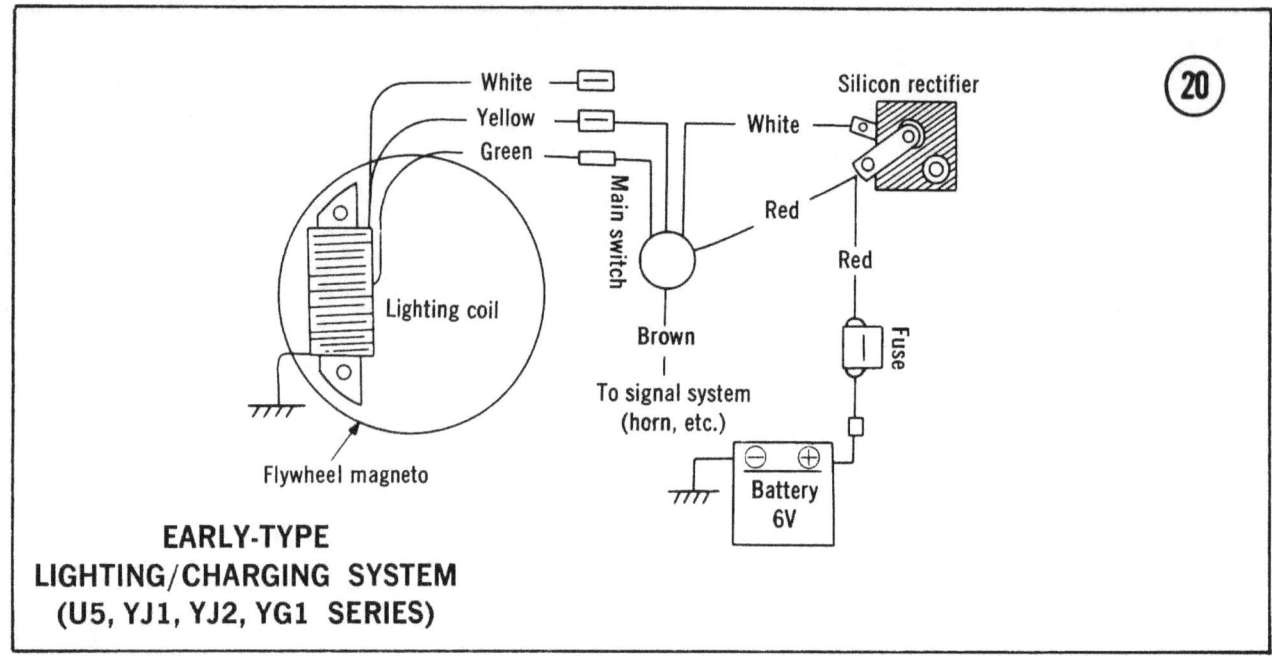

EARLY-TYPE LIGHTING/CHARGING SYSTEM (U5, YJ1, YJ2, YG1 SERIES)

Disconnect the battery red wire and hook an ammeter in series with the red wire, hook meter leads to each separated red wire end. With engine running and lights off, plus battery fully charged, DC amperage should be approximately as shown in **Table 3**.

Table 3 BATTERY CHARGING

Lead	Remarks
Green	Charging starts @ 2,500 rpm 2.0 amperes or less @ 8,000 rpm
White	0.15 amperes or more @ 2,500 rpm 4.0 amperes or less @ 8,000 rpm

Late Type

All models not listed under the old style are covered in this late type procedure.

Figure 21 illustrates the typical wiring diagram for this style charging/lighting system. As shown, the headlight and meter lights are AC volt powered from the yellow (or yellow/white) wire. All other lighting/charging circuits are DC voltage battery powered.

The green (or green/white) magneto wire provides daytime battery charging voltage. The green/red striped magneto wire provides nighttime battery charging voltage. Both charging wires supply AC voltage to the rectifier, where it is changed to DC voltage and passed to the battery and other DC-operated circuits (horn, stoplight, taillight, turn signals).

Battery Charging Circuit Test—Voltage

To test for sufficient DC voltage output to the battery, check voltage output at the battery. Hook the red DC voltmeter lead to red battery terminal. Hook black meter lead to black (negative) terminal or wire. With engine running, check first with switch in daytime position and then nighttime position. Check **Table 4** for correct values.

Table 4 BATTERY CHARGING VOLTAGE

RPM	DC Voltage	
	Lights on	Lights off
2,000	6-8±.5	6-8.5±.5
8,000	8.5±.5	8.5±.5

Battery Charging Circuit Test—Amperage

Separate the battery red wire and connect a DC ammeter in series, a meter lead to each separated red wire end.

With the engine running, compare actual readings with specifications listed in **Table 5**. If

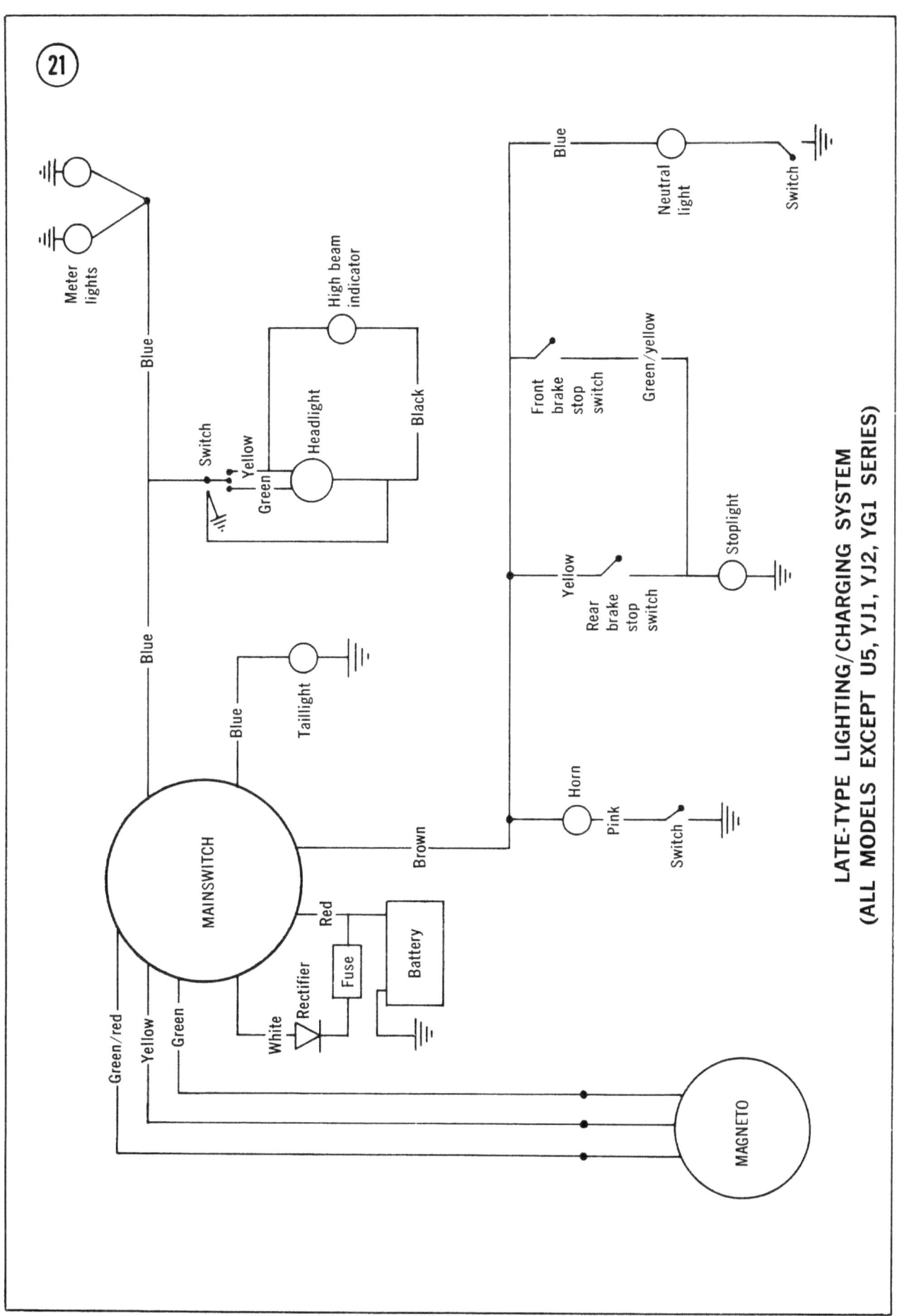

Table 5 BATTERY CHARGING CURRENT

RPM	Amperage (DC) Lights on	Lights off
2,000	1.8±.5	.7±.5
8,000	3.0±.5	1.5±.5

readings are 2 volts or more lower than specified at maximum rpm, check all connections, rectifier, and main switch.

NOTE: *If there is no output, check for disconnected wires, especially solder joints on bottom of main switch (green, green/red, white, and red wires).*

Silicon Rectifier

The rectifier serves 2 purposes. It converts alternating current produced by the magneto into direct current for charging the battery, and also prevents discharge of the battery through the magneto when the engine is not running, or at other times when magneto voltage is less than that of the battery. It is a one-way voltage flow switch.

To check the rectifier, measure its resistance in both forward and reverse directions by measuring resistance in one direction, then reversing ohmmeter leads and measuring resistance again. Forward resistance should be approximately 10 ohms. In the reverse direction, resistance should be essentially infinite. See **Figure 22**.

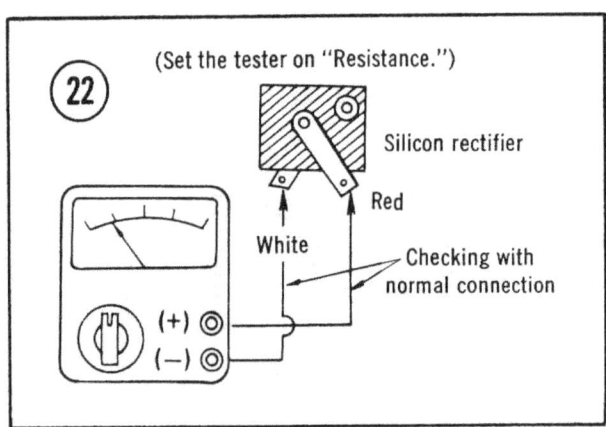

Never connect the rectifier directly to the battery to make a continuity check; doing so will cause instantaneous damage to the rectifier.

LIGHTING/CHARGING SYSTEMS (GENERATOR)

These machines are equipped with a combination starter/generator. **Figure 23** illustrates the electrical system on these models.

Generator Output Test

To check the generator output, proceed as follows.
1. Disconnect the white wire from terminal "A".
2. Disconnect the green wire from terminal "F".
3. Connect terminal "E" to terminal "F" with a jumper.
4. Connect the positive lead of a voltmeter to terminal "A"; connect negative lead to ground.
5. Start the engine and run it at 1,800 rpm. Do not run the engine at a higher speed, as this will damage the coil and other electrical components.
6. If the voltmeter indicates 10 volts or more, the generator is in good condition.

Yoke Inspection

Before checking the yoke, clean it with a rag to remove carbon dust, oil, and other foreign material.
1. With the yoke removed, use an ohmmeter to be sure the positive brush is not shorted to ground.
2. Use the ohmmeter to determine continuity between terminals "M" and "A", and between terminals "A" and "F". If there is no continuity, and coil connections are good, replace the coil. **Figure 24** illustrates this operation.

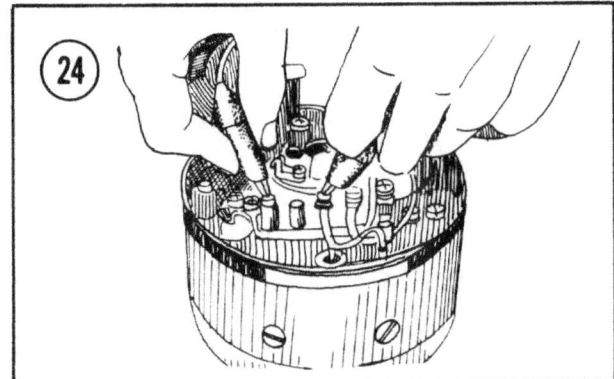

3. Poor brush condition is one of the most frequent causes of generator trouble. Remove the brushes and check them carefully. Each brush

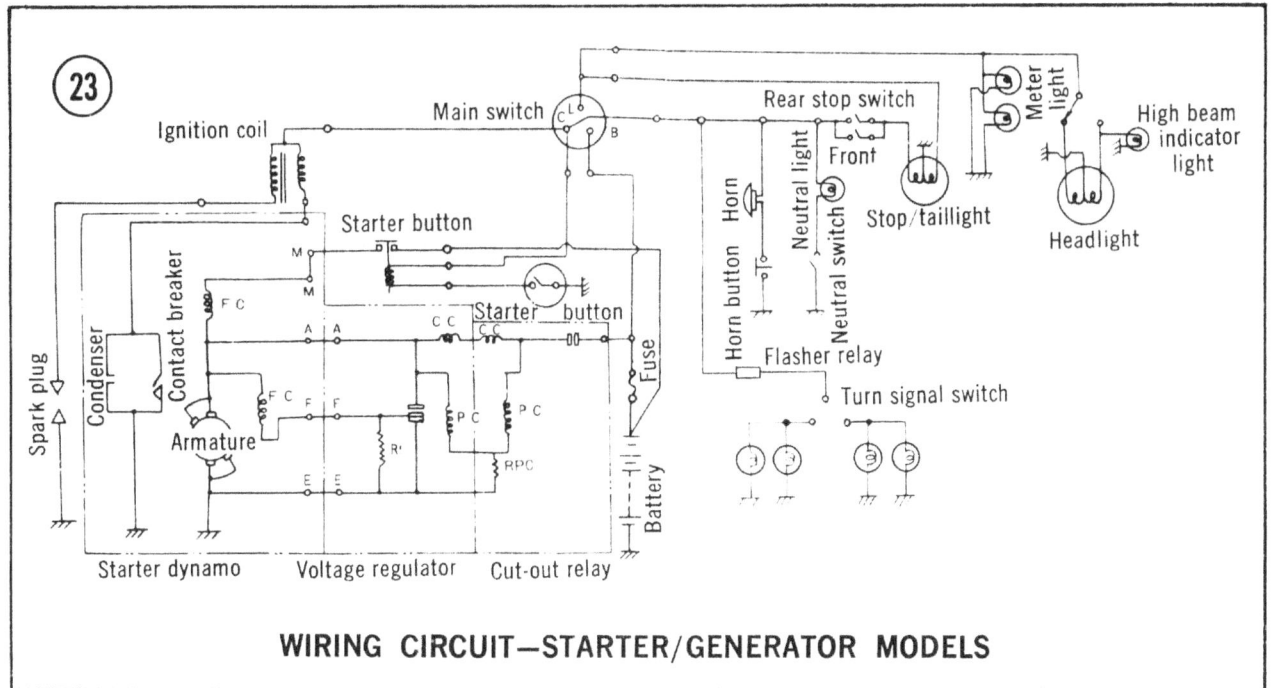

WIRING CIRCUIT—STARTER/GENERATOR MODELS

must contact the commutator with at least three-quarters of its contact surface.

If brushes and commutator are rough, misalignment of the armature and crankshaft may be the cause. Check the tapered bore of the armature and smooth it if any burrs are found. If either brush is worn beyond the minimum length mark, replace both brushes. When you replace brushes, be sure that the positive brush lead doesn't touch the brush holder or the edge of the breaker plate. Also, be sure the negative brush lead doesn't touch the positive brush spring.

Armature Inspection

1. Clean the armature of oil, dust, and foreign material.

2. If the commutator is only slightly rough, it may be polished with No. 400 or 600 emery cloth as shown in **Figure 25**. If the commutator is out-of-round, burned, or too rough to polish, remove it and turn it on a lathe. Do not turn it to a diameter of less than 2.0mm smaller than the original diameter.

3. If the commutator has high mica, undercut the wire segments with a broken hacksaw blade or mica undercutting tool. Be sure that there is no thin mica edge next to the commutator segments. The mica should be undercut 0.02-0.032 inch (0.5-0.8mm). See **Figure 26**.

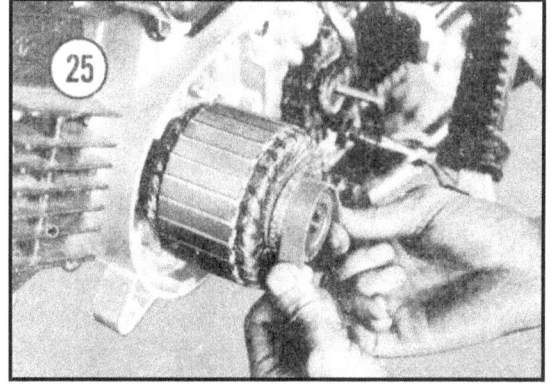

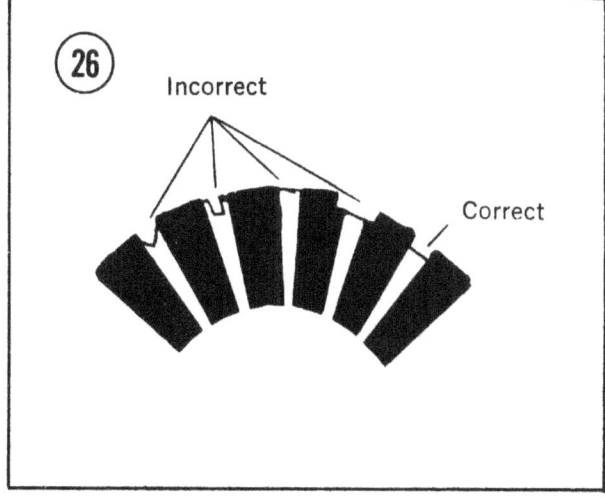

4. Use an ohmmeter or armature growler to determine that no commutator segment is shorted to the shaft. If any short circuit exists, replace the armature (**Figure 27**).

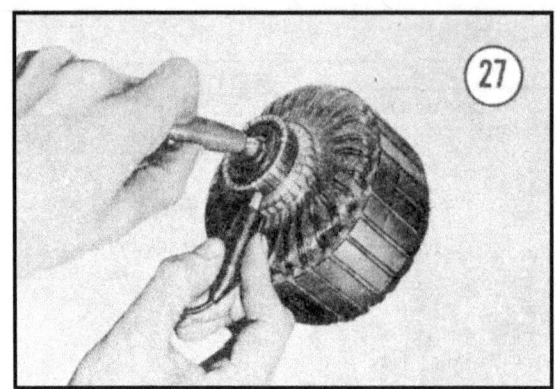

Voltage Regulator Inspection

Varying engine speeds and electrical loads affect output voltage of the generator. The regulator controls output voltage and also disconnects the battery from the generator whenever generator voltage is less than that of the battery, thereby preventing discharge of the battery through the generator.

> NOTE: *Do not attempt to make the following adjustments unless you have a voltmeter of known accuracy.*

To measure no-load voltage, disconnect the red wire from the regulator, then connect red voltmeter probe to the red regulator wire. Ground the negative lead of the voltmeter. Start the engine and allow it to run at 2,500 rpm. **Figure 28** illustrates the connection. If the voltmeter does not indicate 15.8-16.5 volts, adjust the regulator output voltage with the adjustment screw on the regulator shown in **Figure 29**.

To measure cut-in voltage of the cutout relay, disconnect the wire from terminal "A" on the generator. Connect the positive lead of the voltmeter to terminal "A"; ground the negative lead. Start the engine and slowly increase its speed as you observe the voltmeter. The cutout relay should close between 12.5-13.5 volts.

Under normal circumstances, the cutout relay will rarely, if ever, need adjustment. If the contacts are pitted or worn, dress them with fine emery cloth before adjustment.

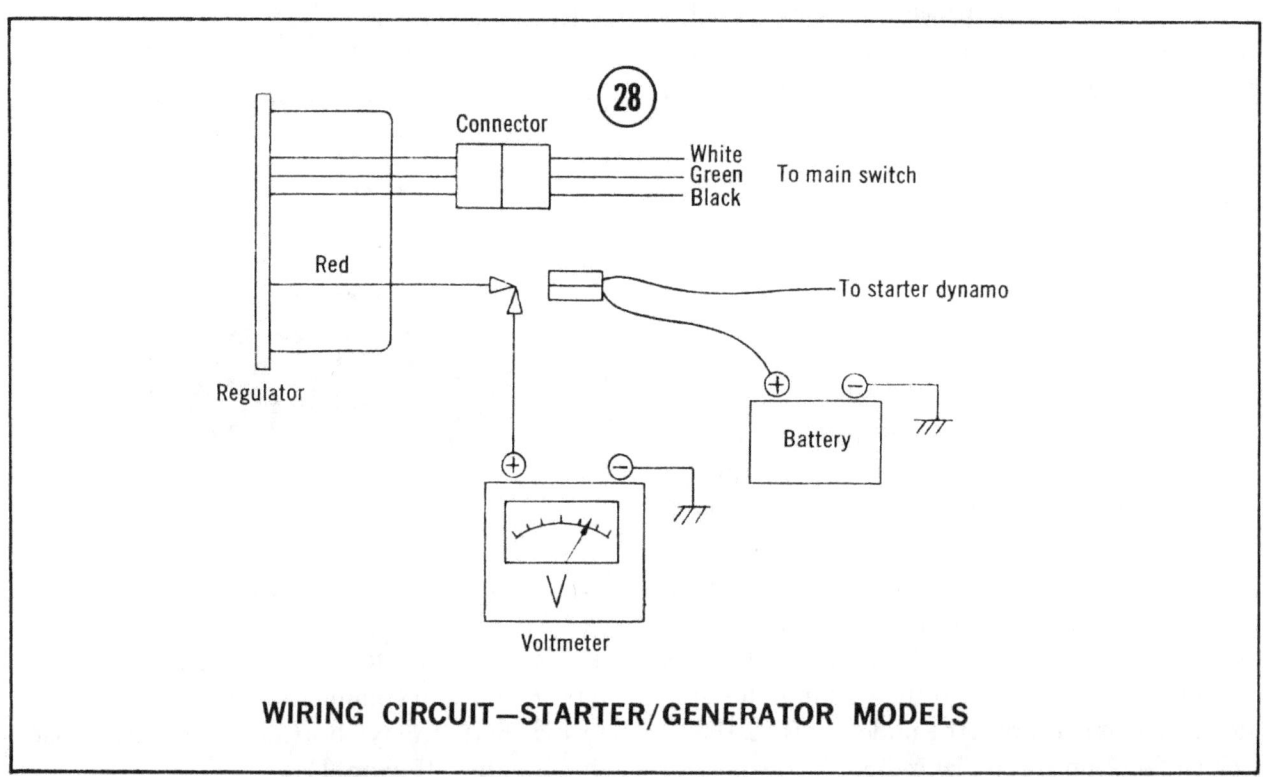

WIRING CIRCUIT—STARTER/GENERATOR MODELS

Battery

All models except those with electric starters have 6-volt batteries which supply power for the horn, stoplight, and turn signals on machines so equipped. Machines with self-starters are equipped with a 12-volt battery.

Check the battery occasionally for sulfation or deposits in the bottom of the cells. If any such conditions are noted, or if the battery will not accept a charge, it should be replaced.

Normal battery life is two to three years. This can be shortened by any of the following.

1. Overcharging. Do not use any charger rated over 1 amp-hour. This includes most auto battery chargers (**Table 6**).
2. Leaving the battery in a discharged condition.
3. Freezing.
4. Allowing the electrolyte level to drop below the plates.
5. Adding anything but distilled water to the electrolyte.

If the motorcycle is inactive for an extended period, the battery should be removed, fully charged, and stored in a cool, dry place. Recharge the battery before returning it to service.

The main switch is a self-contained unit. Most inspection and troubleshooting is directed to the soldered wire connections on the bottom of the main switch. Physically pull at each connection to determine that each solder joint is firmly anchored. Any wire with a broken solder joint will result in no battery charging voltage to the battery. In addition, the battery charging voltage will be redirected in the magneto and sent to the headlight. The headlight will burn out if the battery charging circuit is disconnected.

Carefully try to solder the connection that is broken. Avoid extended heating on this main switch.

WIRING

Figure 30 is a wiring diagram of a typical old-style electrical system.

Figure 31 is a typical wiring diagram for flywheel magneto electrical systems used on all models except those listed for Figure 30.

Table 6 BATTERY STANDARDS

Item	Standard
Specific gravity	1.26 to 1.27
Initial charging current	0.2 amp for 25 hours
Charging current	0.2 amp for 13 hours

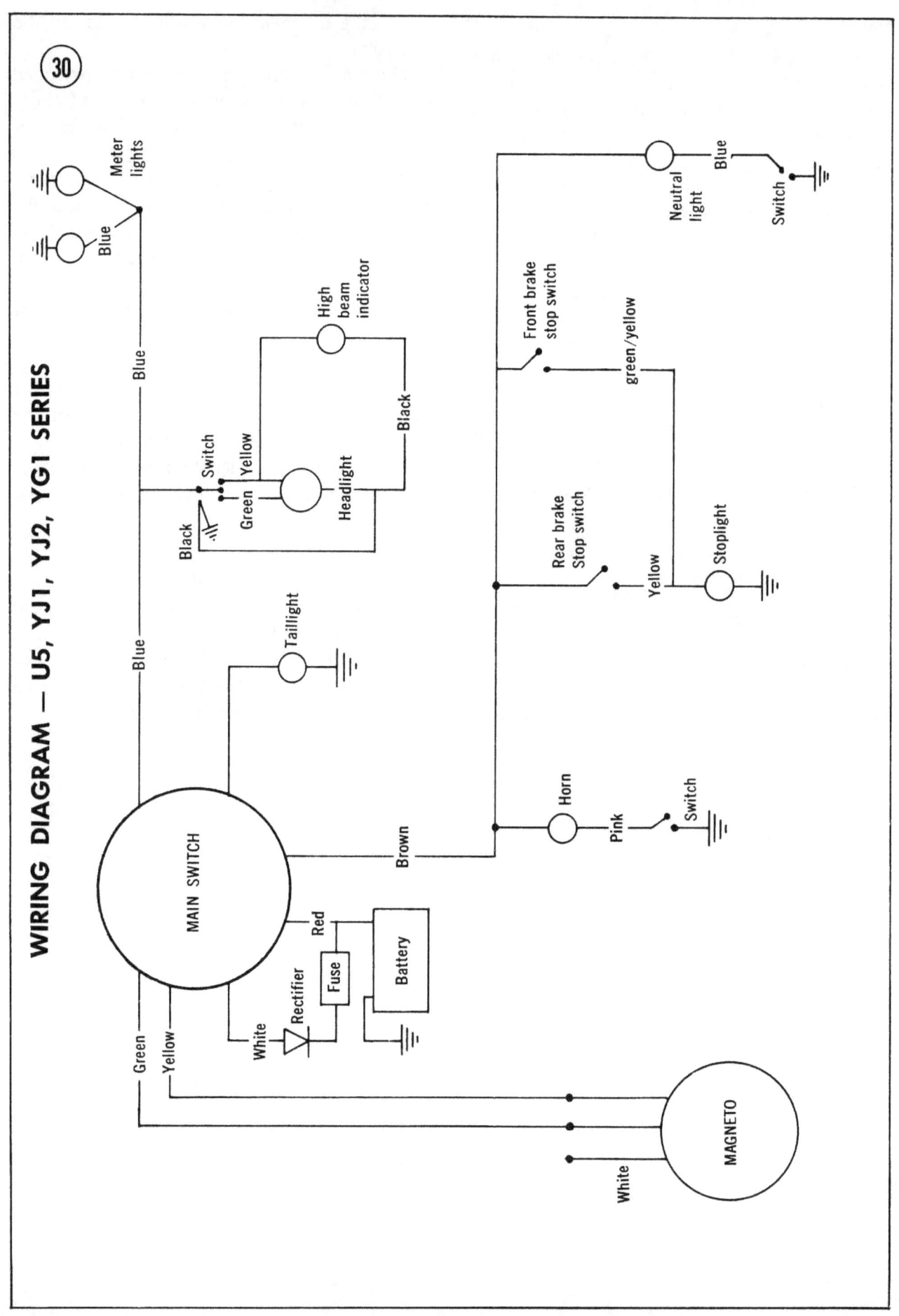

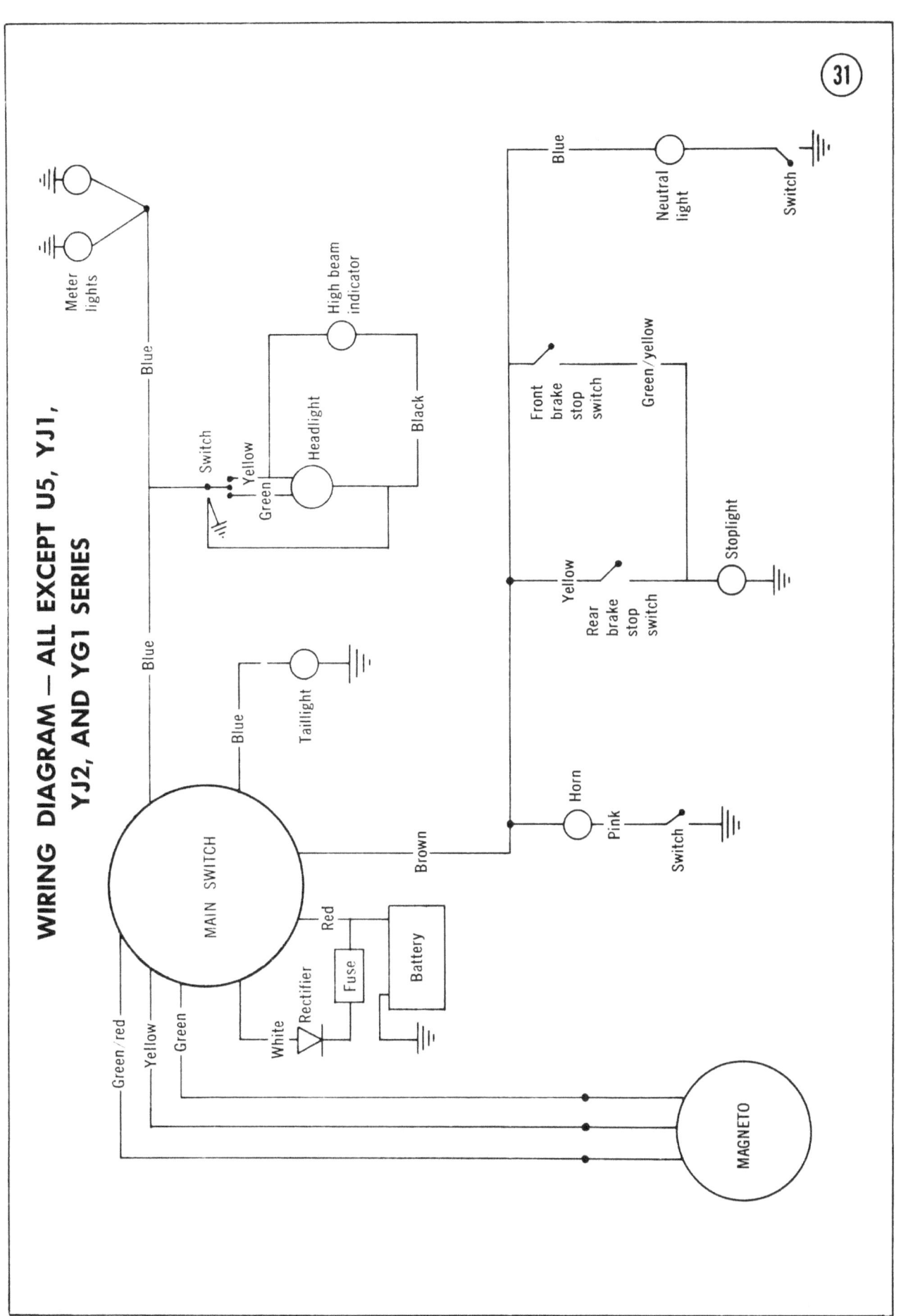

CHAPTER SEVEN

CHASSIS

FRONT WHEEL (ALL MODELS)

Description

Figure 1 identifies the front wheel assembly for the YG1 series. **Figure 2** identifies all parts of the front wheel on all other models.

Removal/Installation

1. Disconnect brake cable at front brake lever.
2. Disconnect the brake cable and speedometer cable (if equipped) at the front wheel (**Figure 3**).

3. Place a box or other support under the motorcycle so the front wheel is off the ground.
4. Loosen the axle nut as shown in **Figure 4**.
5. Insert the shank of a screwdriver through the hole in the end of the axle, then simultaneously

twist and pull the axle out. Support the wheel during this procedure as it will drop down with axle removal.

6. Remove axle bolt spacer. See **Figure 5**.
7. Installation is the reverse of these steps. Be sure the spacer listed in Step 6 is installed. Oil its lip edges prior to inserting it through the oil seal.

Runout Inspection

1. To check wheel rim runout, assemble the wheel and axle, then clamp the axle to a table so the wheel spins freely.
2. Mount a dial indicator (**Figure 6**) or use a stationary pointer. If using a pointer, place the tip within ⅛ inch of the rim.

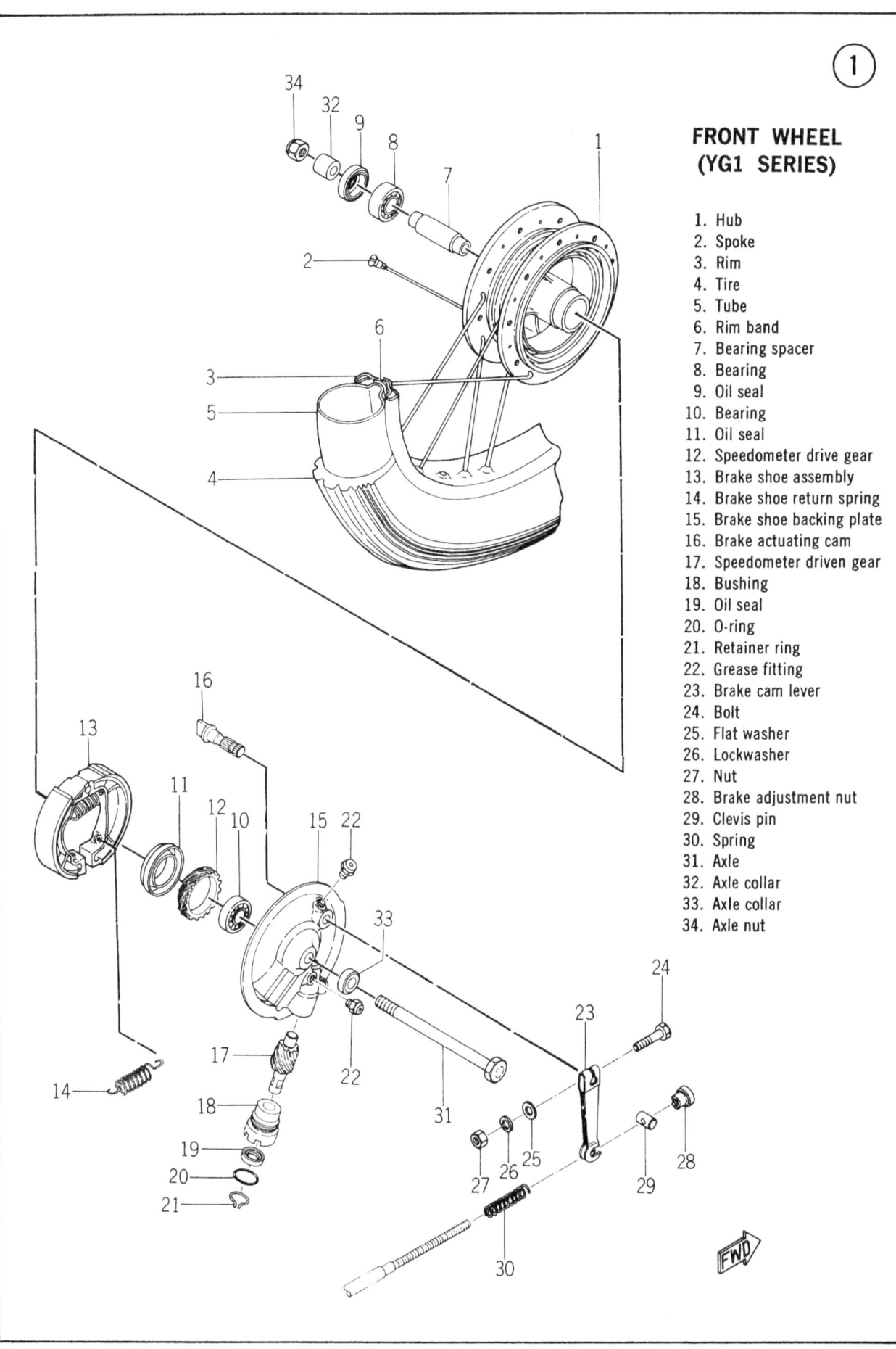

FRONT WHEEL (YG1 SERIES)

1. Hub
2. Spoke
3. Rim
4. Tire
5. Tube
6. Rim band
7. Bearing spacer
8. Bearing
9. Oil seal
10. Bearing
11. Oil seal
12. Speedometer drive gear
13. Brake shoe assembly
14. Brake shoe return spring
15. Brake shoe backing plate
16. Brake actuating cam
17. Speedometer driven gear
18. Bushing
19. Oil seal
20. O-ring
21. Retainer ring
22. Grease fitting
23. Brake cam lever
24. Bolt
25. Flat washer
26. Lockwasher
27. Nut
28. Brake adjustment nut
29. Clevis pin
30. Spring
31. Axle
32. Axle collar
33. Axle collar
34. Axle nut

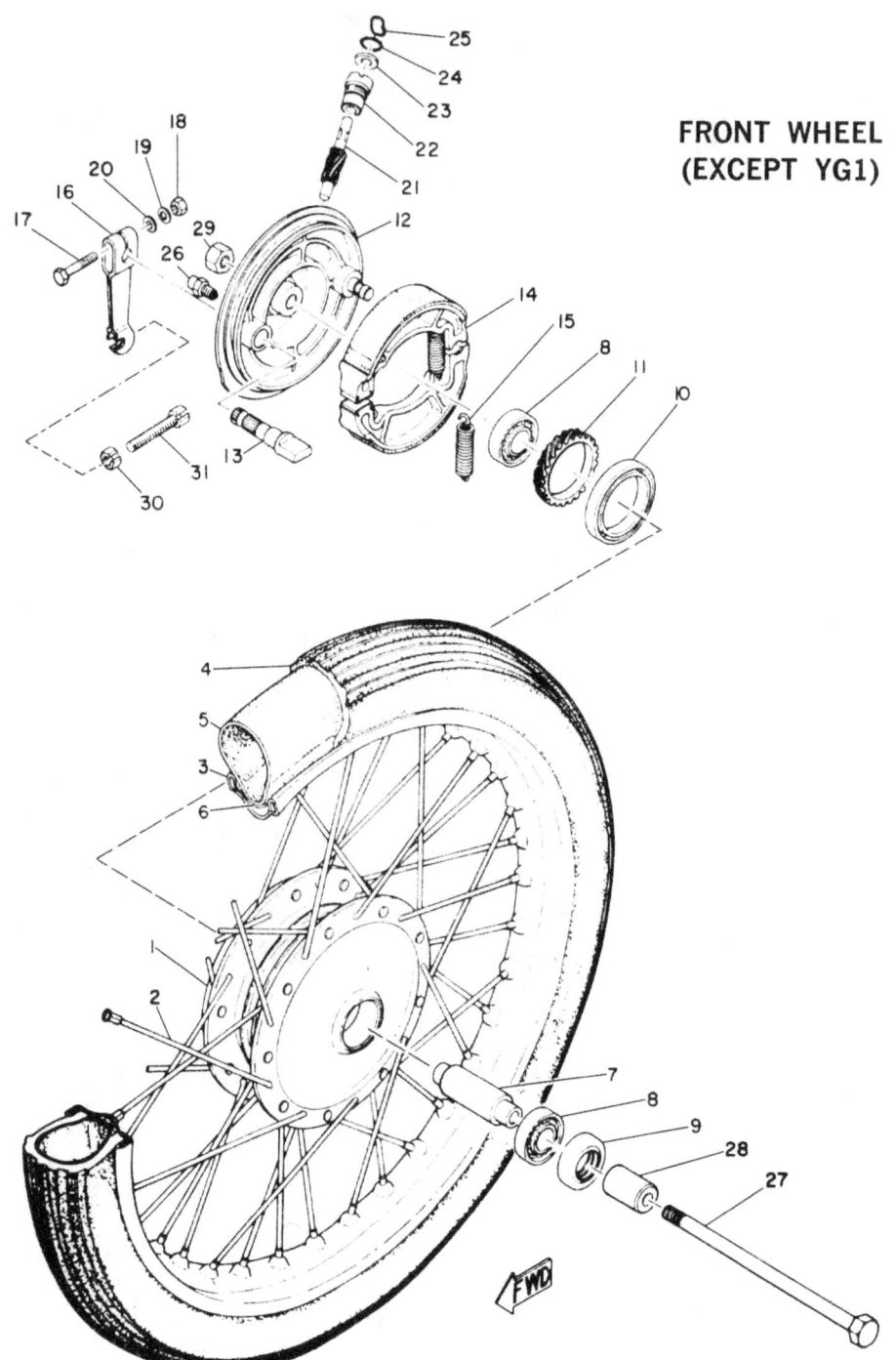

FRONT WHEEL (EXCEPT YG1)

1. Hub
2. Spoke
3. Rim
4. Tire
5. Tube
6. Rim band
7. Bearing spacer
8. Bearing
9. Oil seal
10. Oil seal
11. Speedometer drive gear
12. Brake shoe backing plate
13. Brake actuating cam
14. Brake shoe assembly
15. Brake shoe return spring
16. Brake cam lever
17. Bolt
18. Nut
19. Lockwasher
20. Flat washer
21. Speedometer driven gear
22. Bushing
23. Oil seal
24. O-ring
25. Retainer ring
26. Grease fitting
27. Axle
28. Axle collar
29. Nut
30. Brake adjustment nut
31. Brake adjustment bolt

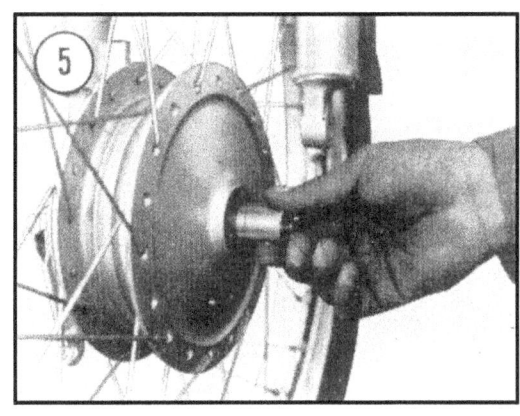

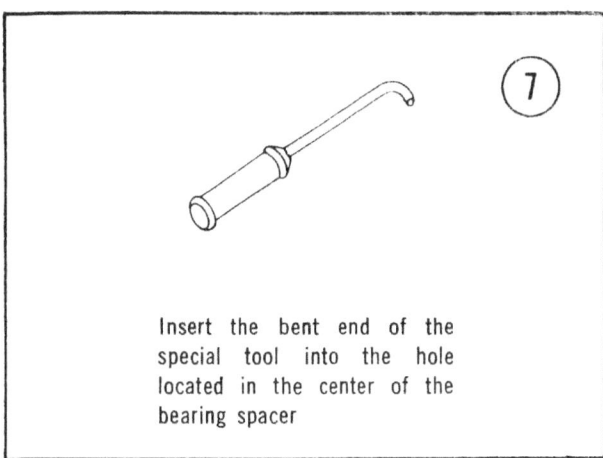

Insert the bent end of the special tool into the hole located in the center of the bearing spacer

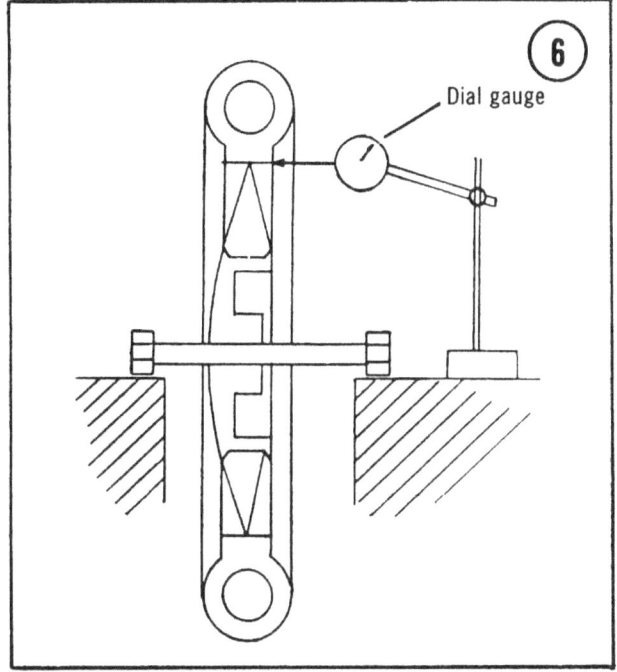

Dial gauge

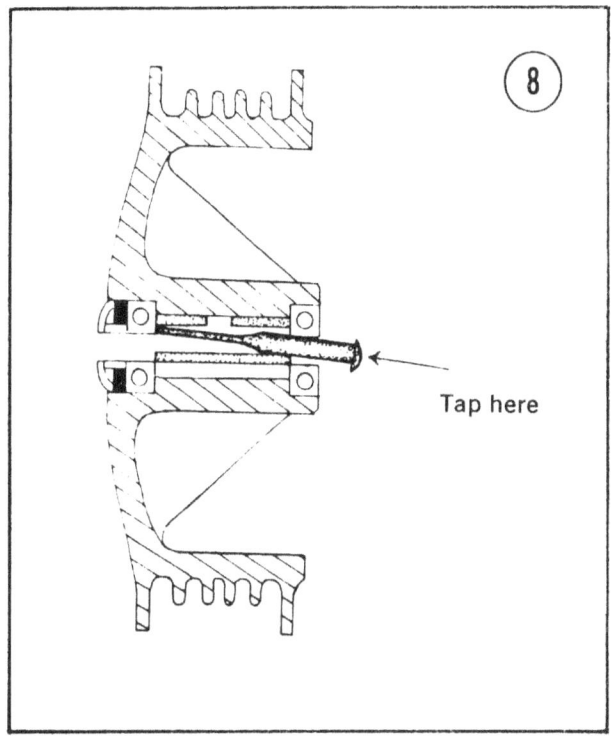

Tap here

3. Slowly rotate the wheel through one revolution. The runout limit is 0.08 in. (2.0mm).

4. If excessive wheel runout exists, have a shop adjust spoke tension to align the rim. If runout is caused by a bent rim, then runout might be impossible to remove.

Wheel Bearing Replacement

1. Clean all dirt from the wheel hub.

2. If possible, make a tool shaped as shown in **Figure 7**; otherwise, use a long thin punch. Place the end of this tool into the hole in the center of the bearing spacer (**Figure 8**). Tap on the spacer to drive the bearing out, then remove the spacer.

3. Drive the remaining bearing out from the opposite side of the hub with a hammer and punch.

4. To install the wheel bearings, reverse the previous steps. Grease each bearing before installation. Make sure no dirt enters the bearings or sticks on the grease. Use hammer and punch to tap around the outer race slowly until the bearing is fully seated.

CAUTION
Failure to install the spacer flange can lead to premature bearing failure.

Spoke Tension

Check all spokes frequently for looseness and bends. Loose spokes should be tightened and bent spokes replaced.

If all spokes are equally tight, they should all produce nearly the same sound when tapped with a screwdriver. If one spoke sounds dull, it is loose and must be tightened. If one produces a higher pitched sound than the others, the spoke should be loosened until the sound approximately equals the rest. After any adjustment, recheck rim runout.

Spoke Replacement

When replacing spoke or relacing a rim, note there are two kinds of spokes used. See **Figure 9**. When lacing up a new wheel, install the inside spokes first, then true the wheel. Install the outside spokes and then give the wheel a final truing.

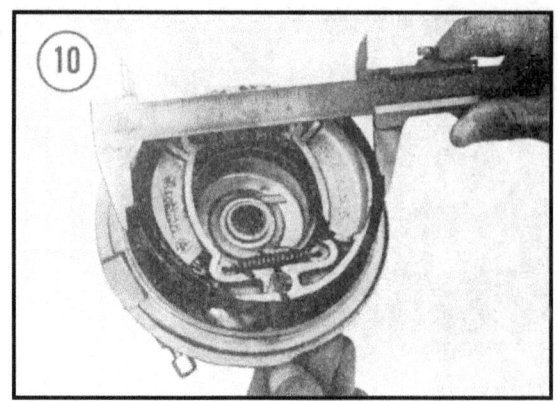

performance or result in abnormal noise. Remove minor scratches with No. 400 emery cloth, then clean with lacquer thinner or other non-petroleum-based solvent.

Brake Shoe Replacement

With brake shoe plate flat, hold 1 shoe securely, then *carefully* lift the center section of the other shoe until it pivots over the anchor cam on each end. Spring tension is strong.

1. To install a new brake shoe, lay both shoes flat on a counter, forming a circle (installed position).

2. Hook both return springs to the shoes.

3. Lift the assembled shoes and place 1 shoe fully into position, its flat end against the actuating cam and its radiused end against the stationary anchor pin.

4. Firmly hold the positioned shoe, then slip the remaining shoe ends over anchor pin and cam, and push the shoe until it is flat with the brake shoe plate (**Figure 11**).

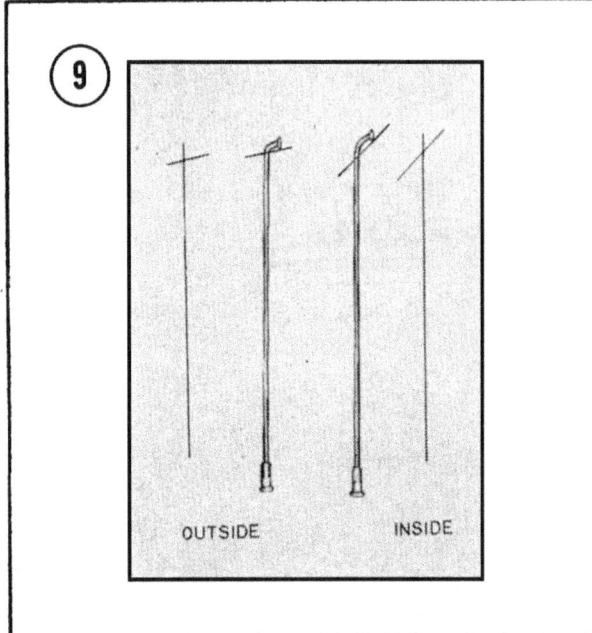

FRONT BRAKE

Remove front wheel as described earlier to get to the front brake.

Brake Inspection

1. To check for front brake wear, measure the outside diameter of the brake shoe assembly shown in **Figure 10**. If it is less than 4.09 inches (104mm), replace the shoes.

2. If brake shoe surfaces are not worn, but appear glazed and shiny, scrub the surfaces with No. 320 sandpaper to rough up the surface.

3. Examine the brake drum contact surface. Oil, grooves, or scratches will impair braking

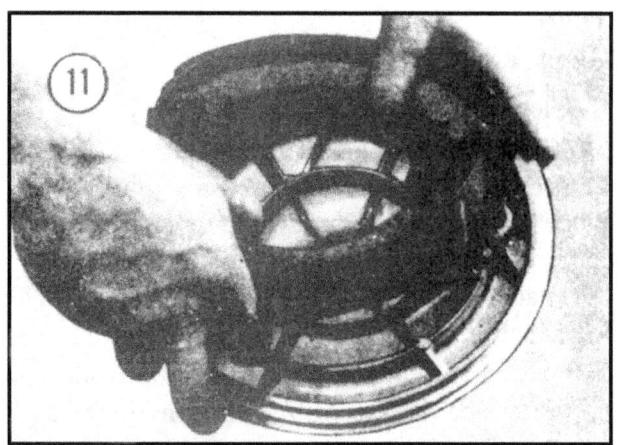

5. Rotate the cam as shown in **Figure 12** and place a little grease on both sides of the actuating cam. *Do not* get grease on any part of the brake lining. This will ruin the lining.

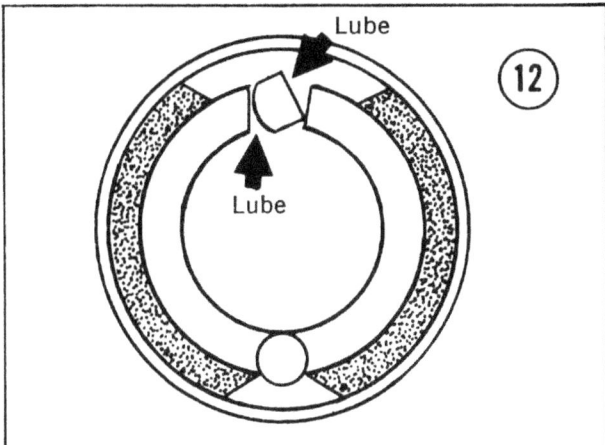

Brake Adjustment

As shown in **Figure 13**, proper brake cable adjustment results in approximately ¼ inch (5-8mm) brake lever clearance at the mounting bracket when the lever is pulled and all cable slack is taken up.

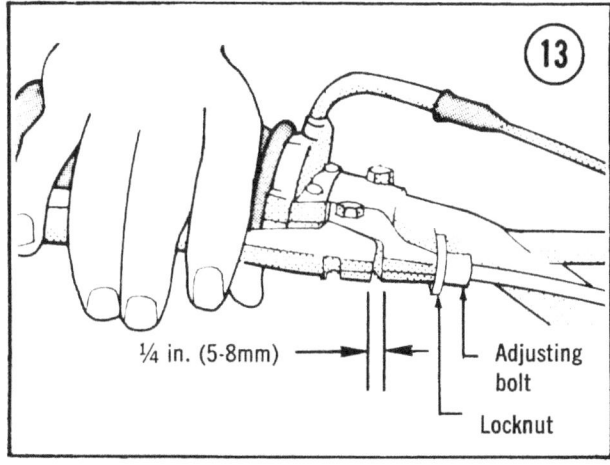

Make this adjustment at the front wheel where the brake cable terminates. Loosen the adjuster locknut, then turn the adjuster to take up or add cable slack. Retighten the locknut; do not tighten with pliers.

FRONT FORKS
(JT1/2, 80cc, 100cc, AND YJ1/2)

All models have oil damped telescopic front forks. **Figures 14, 15, and 16** (pages 96-98) are exploded views of the JT series, YG1 series, and all other remaining model front fork units, respectively. One of these illustrations will match your machine.

Removal

1. To remove the front forks, take off the front fender and remove the inner tube cap bolt (**Figure 17**).

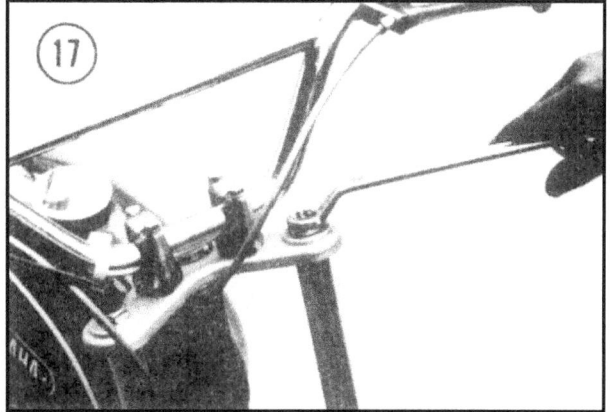

2. Loosen the inner tube clamping bolt on the underbracket (**Figure 18**).

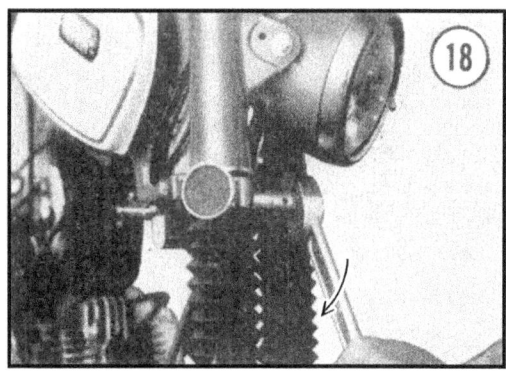

3. Draw the outer tube downward to remove the assembly (**Figure 19**).

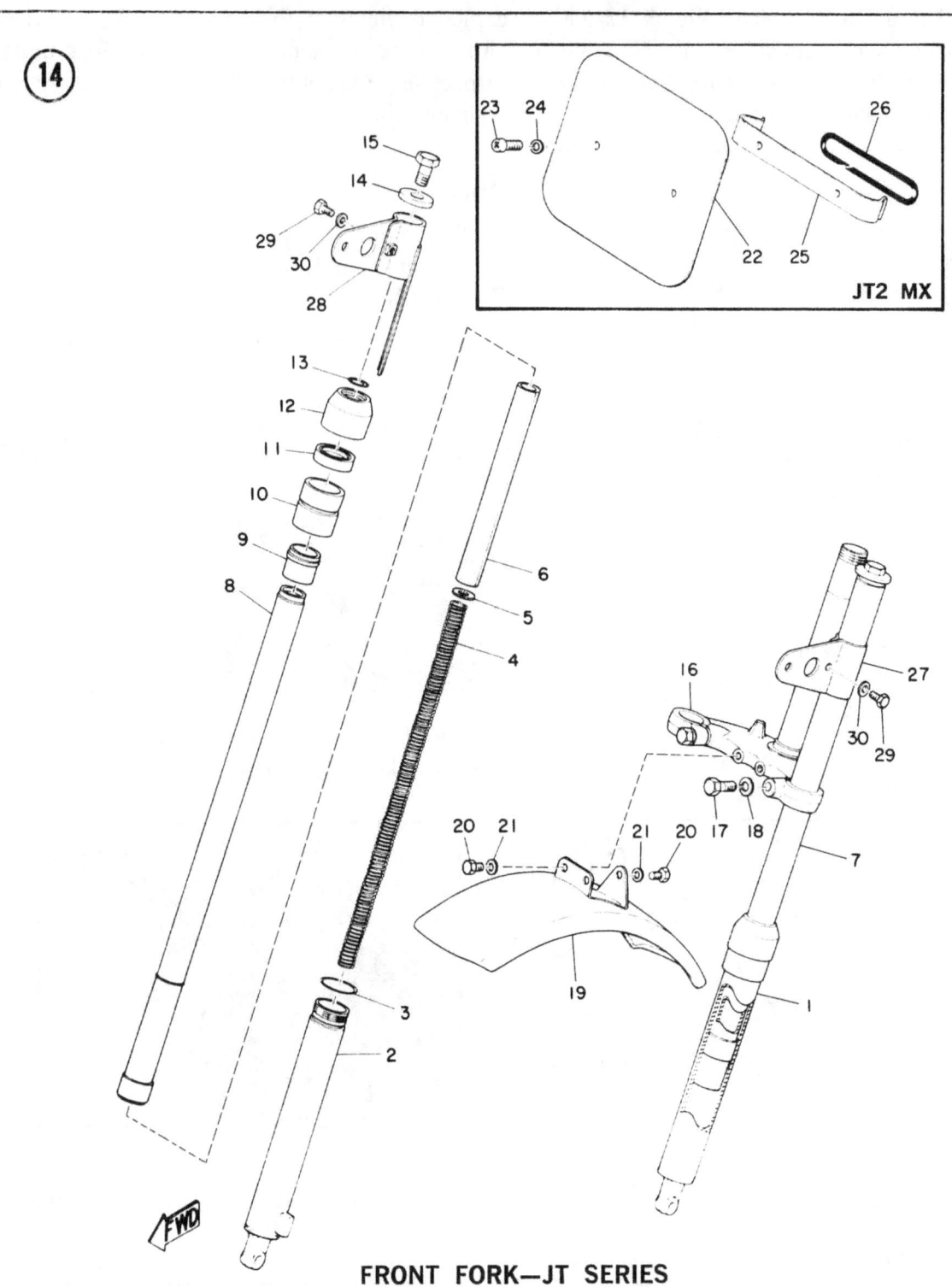

FRONT FORK—JT SERIES

1. Outer left tube
2. Outer right tube
3. O-ring
4. Fork spring
5. Spring upper washer
6. Spacer
7. Left inner tube
8. Right inner tube
9. Slide metal (bushing)
10. Outer nut
11. Oil seal
12. Dust cover
13. Gasket
14. Washer
15. Cap bolt
16. Underbracket
17. Bolt
18. Lockwasher
19. Front fender
20. Bolt
21. Flat washer
22. Number plate (JT2-MX3)
23. Pan head screw
24. Flat washer
25. Plate stay
26. Band
27. Left headlight support
28. Right headlight support
29. Bolt
30. Flat washer

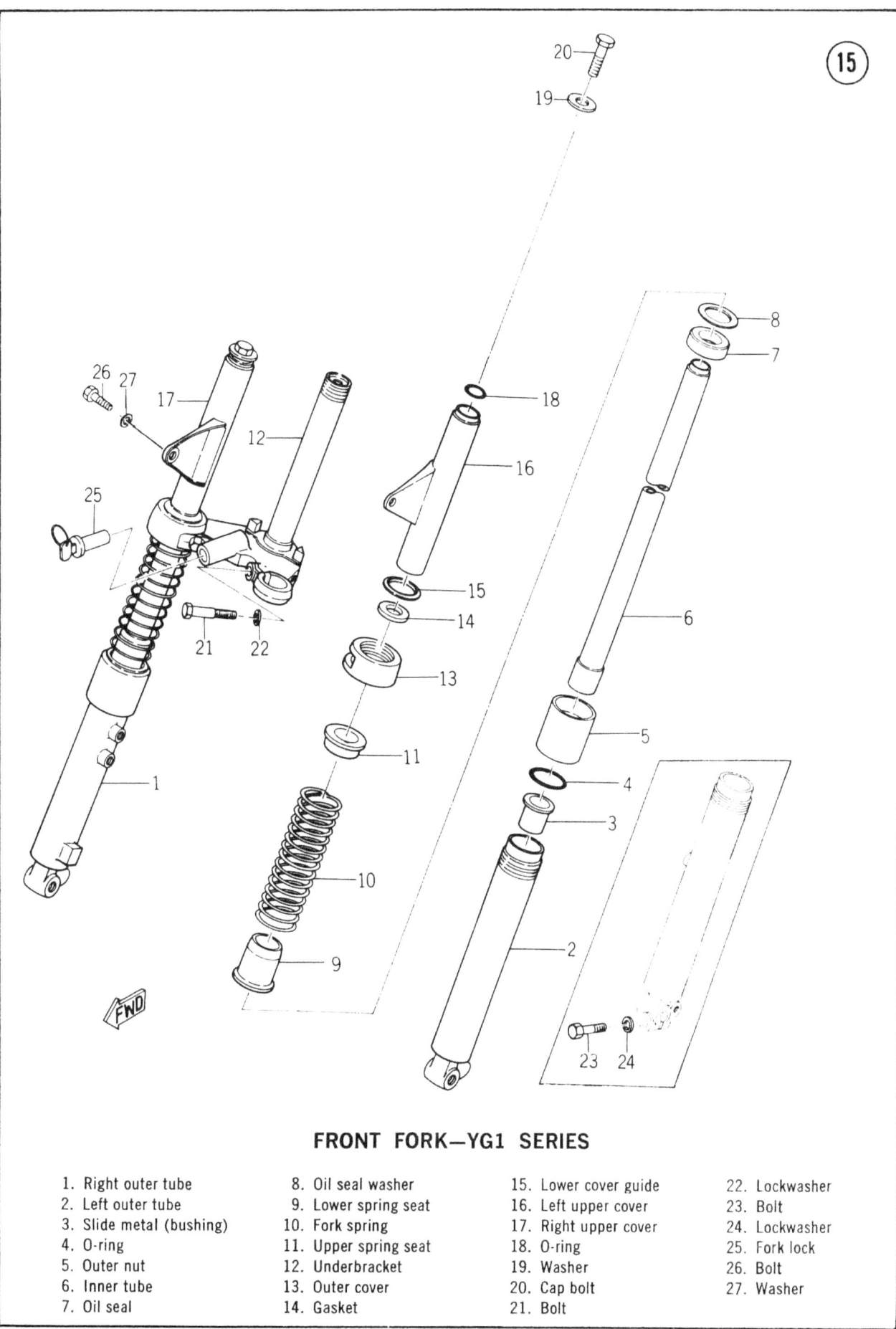

FRONT FORK—YG1 SERIES

1. Right outer tube
2. Left outer tube
3. Slide metal (bushing)
4. O-ring
5. Outer nut
6. Inner tube
7. Oil seal
8. Oil seal washer
9. Lower spring seat
10. Fork spring
11. Upper spring seat
12. Underbracket
13. Outer cover
14. Gasket
15. Lower cover guide
16. Left upper cover
17. Right upper cover
18. O-ring
19. Washer
20. Cap bolt
21. Bolt
22. Lockwasher
23. Bolt
24. Lockwasher
25. Fork lock
26. Bolt
27. Washer

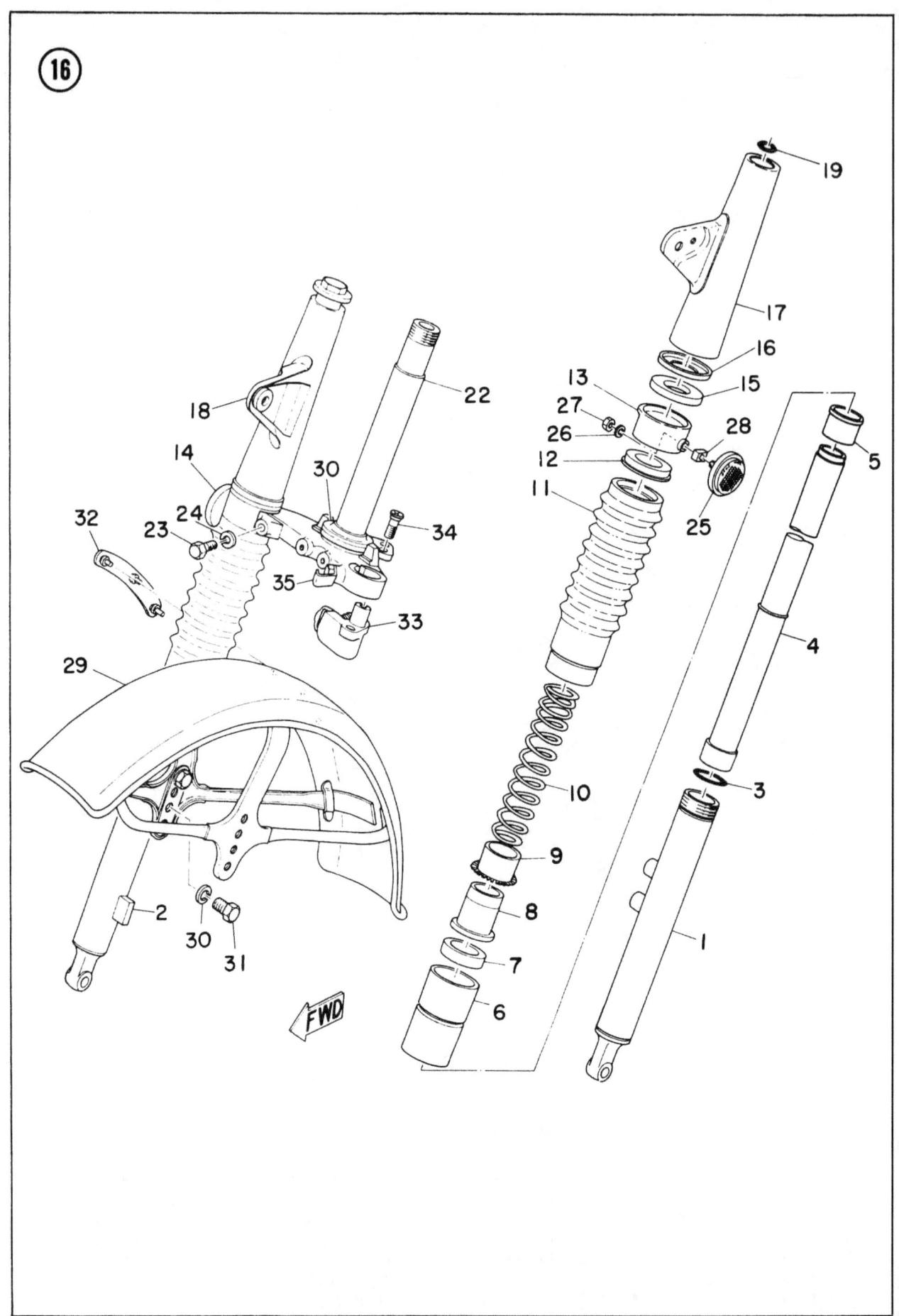

FRONT FORK—80, 100cc (EXCEPT JT, YG1 SERIES)

1. Outer left tube
2. Outer right tube
3. O-ring
4. Inner left tube
5. Inner right tube
6. Outer nut
7. Oil seal
8. Lower spring seat
9. Spring guide
10. Fork spring
11. Dust cover
12. Upper spring seat
13. Left outer cover
14. Right outer cover
15. Gasket
16. Lower cover guide
17. Upper left cover
18. Upper right cover
19. Gasket
20. Washer
21. Cap bolt
22. Underbracket
23. Bolt
24. Lockwasher
25. Reflector
26. Spring washer
27. Nut
28. Reflector stay cover
29. Fender
30. Lockwasher
31. Bolt
32. Cable guide
33. Fork lock
34. Screw
35. Cable holder

Disassembly

To disassemble the outer and inner tubes, drain oil from the forks, then wrap a piece of tire tube around the outer tube nut and remove the nut. See **Figure 20**. Disassemble the tubes by turning the outer tube counterclockwise (**Figure 21**).

NOTE: *Replace oil seals any time the forks are disassembled.*

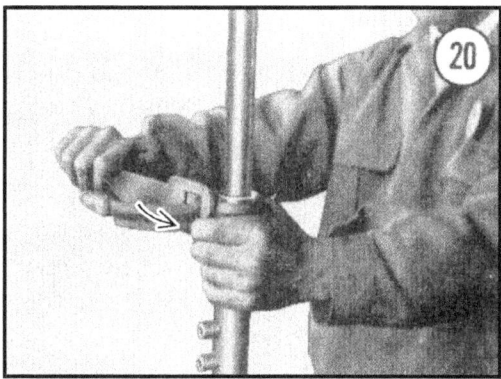

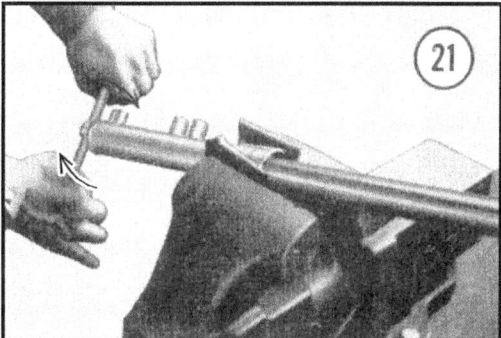

Assembly

1. To assemble, reverse the removal procedure. Check the sliding action of the 2 tubes as shown in **Figure 22**.

2. Push the front fork into place and tighten the underbracket clamping bolt.

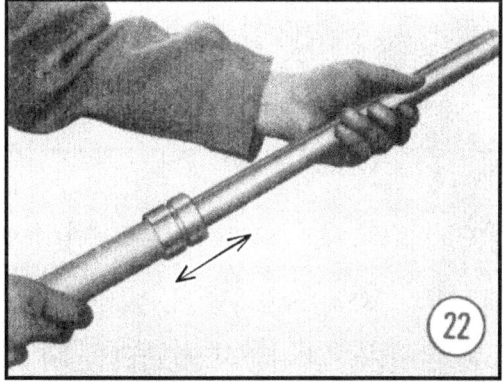

3. Fill the inner tube with fork oil through the top opening of the tube.

Inner Tube Inspection

Check the inner tube for straightness. If it is slightly bent, the tube may be straightened in a press. If the tube has buckled, it is structurally weakened and should be replaced as a safety precaution.

Spring Inspection

These springs become fatigued, resulting in slow or incomplete fork extension. Compare overall spring length with a new one. If the used spring is shorter by more than ¼ inch, replace it.

> NOTE: *JT1/2 series—only 1 fork leg has a spring. The other leg contains only oil.*

Fork Seal Replacement

Oil seepage past the seal and onto the dust cover or fork leg indicates a leaking seal.

An outer ring nut holds inner and outer tubes together. The seal is located inside this ring nut.

1. Carefully pry out the old oil seal with a screwdriver as demonstrated in **Figure 23**. Place a piece of wood or cloth against the outer edge to protect this edge. Do not clamp the ring nut in a vise to hold it; it will bend.

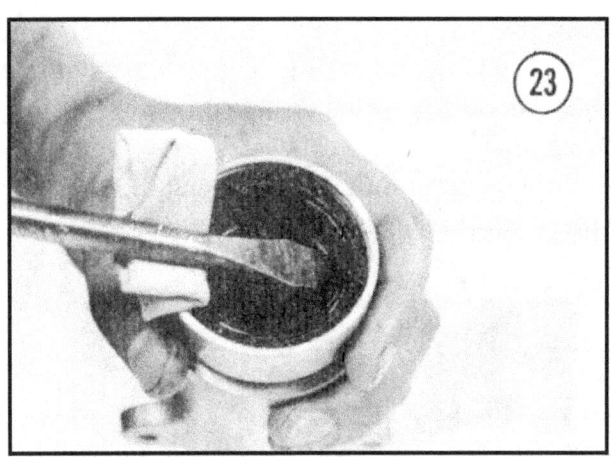

2. To install the seal, place it open-end down. Gently tap around the exposed edge to start it in. When the seal is flush with the ring nut edge, use a large socket to tap it on until the seal is seated.

3. Lubricate the inner seal lip so the inner tube will not damage the seal during installation.

4. Assemble the fork leg.

Fork Oil Change

Aluminum, dirt particles, and water gradually build up in the fork oil. Change it occasionally.

1. Remove the special fork oil drain screw as shown in **Figure 24**.

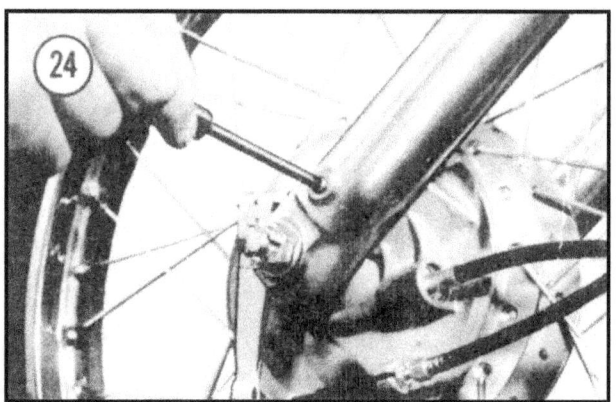

2. Place a pan beneath the drain hole, lock the front brake, then pump the forks until all oil drains out. Repeat for other fork leg.

3. Install the drain screw. Be careful; it is extremely easy to cross-thread this screw.

4. Remove the cap bolt from the top of the fork leg. On some models this requires instrument and handlebar removal.

> CAUTION
> *The cap bolt is under considerable spring tension. Hold palm of hand securely over the top of this cap during final removal stage to prevent the bolt from springing out.*

5. Slowly add the proper amount of fork oil. Refer to Chapter Eight for specifications. Use SAE 10W-30 oil. Change oil weight as needed to gain fork reaction to suit your needs. During hot weather, or severe usage, 20 or 30 weight oil might be required. If possible, use special non-foaming fork oil.

6. Lightly pump the forks until all oil has drained down, then install and tighten the cap bolt. Tighten the pinch bolt.

7. Repeat this procedure for the other fork leg.

FRONT FORKS (U5 SERIES)

1. The front suspension is not meant to be disassembled farther than shown in **Figure 25** unless springs, etc., need checking. In that case, consult the section on rear shocks.

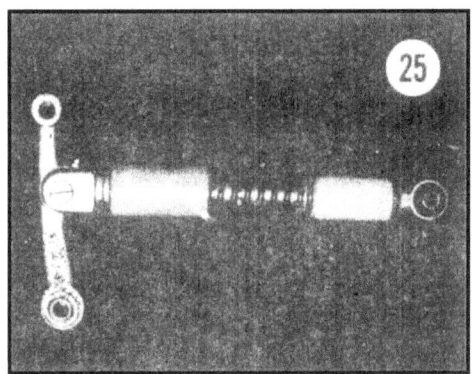

2. To remove the front forks, pull out the speedometer cable by taking off its clips (**Figure 26**).
3. Take off the brake cable (**Figure 27**).

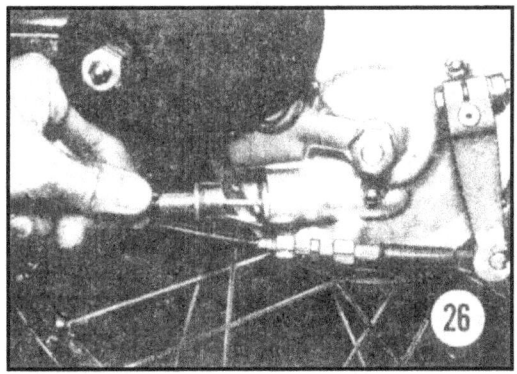

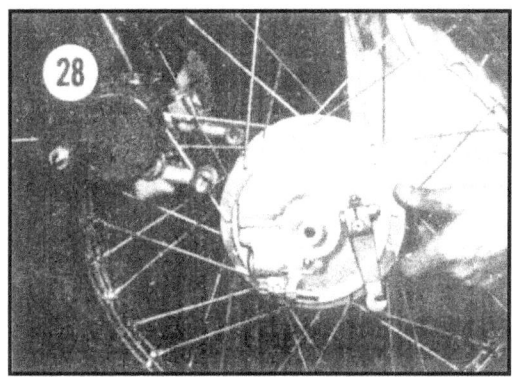

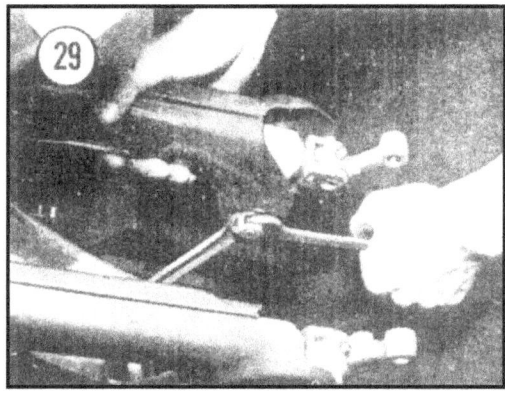

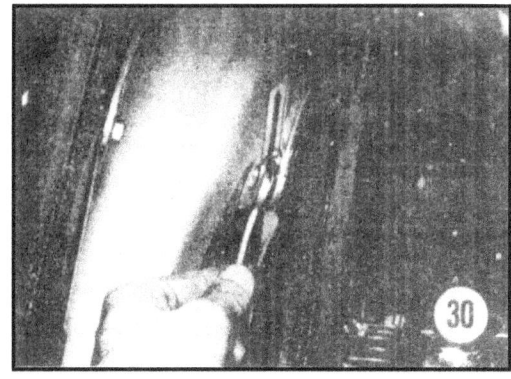

4. Pull out the front wheel axle and remove the front wheel (**Figure 28**).
5. Remove the front arm bolts (**Figure 29**).
6. Remove the front suspension unit upper bolts (**Figure 30**).

FRONT FORKS (MJ1/2)

Refer to **Figure 31**.

1. Before disassembling the front forks, block up the motorcycle under the engine to keep the front wheel in the air.
2. Take off the front fender. Remove the handlebar upper cover, the steering hub clamping bolt, and the under cover and front panel.
3. Remove the steering locknut and the forks will come off.
4. Loosen the hexagonal bolt, the spring, washer, and stem set washer, and take out the square stem.

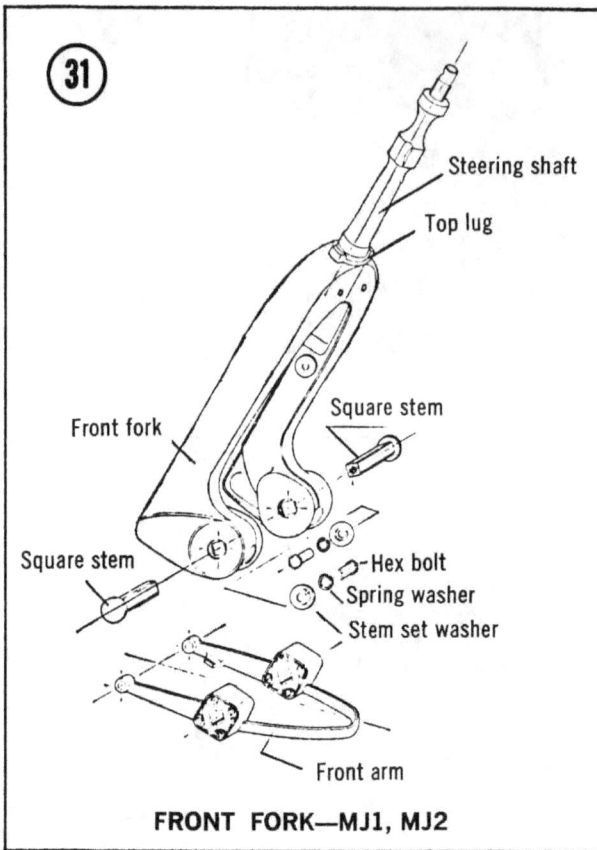

FRONT FORK—MJ1, MJ2

5. Remove the front arm assembly from the forks. Unless the rubber cushions are worn out, do not disassemble any further.

FRONT END (MJ1/2)

Figure 32 identifies all parts directly related to the front end. Refer to it for identification and parts location as needed.

STEERING HEAD

Figure 33 is an exploded view of a typical steering head. Occasionally check the ball races and balls for pitting, cracks, rust, or any other wear. If any of these conditions exist, replace all balls and races as a unit. Do not use a combination of new and used parts.

Bearing Race/Ball Replacement and Adjustment

1. Disconnect clutch cable, throttle cable, and front brake cables from the handlebar.

2. If applicable, remove the headlight from its shell and disconnect any wiring to handlebar switches.

3. Remove the handlebar.

4. If applicable, disconnect tachometer and speedometer cables from meters, then remove the meters.

5. Remove front wheel assembly.

6. It is advisable to remove both front fork legs. Do not disassemble; just loosen all underbracket pinch bolts, remove each cap bolt (on top), then pull fork legs down and out.

7. If equipped with a steering head damper, remove it.

8. Remove the bolt located in the center of the top bracket; it anchors the top bracket. Now lift off the top bracket.

9. Loosen ring nut (8, Figure 33). Tap it with hammer and punch in a counterclockwise direction. As this ring is loosened, the bottom bracket (underbracket) will start to drop down. Hold this bracket up to prevent steering head bearings from falling out.

10. Remove the ring nut, then lift off race protector, top race, and remove all balls. A magnet is helpful.

11. Lower the underbracket until you can remove the bottom balls. Keep a rag or container under the bracket to catch any balls that fall.

12. To remove the ball races inside the steering head (4 and 5, Figure 33), tap each one out from the opposite end with hammer and punch. To remove the bottom most ball race, carefully wedge it up over the underbracket stem.

13. When installing new inner races, carefully tap them down until fully seated.

14. To begin reassembly, grease the bottom bearing race (on underbracket), push all balls firmly into the grease, then apply more grease. Slide the underbracket up and hold in place.

15. Grease the top inner bearing race (in top of frame), push all bearings into the grease, apply more grease, then fit the top bearing race.

16. Install the bearing protector, then install and tighten the ring nut until all underbracket free-play is removed.

17. Install the top bracket and nut, then install both fork leg units.

18. Make a final steering bearing free-play adjustment. Use hammer and punch to tighten the

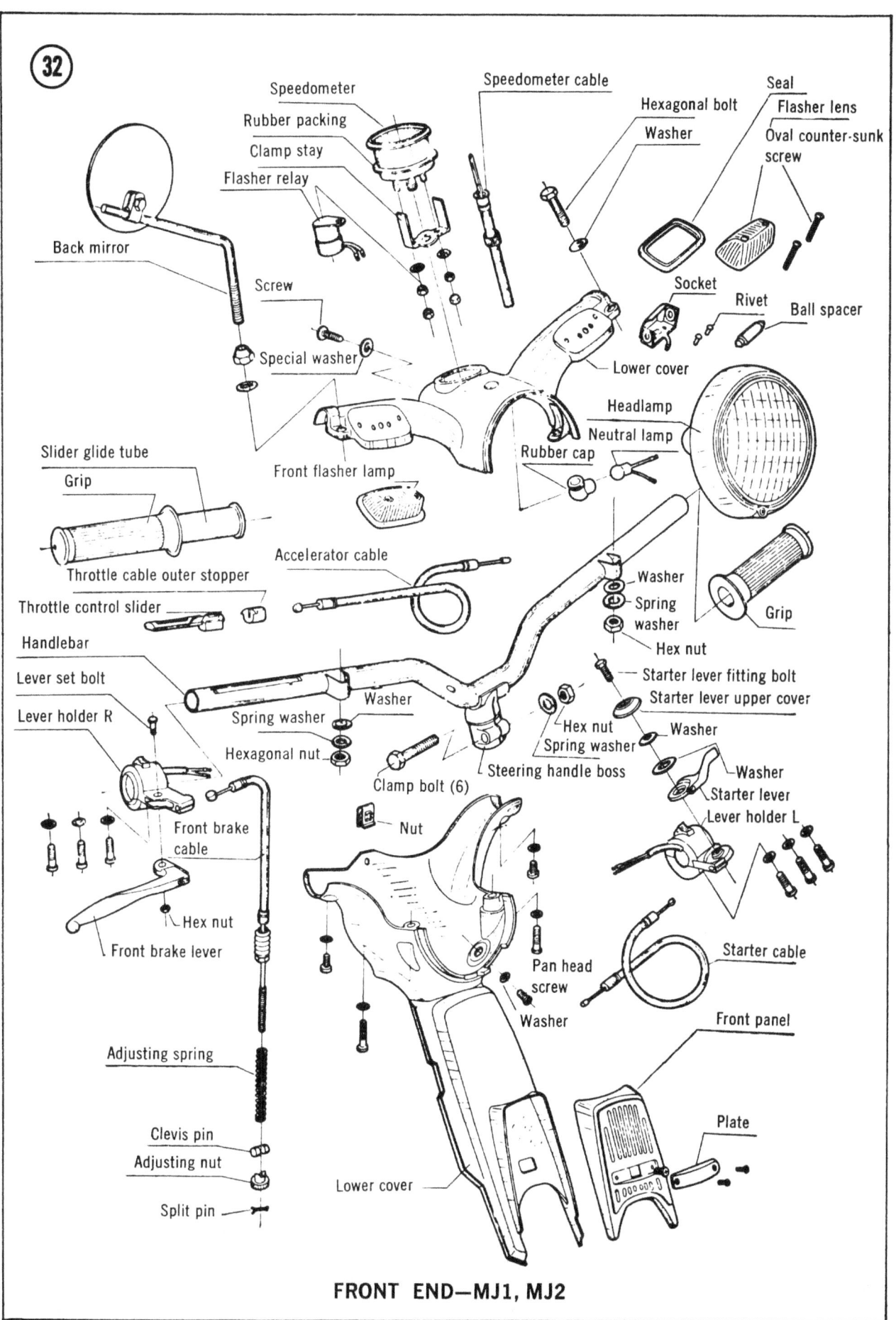

FRONT END—MJ1, MJ2

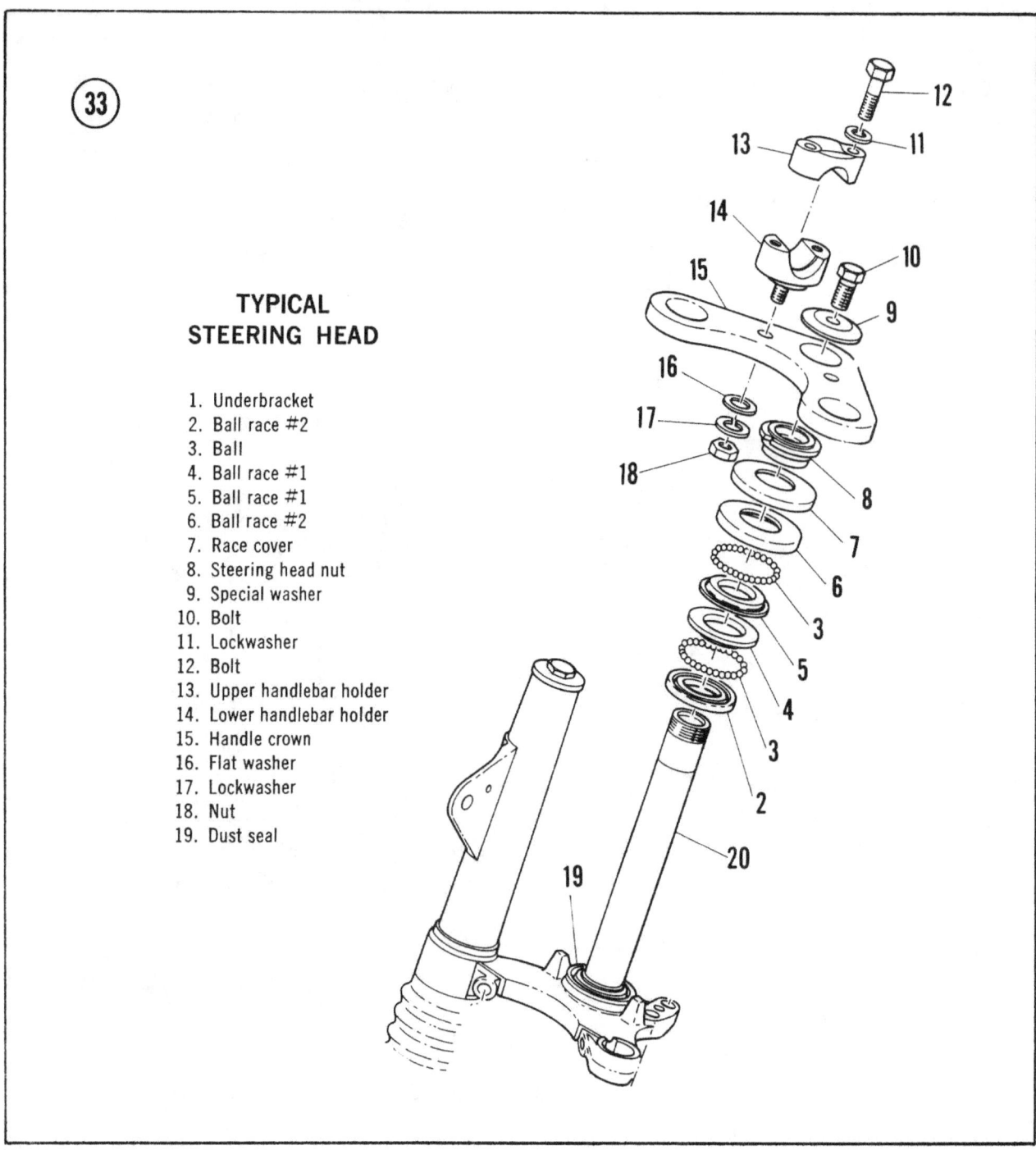

TYPICAL STEERING HEAD

1. Underbracket
2. Ball race #2
3. Ball
4. Ball race #1
5. Ball race #1
6. Ball race #2
7. Race cover
8. Steering head nut
9. Special washer
10. Bolt
11. Lockwasher
12. Bolt
13. Upper handlebar holder
14. Lower handlebar holder
15. Handle crown
16. Flat washer
17. Lockwasher
18. Nut
19. Dust seal

ring nut until the underbracket is not loose, but the forks still swing from lock to lock without binding.

19. Install all remaining parts in reverse order of their removal.

REAR WHEEL

Description

Figure 34 identifies the JT1/2 series rear wheel unit. **Figure 35** (page 106) identifies the YG1 series and 100cc series unit, while **Figure 36** (page 108) identifies all other 80cc model's rear wheel unit.

A labyrinth seal between the wheel hub and brake plate keeps out water and dust.

Removal

1. Unfasten rear tension bar (**Figure 37**).
2. Remove the rear brake rod from the brake lever (**Figure 38**).
3. Disconnect the chain, if not done already.

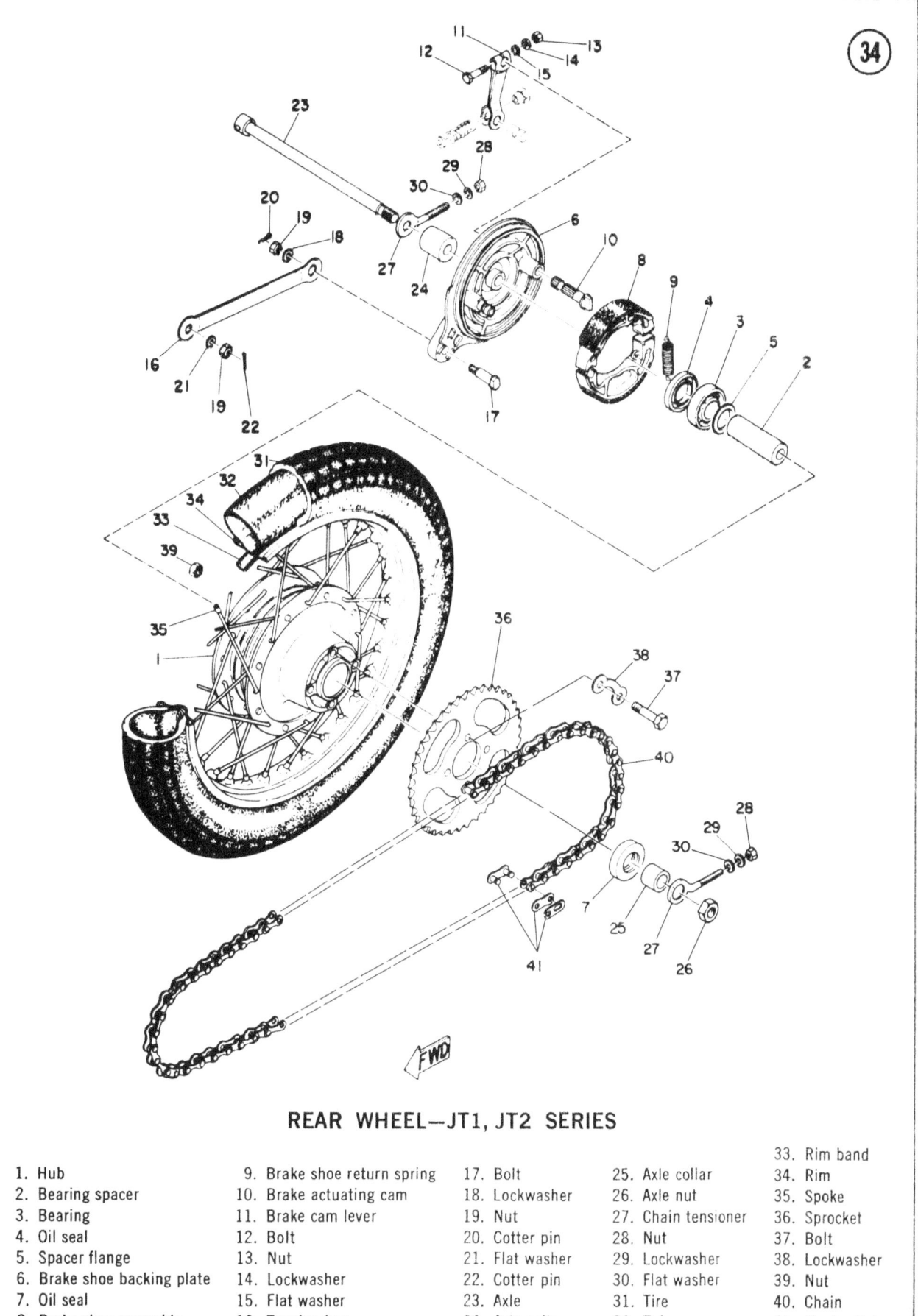

REAR WHEEL—JT1, JT2 SERIES

1. Hub
2. Bearing spacer
3. Bearing
4. Oil seal
5. Spacer flange
6. Brake shoe backing plate
7. Oil seal
8. Brake shoe assembly
9. Brake shoe return spring
10. Brake actuating cam
11. Brake cam lever
12. Bolt
13. Nut
14. Lockwasher
15. Flat washer
16. Tension bar
17. Bolt
18. Lockwasher
19. Nut
20. Cotter pin
21. Flat washer
22. Cotter pin
23. Axle
24. Axle collar
25. Axle collar
26. Axle nut
27. Chain tensioner
28. Nut
29. Lockwasher
30. Flat washer
31. Tire
32. Tube
33. Rim band
34. Rim
35. Spoke
36. Sprocket
37. Bolt
38. Lockwasher
39. Nut
40. Chain
41. Master link

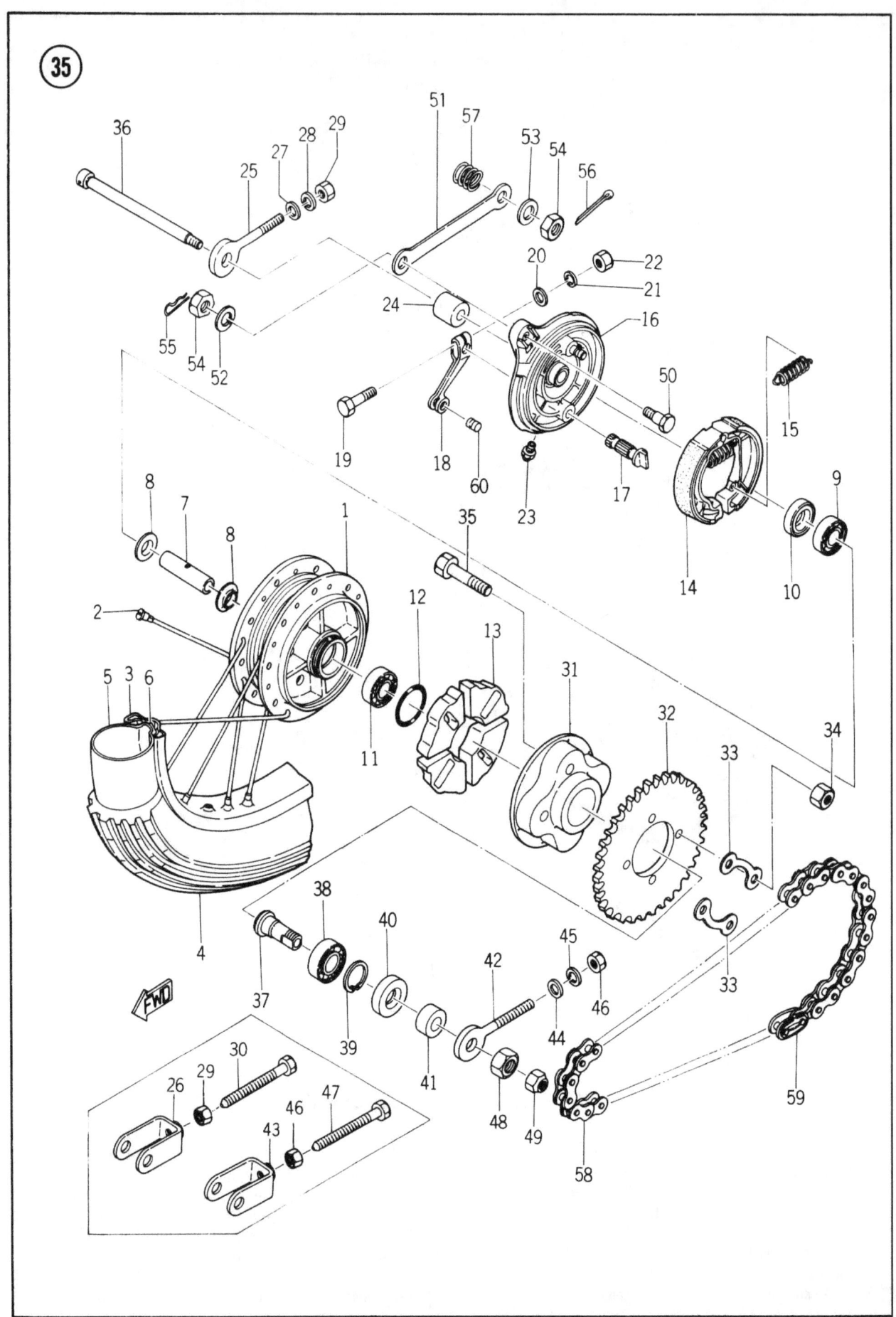

REAR WHEEL
(YG1, 100cc SERIES)

1. Hub
2. Spoke
3. Rim
4. Tire
5. Tube
6. Rim band
7. Bearing spacer
8. Spacer flange
9. Bearing
10. Oil seal
11. Bearing
12. Oil seal
13. Clutch hub cushion
14. Brake shoe assembly
15. Brake shoe return spring
16. Brake shoe backing plate
17. Brake actuating cam
18. Brake cam lever
19. Bolt
20. Flat washer
21. Lockwasher
22. Nut
23. Grease fitting
24. Axle collar
25. Chain tensioner
26. Chain tensioner
27. Flat washer
28. Lockwasher
29. Nut
30. Bolt
31. Hub clutch
32. Sprocket
33. Lockwasher
34. Nut
35. Bolt
36. Axle
37. Sprocket shaft
38. Bearing
39. Circlip
40. Oil seal
41. Axle collar
42. Chain tensioner
43. Chain tensioner
44. Flat washer
45. Lockwasher
46. Nut
47. Bolt
48. Nut
49. Nut
50. Bolt
51. Tension bar
52. Lockwasher
53. Flat washer
54. Nut
55. Tension bar clip
56. Cotter pin
57. Spring
58. Chain
59. Master link
60. Clevis pin

4. Remove the axle nut as shown in **Figure 39**.
5. Pull out the rear axle (**Figure 40**).
6. Remove the axle spacer shown in **Figure 41**.

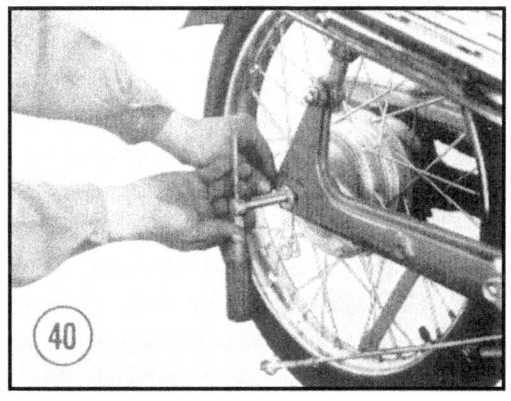

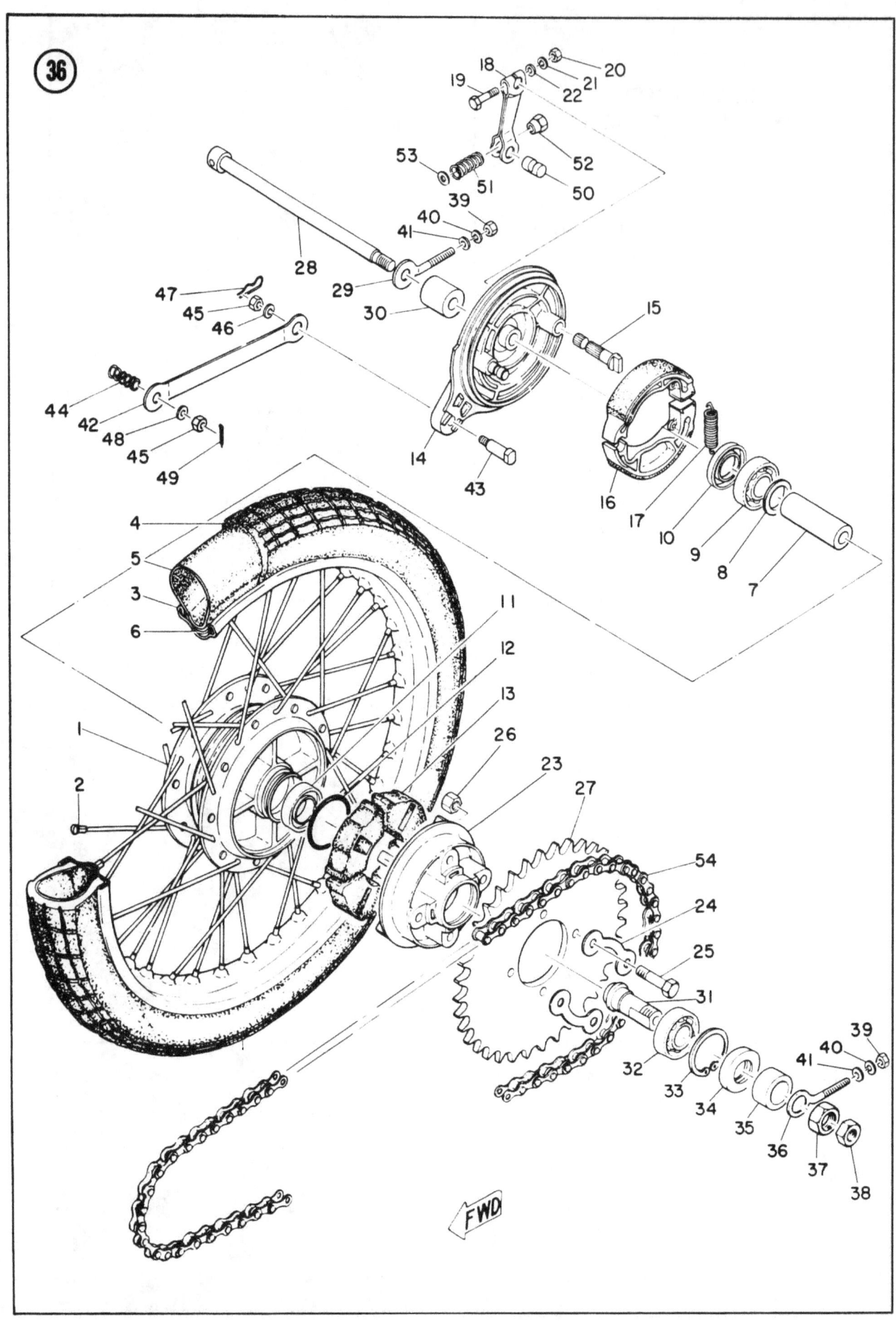

REAR WHEEL — 80cc MODELS

1. Hub
2. Spoke
3. Rim
4. Tire
5. Tube
6. Rim band
7. Bearing spacer
8. Spacer flange
9. Bearing
10. Oil seal
11. Bearing
12. O-ring
13. Clutch hub cushion
14. Brake shoe backing plate
15. Brake actuating cam
16. Brake shoe assembly
17. Brake shoe return spring
18. Brake cam lever
19. Bolt
20. Nut
21. Lockwasher
22. Flat washer
23. Hub clutch
24. Lockwasher
25. Bolt
26. Nut
27. Sprocket
28. Axle
29. Chain tensioner
30. Axle collar
31. Sprocket shaft
32. Bearing
33. Circlip
34. Oil seal
35. Sprocket shaft collar
36. Chain tensioner
37. Nut
38. Nut
39. Nut
40. Lockwasher
41. Flat washer
42. Tension bar
43. Bolt
44. Spring
45. Nut
46. Spring washer
47. Tension bar clip
48. Flat washer
49. Cotter pin
50. Clevis pin
51. Rod spring
52. Adjustment nut
53. Flat washer
54. Chain

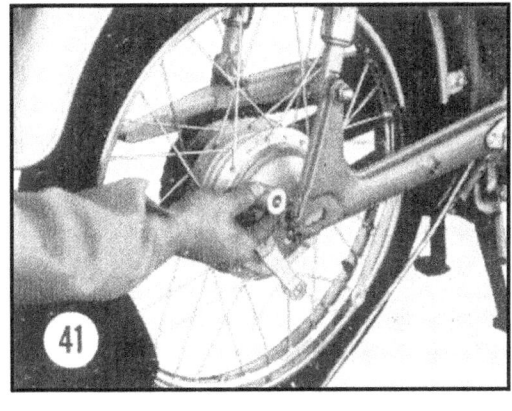

7. Tip the machine to the left, pivoting on its center or side stand, until the rear wheel can be slipped out.

8. On all models except the JT series, the sprocket assembly must be removed from the frame. **Figures 42 and 43** show which nut to remove and how to lift off the assembly.

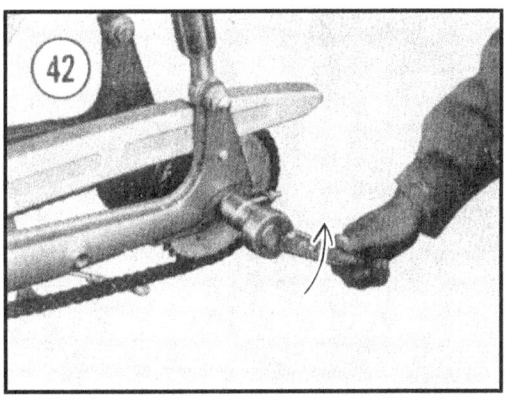

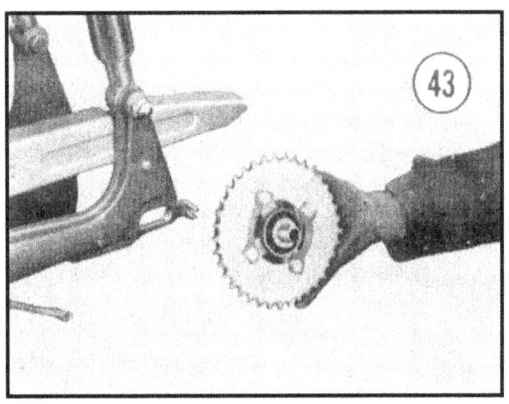

9. Remove the left and right side chain tension adjusters.

Installation

Reverse the previous 9 steps to install this wheel.

Runout Inspection

Refer to *Runout Inspection* in the *Front Wheel* section. The procedure is identical.

Wheel Bearing Replacement

Figure 44 is an exploded view of a typical clutch hub. To replace the bearings, proceed as follows.

1. Push out the sprocket shaft.
2. Pull out the sprocket shaft collar.
3. Remove the oil seal. Be careful not to damage it.
4. Remove the snap ring.
5. Press out the clutch hub bearing.
6. Reverse the procedure to install the clutch hub bearing. Grease the bearing and oil seal before installation.

Spoke Tension

Refer to *Spoke Tension* listed in the *Front Wheel* section. The steps are identical.

Spoke Replacement

Refer to *Spoke Replacement* listed in the *Front Wheel* section. The steps are identical.

Clutch Hub Cushion Replacement

All models in this chapter, except the JT series, have a set of rubber cushions in the rear hub to dampen any sudden torque shock to the transmission and rear wheel. Refer back to Figures 35 and 36 for identification.

If your model has the 2-piece rear hub (hub and clutch hub), with rubber cushions between, inspect these cushions on occasion. Gradually they break up and wear. There will be a metallic

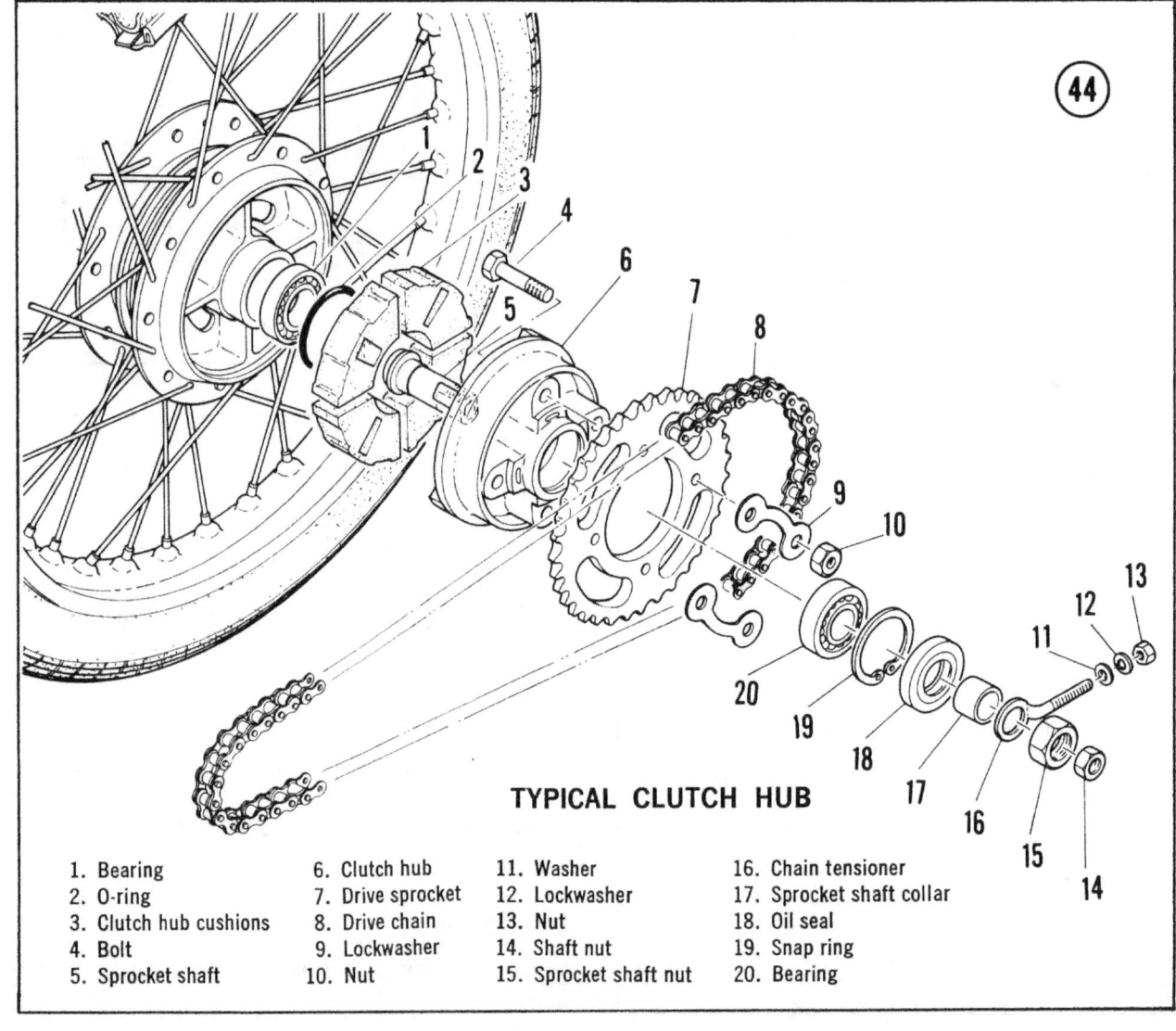

TYPICAL CLUTCH HUB

1. Bearing
2. O-ring
3. Clutch hub cushions
4. Bolt
5. Sprocket shaft
6. Clutch hub
7. Drive sprocket
8. Drive chain
9. Lockwasher
10. Nut
11. Washer
12. Lockwasher
13. Nut
14. Shaft nut
15. Sprocket shaft nut
16. Chain tensioner
17. Sprocket shaft collar
18. Oil seal
19. Snap ring
20. Bearing

clunking noise during acceleration and deceleration if the cushions are completely broken up. Also, the clutch hub will have considerable forward and backward free-play inside the hub if the cushions are damaged. Perform the following procedure to inspect and/or replace cushions.

1. Remove the rear wheel assembly.
2. To protect hub surfaces, support the wheel on a box, sprocket facing up.
3. Remove the clutch hub retainer circlip identified in **Figure 45**. The clutch hub can now be lifted off the hub. This exposes all cushions in the hub.

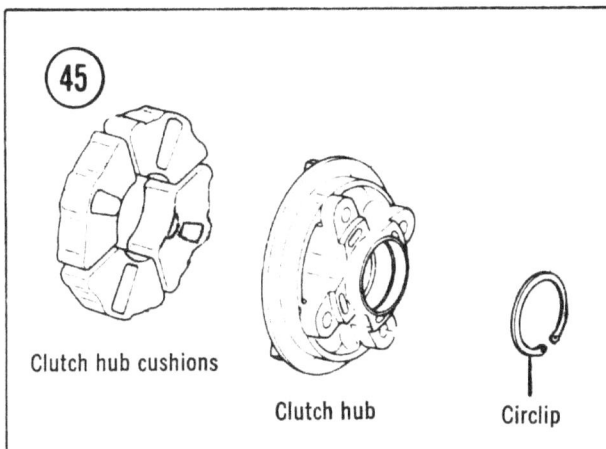

4. Inspect and replace cushions as needed. They are pie-shaped so they fit only one way into their individual hub cavities.
5. Inspect the cushion cavities and circlip groove for cracks. If found, replace the hub.
6. Slip the clutch hub down into the hub. Protrusions on the clutch hub bottom must slip into the center of each cushion.
7. Use circlip pliers to spread the circlip end, then install into the hub groove.

NOTE: *If the circlip was bent during removal, replace it.*

REAR BRAKE

Remove rear wheel to get to rear brake.

Brake Inspection

Refer to *Brake Inspection* in the *Front Wheel* section. It is identical except for the measurements. The JT series must measure more than 4.9 in. (124mm). All other models must measure more than 4.09 in. (104mm).

Brake Shoe Replacement

Refer to *Brake Shoe Replacement* in the *Front Wheel* section. The step is identical.

Brake Adjustment

1. Proper rear brake adjustment results in approximately 1 inch (25mm) of brake pedal down travel free-play before the brake starts working.
2. **Figure 46** identifies the rod that connects brake pedal to rear brake and the adjuster nut that can be screwed forward or backward to change pedal free-play.

NOTE: *There is no locknut. Be sure the special spring is in place on the rod, just forward of the rear brake lever.*

TIRES AND TUBES

Tire Pressure

Normal tire pressure is 22-24 pounds front, and 26-34 pounds rear, depending on load and terrain conditions. This is cold pressure. As the machine is run, the tires will become warm and the pressure will rise. This rise is normal. Do not bleed air out of a hot tire, nor check it when it is hot.

Dirt riding may require a tire pressure change. Less pressure affords better tire traction. However, do not deflate too much, as the tube could be pinched or the valve stem pulled off during hard usage.

Tire and Tube Removal/Installation

1. Remove the valve cap and locknut from the tire valve, then deflate the tire.

2. Use 2 tire irons to remove the tire from the rim. Take care that you do not damage the inner tube with the tire irons.

3. If only the inner tube is to be replaced, it is not necessary to remove the tire entirely from the rim.

4. To install, work 1 tire bead onto the rim, using 2 tire irons.

5. Insert the inner tube valve stem through the hole in the rim. Then insert the inner tube between the tire and wheel rim.

6. Partially inflate the inner tube to remove creases, then deflate the tube.

7. Using 2 tire irons, work the remaining tire bead onto the wheel rim. This operation will be easier if the bead on the other side of the tire is pushed in toward the rim flange. Soaping the bead to be installed also helps.

8. While the tire is still partially inflated, tap the tire with a hammer to avoid pinching the tube between the tire and rim.

9. Install the tire valve locknut. Inflate the tire to the recommended pressure and install the valve cap.

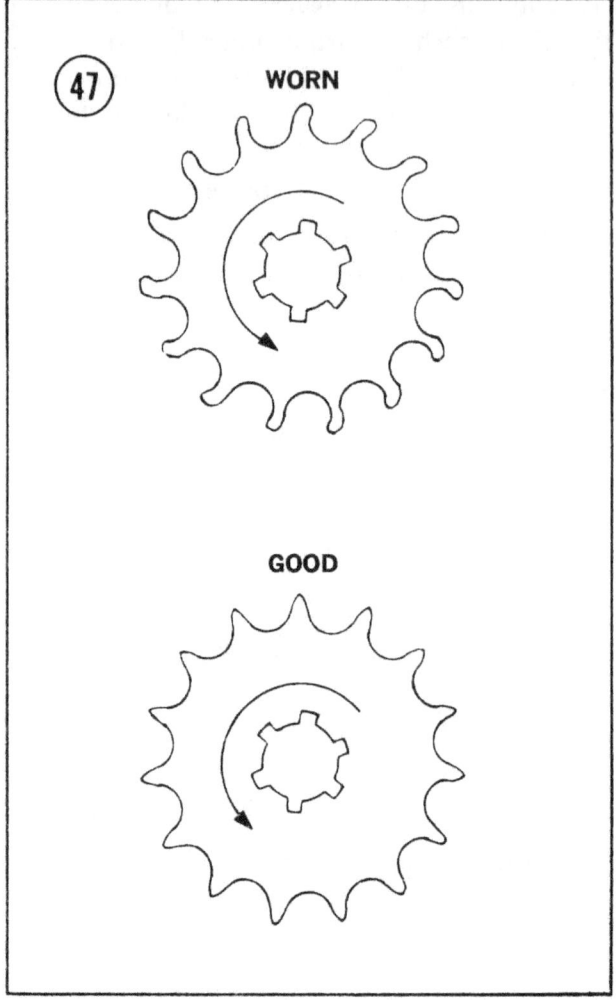

REAR SPROCKET (ALL EXCEPT MJ1/2)

Removal

1. Place the rear wheel on a level surface with the sprocket facing upward.

2. Using hammer and punch, bend the lock tabs flat that secure the sprocket bolts (or nuts).

3. Loosen the sprocket securing bolts (or nuts, if your model has a nut on the outer surface), then lift off the sprocket.

4. Thoroughly tighten the securing bolts (nuts) to 15 ft.-lb. (2.0 mkg) and bend up the lock tabs.

Inspection

Constant rubbing and pulling on the sprocket by the chain results in tooth wear. **Figure 47** identifies a serviceable and a worn out sprocket. Replace the sprocket if its teeth are bent and worn as shown.

REAR SPROCKET ASSEMBLY

Refer to **Figure 48** for this procedure.

1. To remove the rear sprocket assembly, take off the rear wheel. Remove the bottom chain case and the chain. Remove the rear shock, the upper chain case, and the special nut. The clutch assembly can now be removed.

2. Inspect all parts, paying particular attention to the bearing, oil seal, and sprocket.

3. When assembling, be careful to get the bearing pressed squarely in place. Grease the bearing and oil seal liberally. The locking tabs on the sprocket nuts should be bent up around the nuts. Install the clutch and sprocket, but do not tighten them fully until chain adjustment has been made.

CHAIN

Inspection

1. The chain is a series of connecting plates, pins, and bushings. Dirt causes pin and bushing

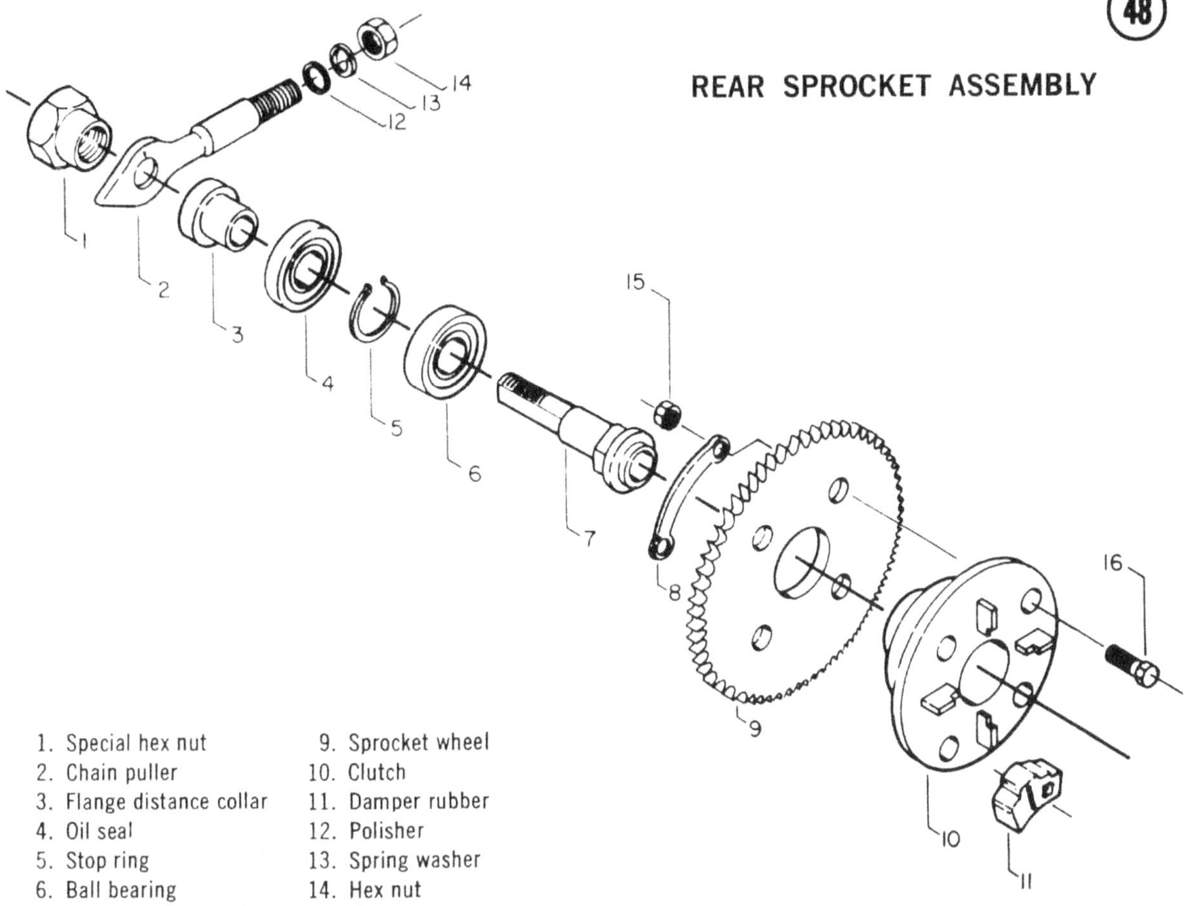

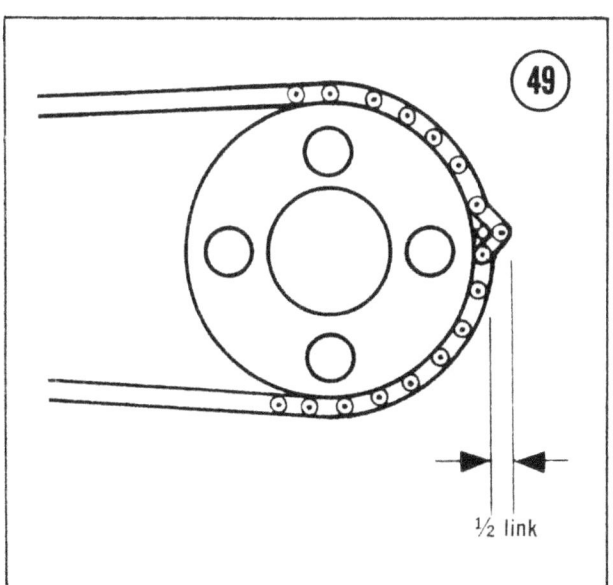

REAR SPROCKET ASSEMBLY

1. Special hex nut
2. Chain puller
3. Flange distance collar
4. Oil seal
5. Stop ring
6. Ball bearing
7. Sprocket wheel shaft
8. Lockwasher
9. Sprocket wheel
10. Clutch
11. Damper rubber
12. Polisher
13. Spring washer
14. Hex nut
15. Hex nut
16. Hex bolt

wear. As shown in **Figure 49**, the chain should be replaced if you can pull the chain away from the sprocket more than ½ the length of a link.

2. Check for links that are binding. Hang the chain straight down. The chain will not hang straight if there are kinks. If any kinks are found, thoroughly clean, oil, and work the connecting links to free them. If binding persists, replace the chain.

3. Rust causes rapid pin and bushing wear. If any rust is found, immediately clean the chain and soak in oil for full penetration.

4. Frequently wipe all dirt away with a rag, then lubricate with one of several commercially-available aerosal can lubricants. Lubricate the chain every 300-400 miles maximum if you street ride. If you dirt ride, wipe and lube after each day in the dirt.

Chain Maintenance

The chain requires periodic removal and cleaning. If you dirt ride, and do not have an enclosed chain, remove and clean after each day's use. This applies to races as well. If you street ride, clean once a month.

1. Scrub off dirt with a wire brush.
2. Soak the chain in clean solvent, then use a bristle brush to remove remaining dirt.
3. Hang until dry.
4. Immediately lubricate. Spray can lubricants usually have a dry lubricant base that does not pick up dirt as readily as oil. If desired, you can soak the chain in oil, moving the chain occasionally to permit full penetration. Hang the chain until excess oil drains. Each pin and bushing must receive lubrication.

CAUTION
Do not use high pressure water or coin-operated car wash to clean dirt off the chain. Water and soap enter the chain links, drive out lubrication, and cause rapid rust formation.

Adjustment

Figure 50 illustrates that the chain should have ¾-1 inch of up-and-down free-play on the bottom chain run, measured half-way between both sprockets, with both wheels on the ground and rider in position. Push up lightly only until obvious free-play is gone. Follow this procedure if adjustment is needed.

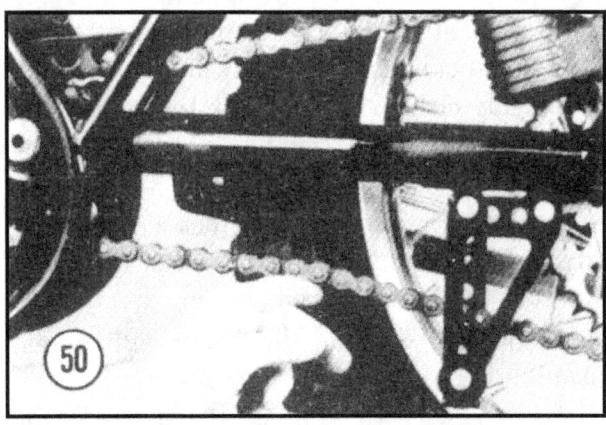

1. Loosen the axle locknut. If your machine has rubber hub cushions, there is an additional nut that must be loosened.
2. Loosen both chain adjuster locknuts, then turn both left and right adjuster bolts to pull the axle until you get correct free-play.

3. Now check rear wheel alignment. **Figure 51** shows that each adjuster has a single alignment mark. Just above each adjuster, stamped into the swing arm, are several corresponding alignment marks. Both adjuster marks must line up with identical swing arm marks on each side, or equally between the marks. For example, the left adjuster mark lines up with third swing arm mark from the front. The right adjuster mark must line up with third swing arm mark from the front also. Turn 1 adjuster to align it with the other. Recheck chain free-play. If changed, turn both adjusters in or out equally to maintain rear wheel alignment until proper chain free-play is achieved.

4. Tighten the axle nut(s) and the chain adjuster locknuts.

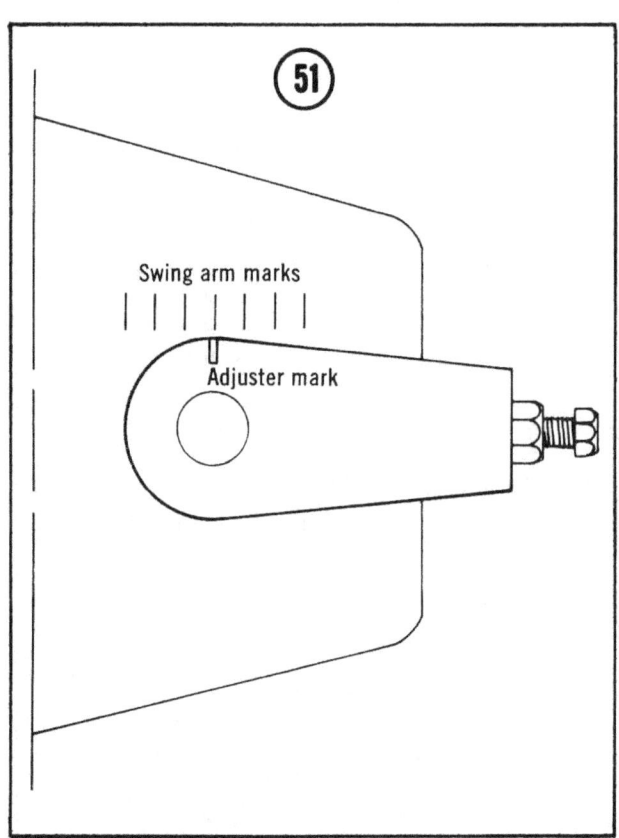

REAR SHOCKS (U5 SERIES)

Refer to **Figure 52**.

1. Built-in parts such as the spring and rubber bumpers of these shocks are the only parts designed to be replaced.
2. For disassembly, pull the roll pin out of each bottom bracket.

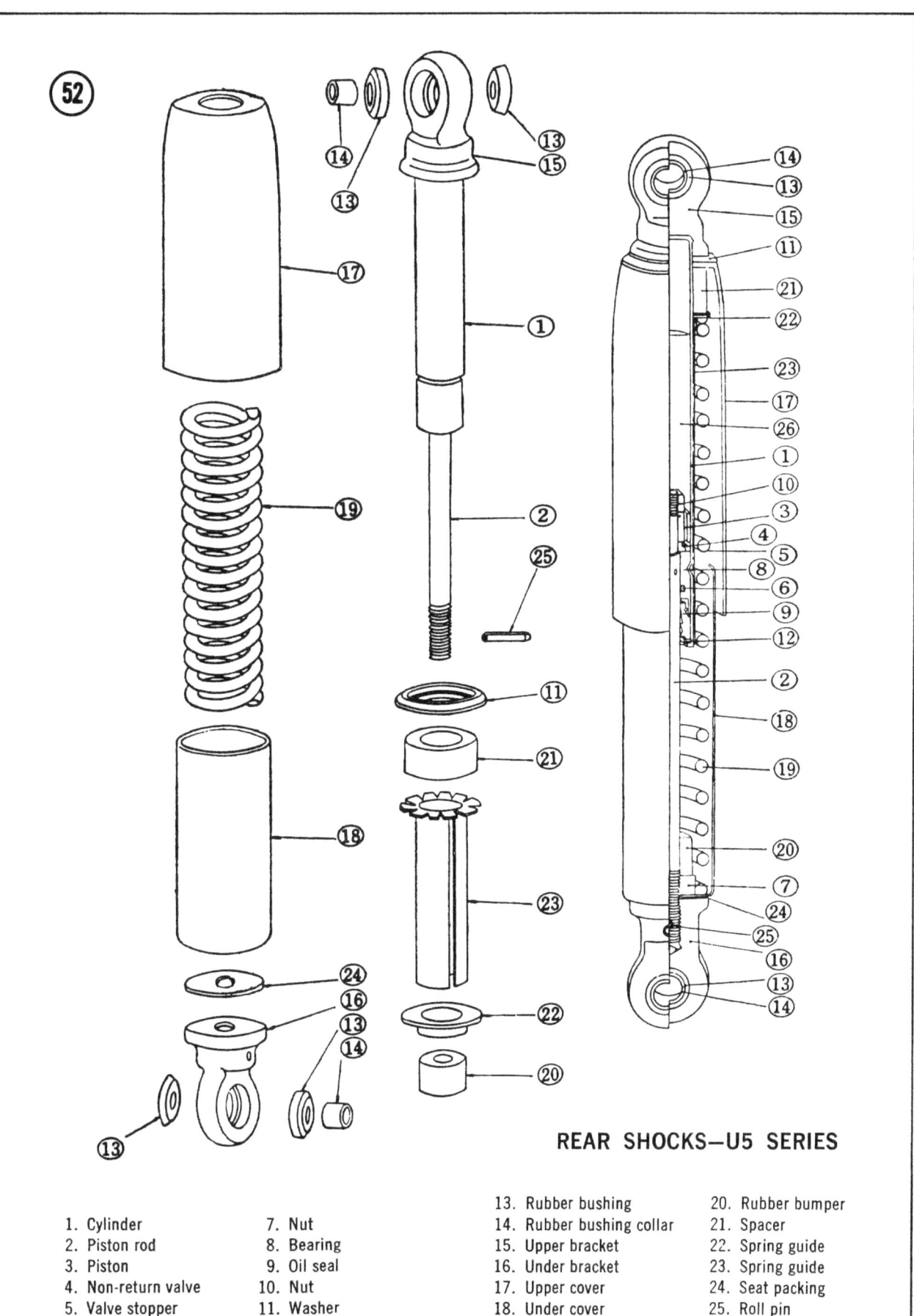

REAR SHOCKS—U5 SERIES

1. Cylinder
2. Piston rod
3. Piston
4. Non-return valve
5. Valve stopper
6. O-ring
7. Nut
8. Bearing
9. Oil seal
10. Nut
11. Washer
12. Washer
13. Rubber bushing
14. Rubber bushing collar
15. Upper bracket
16. Under bracket
17. Upper cover
18. Under cover
19. Spring
20. Rubber bumper
21. Spacer
22. Spring guide
23. Spring guide
24. Seat packing
25. Roll pin
26. Oil

3. Cover the undercover with a piece of inner tube or thick rag and secure in a vise. Turn the bottom bracket counterclockwise until it comes free.

4. Hold the split groove in the end of the piston rod with a screwdriver and unscrew the undercover.

5. Reverse the above procedure for reassembly. Inspect the shock for free compression and extension motion.

REAR SHOCK ABSORBERS (JT1/2, 80cc, 100cc, YJ1/2)

The rear shocks are not designed to be disassembled, but they can be checked for oil leakage and failure. Oil seepage can be sometimes seen on the lower part of the outer cover. In most cases, this results from melting grease applied to the spring inside and will not impair the shock action. To check the shocks, remove them and depress them fully as shown in **Figure 53**. If they rebound quickly half-way, and slowly the remaining distance, the dampening mechanism is functioning. If they rebound quickly the full distance, they must be replaced.

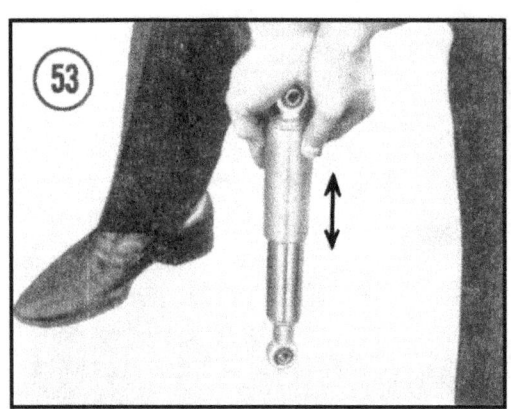

REAR SHOCKS (MJ1/2)

Refer to **Figure 54**.

1. To disassemble the shock absorbers, follow these steps: Pull out the roll pin. Protect the inner cover with a piece of inner tube or the like and secure the shock in a vise. Loosen the underbracket with a wrench and take it off the piston rod.

2. Remove the inner cover from the piston rod. Remove the spring, the spring guide, fiber tube outer cover, and cushion rubber. This is as far as the shock should be disassembled.

3. If the spring is bent or shorter than 7¾ inch (197mm), it should be replaced. If the shock is leaking oil or if the piston rod is damaged, the entire shock should be replaced. Inspect rubber components for elasticity.

4. Assemble in reverse order of disassembly. When installing shocks on the motorcycle, note that the bottom bracket is offset by 0.08 inch (2mm). The inset side should go next to the swing arm.

REAR SWING ARM

The rear swing arm holds the rear wheel to, and in line with, the frame, yet allows the wheel to move up and down independently of the frame. **Figures 55 (page 118) and 56 (page 119)** are exploded views of typical rear swing arms. Although different in appearance, they function identically. Removal and inspection procedures are also basically the same.

Removal

Figure 57 shows how to remove the swing arm shaft nut, pull out the shaft, and remove the swing arm.

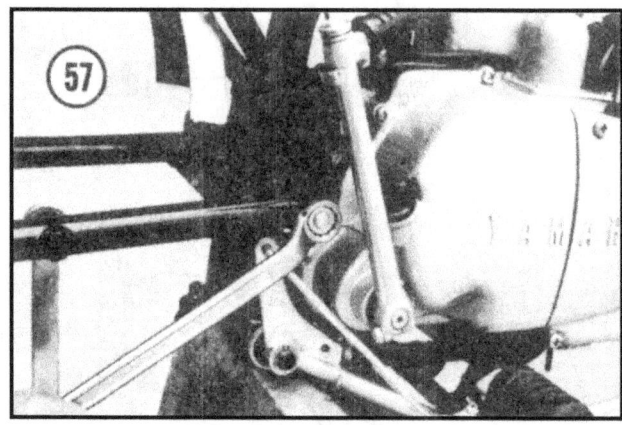

Inspection

1. Check swing arm play by shaking it as shown in **Figure 58**. If there is noticeable looseness, replace the swing arm bushings or shaft (if it is worn).

2. Insert the bushing as shown in **Figure 59** and check for looseness. Replace the bushing if it is looser than a slip fit. Grease the shaft periodically. Bushings should be checked at least

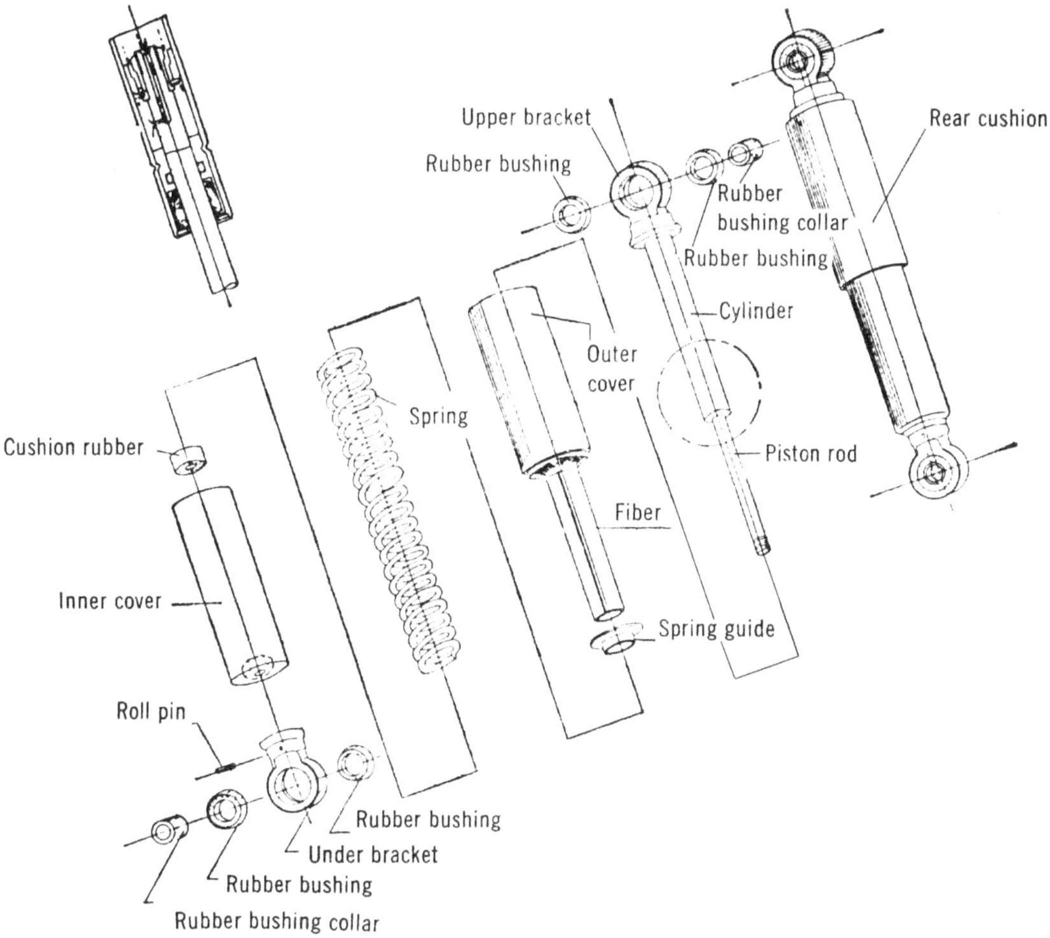

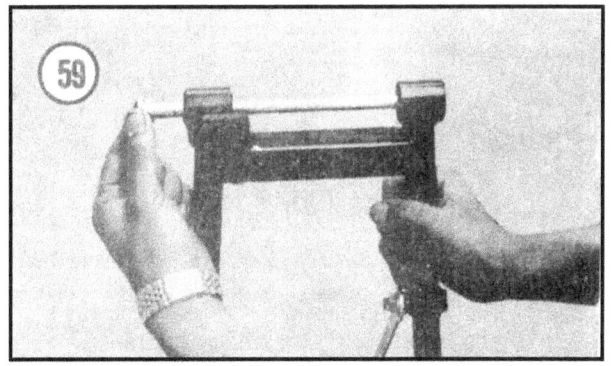

REAR SHOCKS—MJ1, MJ2

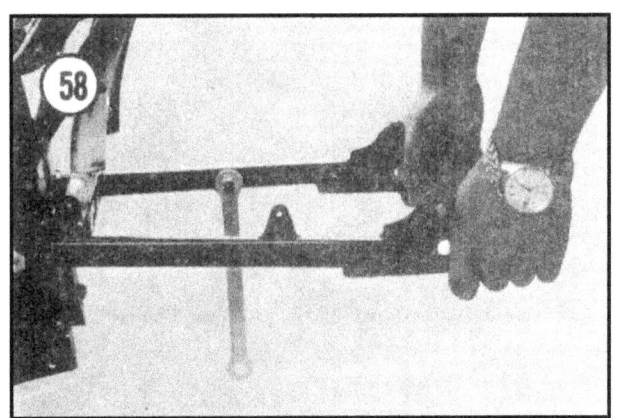

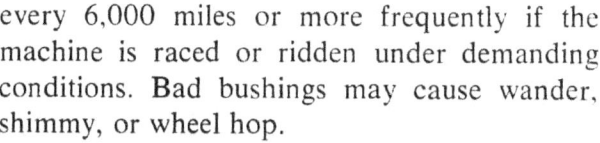

every 6,000 miles or more frequently if the machine is raced or ridden under demanding conditions. Bad bushings may cause wander, shimmy, or wheel hop.

REAR SWING ARM (MJ1/2)

Refer to **Figure 60** on page 120.

1. To take off the swing arm, remove the lower left shock absorber bolt and turn the shock up and out of the way.

117

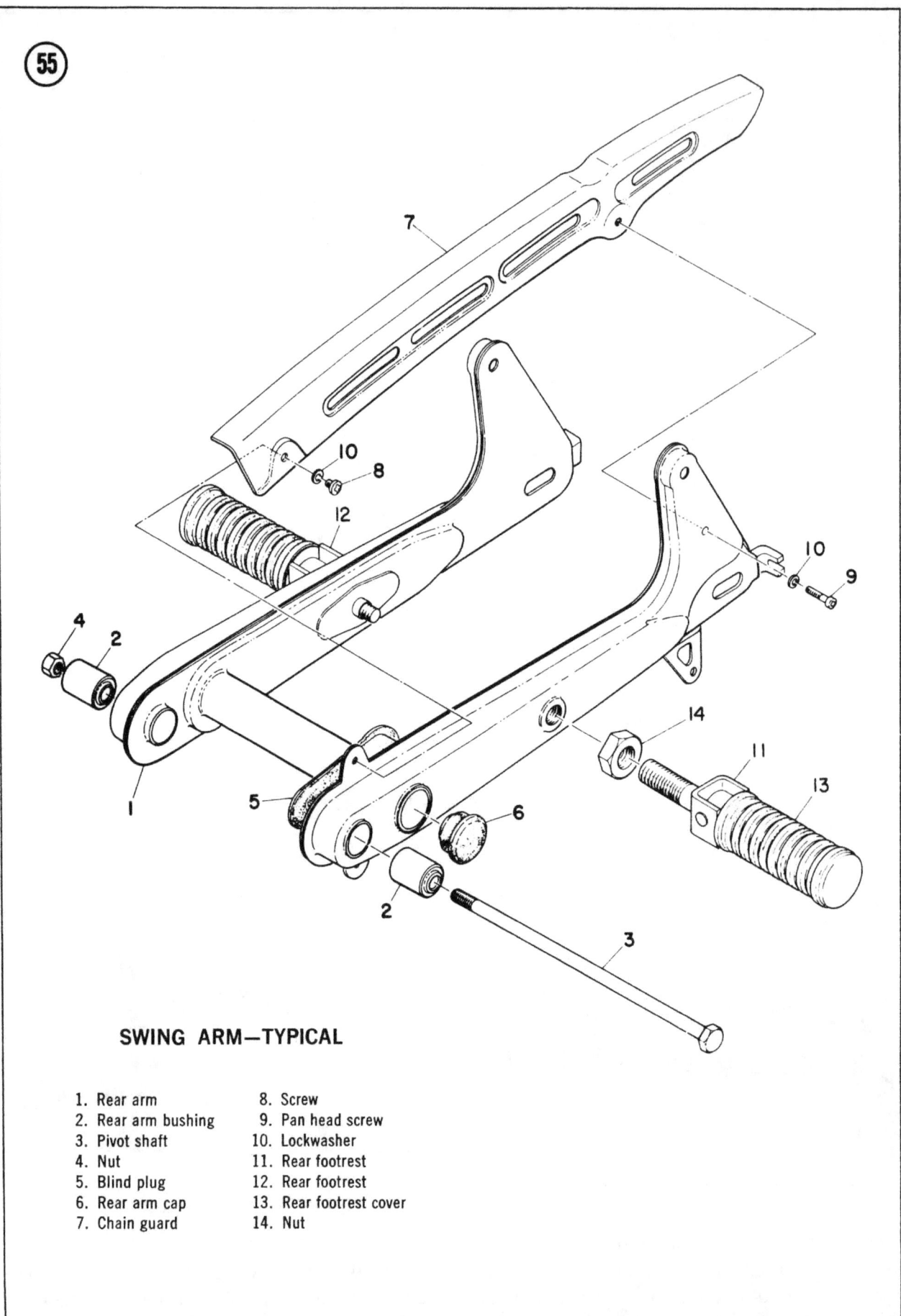

SWING ARM—TYPICAL

1. Rear arm
2. Rear arm bushing
3. Pivot shaft
4. Nut
5. Blind plug
6. Rear arm cap
7. Chain guard
8. Screw
9. Pan head screw
10. Lockwasher
11. Rear footrest
12. Rear footrest
13. Rear footrest cover
14. Nut

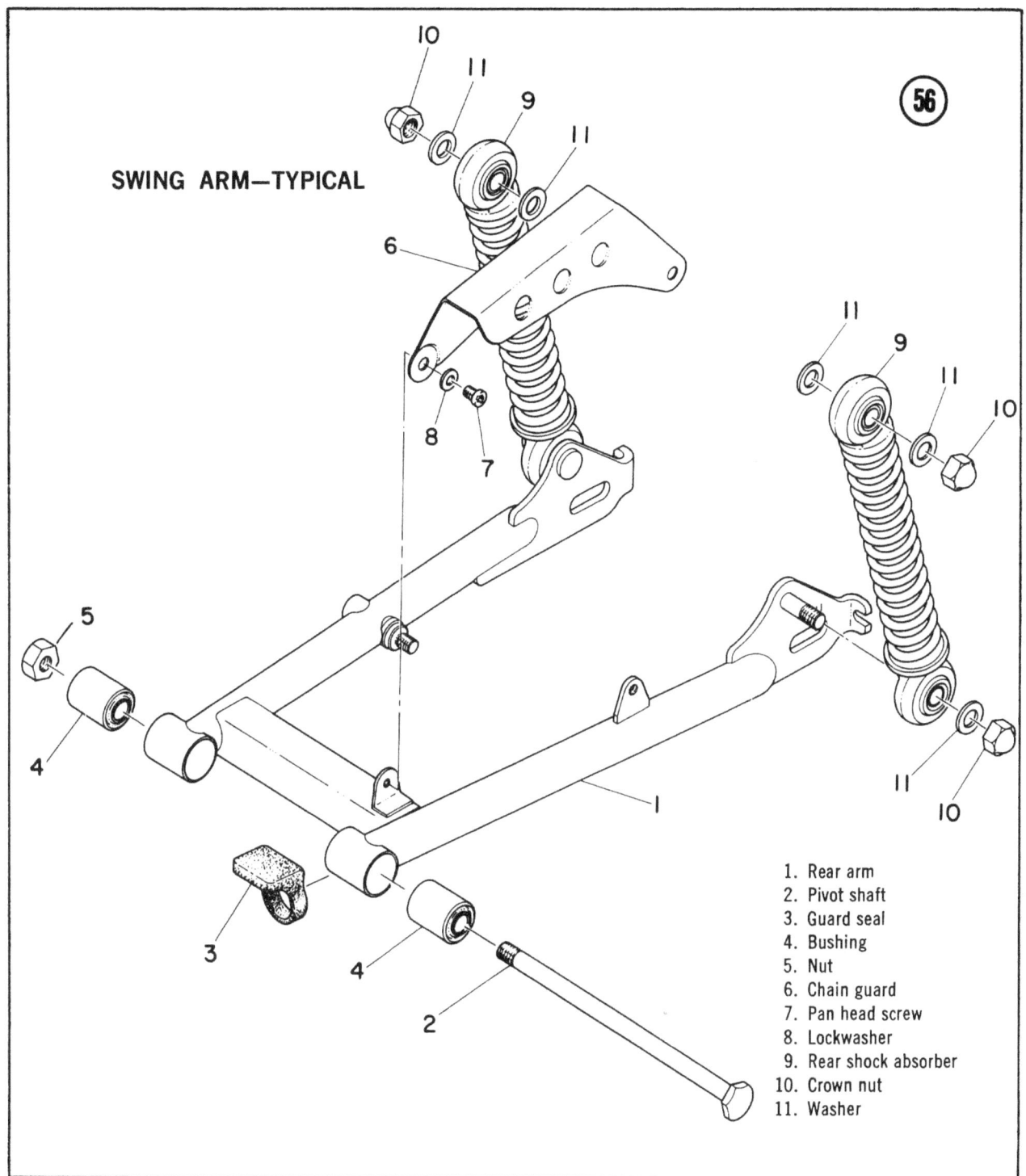

SWING ARM—TYPICAL

1. Rear arm
2. Pivot shaft
3. Guard seal
4. Bushing
5. Nut
6. Chain guard
7. Pan head screw
8. Lockwasher
9. Rear shock absorber
10. Crown nut
11. Washer

2. Remove the upper and lower chain cases.

3. Remove the rear wheel, the anchor bar, and the chain.

4. Remove the right shock absorber, loosen the pivot shaft bolt, and take out the pivot shaft. The rear swing arm can then be removed.

5. Check the rear arm rubber guard, the anchor bar, and anchor bar spring for wear and replace if necessary.

6. To assemble the arm, press in the pivot shaft bushing into the bearing pipe. Install the rubber guard slowly from the rear.

7. Hold the swing arm in place and fit the shaft through it, lightly screwing on its securing nut.

8. Install the right shock absorber and the rear wheel hub and sprocket. Install the chain and the chain guard.

9. Install the left shock absorber.

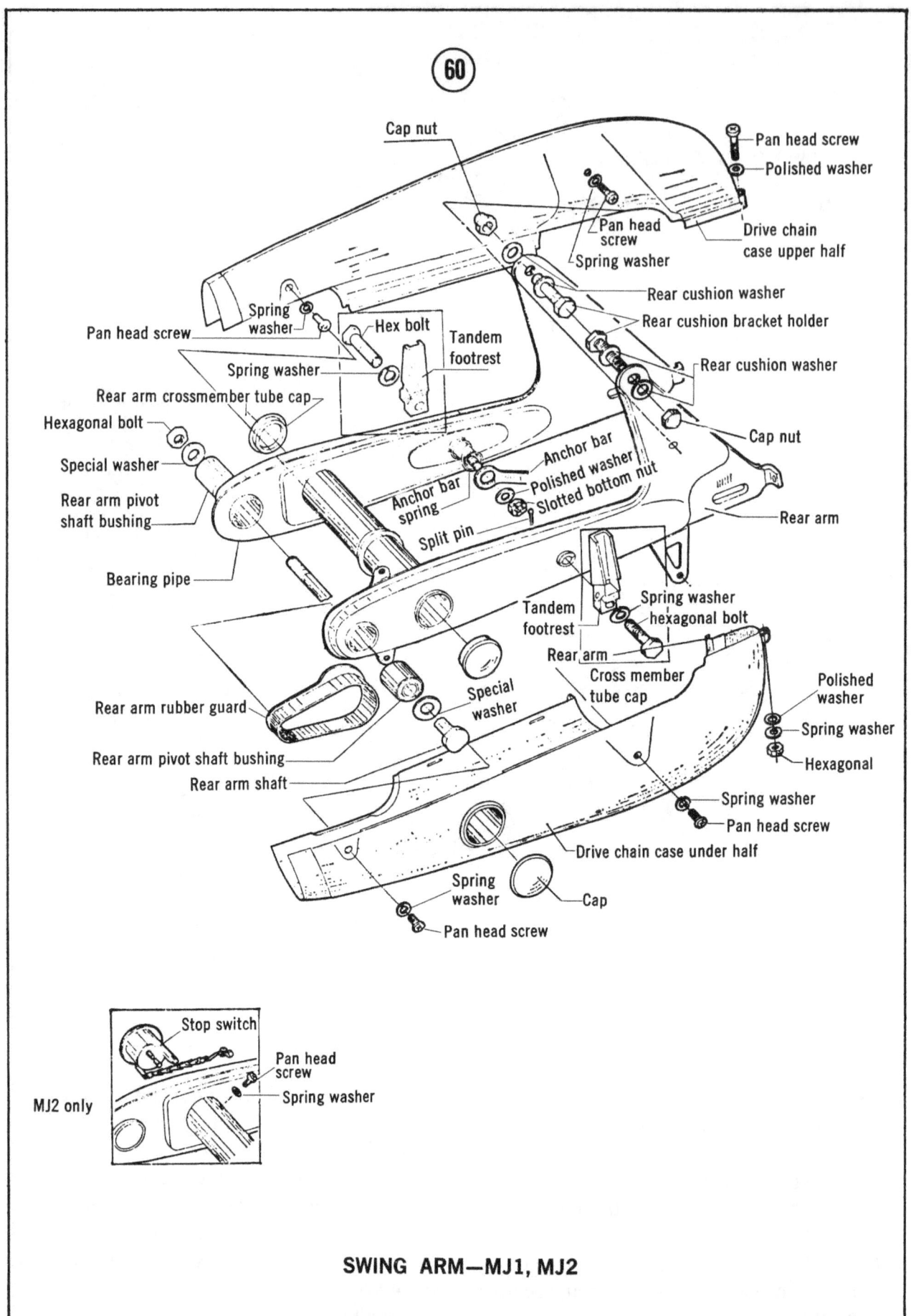

SWING ARM—MJ1, MJ2

10. Be sure the rubber guard and chain case do not interfere with each other.

FRAME

Figure 61 identifies major frame construction for the JT1/2 series and **Figure 62** provides a view of all other frames covered in this chapter.

The JT1/2 series has a tube-type frame with detachable front down tube members. The other frame uses pressed sheet metal.

FRAME (MJ2)

1. The frame, identified in **Figure 63**, is a combined tubing and pressed steel, monocoque type.

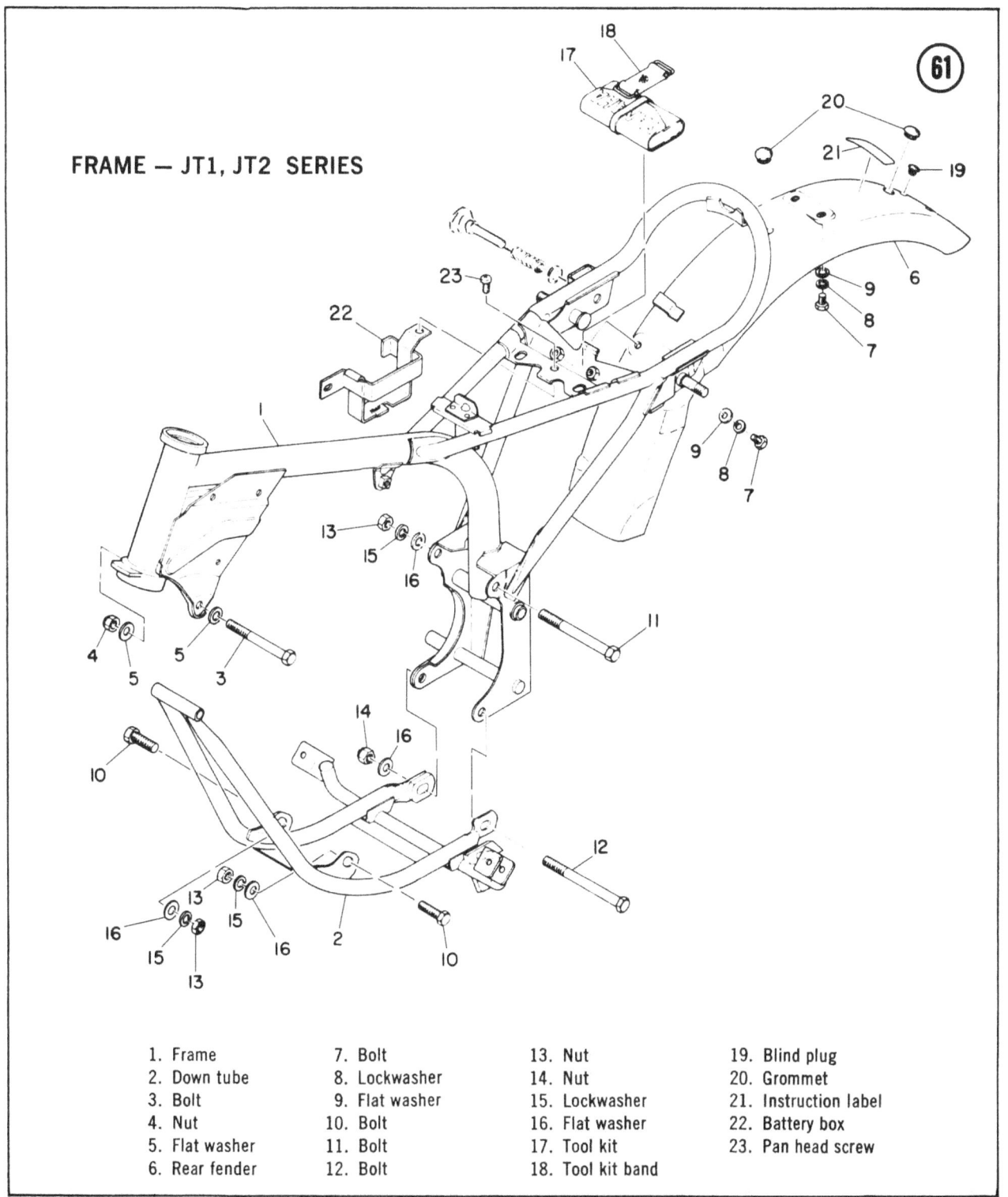

FRAME — JT1, JT2 SERIES

1. Frame
2. Down tube
3. Bolt
4. Nut
5. Flat washer
6. Rear fender
7. Bolt
8. Lockwasher
9. Flat washer
10. Bolt
11. Bolt
12. Bolt
13. Nut
14. Nut
15. Lockwasher
16. Flat washer
17. Tool kit
18. Tool kit band
19. Blind plug
20. Grommet
21. Instruction label
22. Battery box
23. Pan head screw

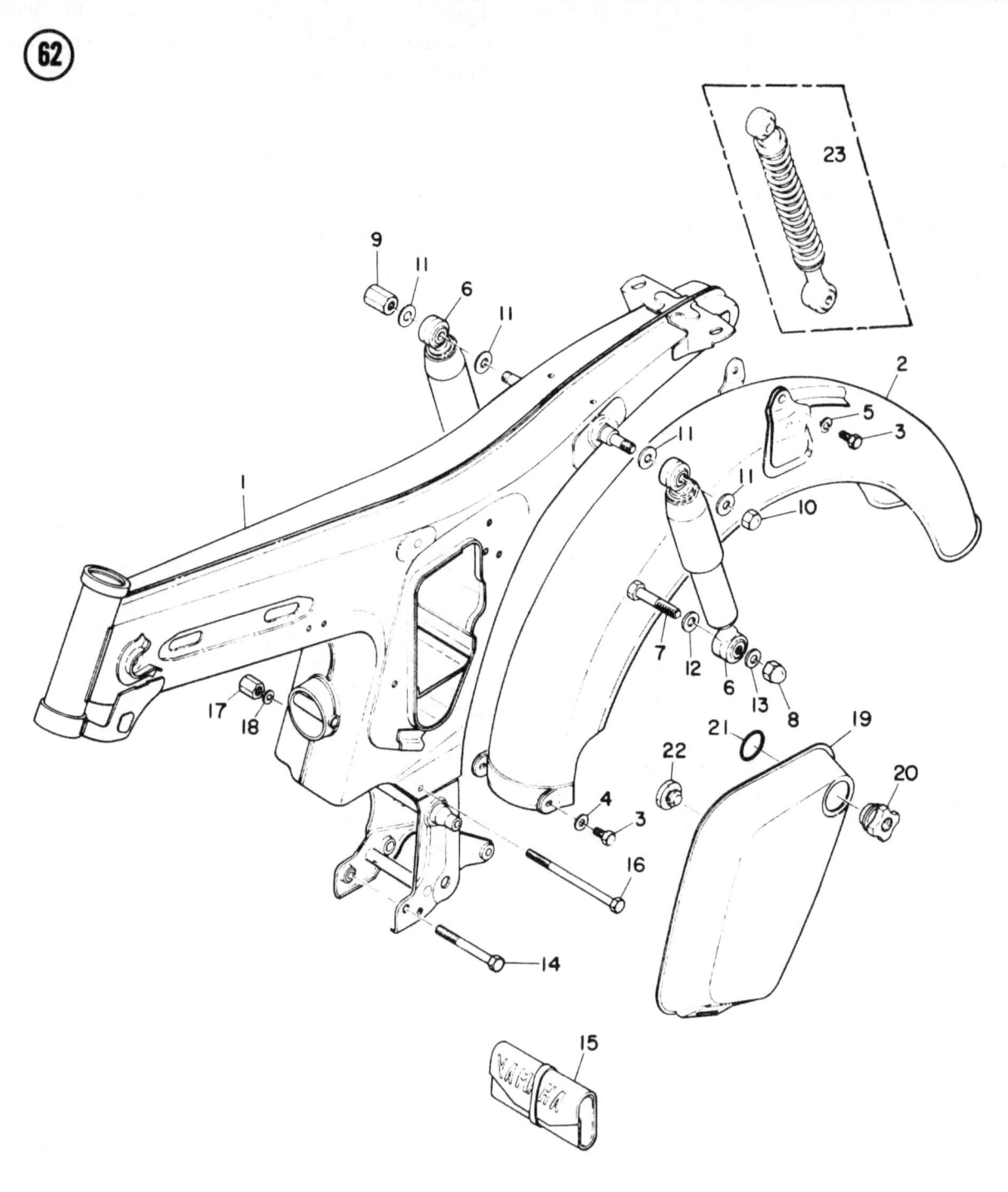

FRAME—ALL EXCEPT JT1, JT2 SERIES

1. Frame
2. Rear fender
3. Bolt
4. Flat washer
5. Lockwasher
6. Rear shock absorber
7. Shock absorber bolt
8. Acorn nut
9. Nut
10. Acorn nut
11. Flat washer
12. Flat washer
13. Flat washer
14. Engine mounting bolt
15. Tool kit
16. Bolt
17. Nut
18. Lockwasher
19. Left side cover
20. Cover knob
21. Cover knob ring
22. Side cover damper
23. Rear shock absorber (accessory)

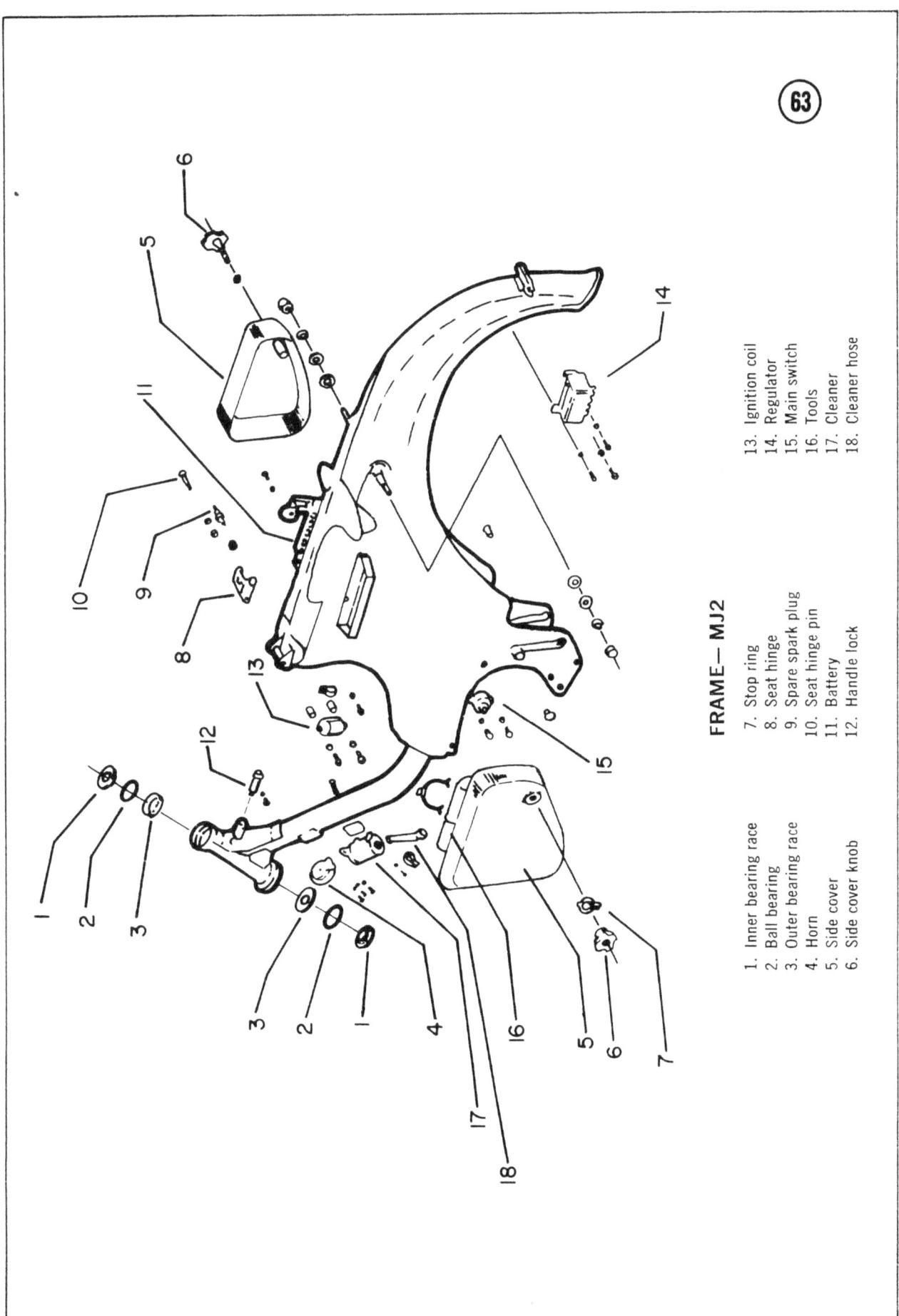

FRAME— MJ2

1. Inner bearing race
2. Ball bearing
3. Outer bearing race
4. Horn
5. Side cover
6. Side cover knob
7. Stop ring
8. Seat hinge
9. Spare spark plug
10. Seat hinge pin
11. Battery
12. Handle lock
13. Ignition coil
14. Regulator
15. Main switch
16. Tools
17. Cleaner
18. Cleaner hose

The gas tank is located inside the frame, underneath the seat.

2. Welded joints on the frame should be checked occasionally for cracking, especially if handling problems occur. Frame alignment must be checked if the motorcycle has been involved in a collision.

FRAME (YJ1/2)

The frame shown in **Figure 64** is of the backbone type and incorporates the rear fender for rigidity. Occasionally check each welded joint for cracking or flexing. If the motorcycle has been involved in a collision, it should be checked carefully for frame and steering head alignment.

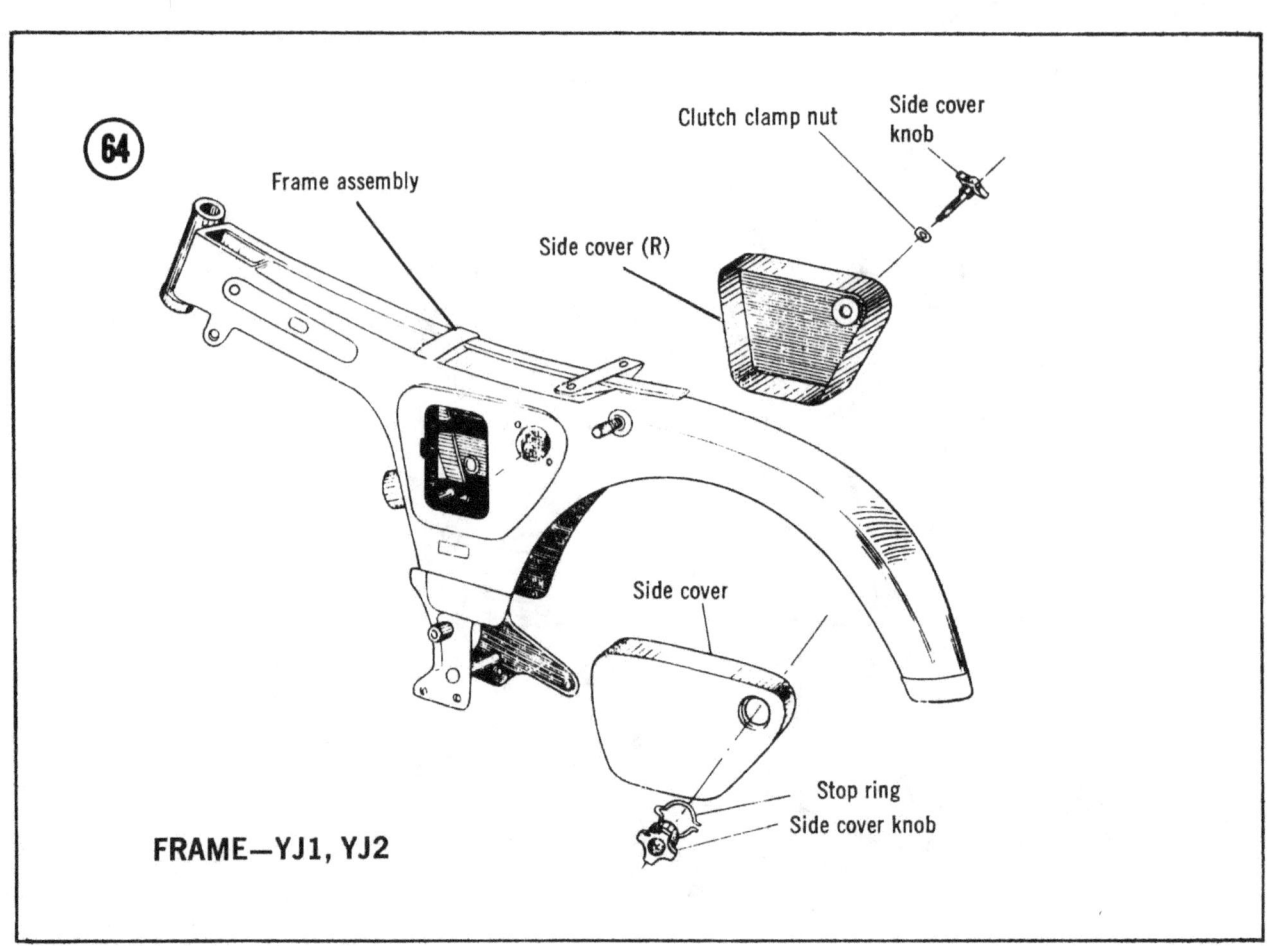

FRAME—YJ1, YJ2

CHAPTER EIGHT

SPECIFICATIONS

This chapter contains specifications and performance figures for the various Yamaha models covered by this book. The tables are arranged in order of engine size. Since there are differences between the various models, be sure to consult the correct table for the motorcycle in question.

MODELS U5, U5E, AND U5L

DIMENSIONS
  Overall length   71.1 in.
  Overall width   24.4 in.
  Overall height   39.6 in.
  Wheelbase   44.9 in.
  Road clearance   5.1 in.

WEIGHT   161 lb.

PERFORMANCE
  Maximum output   4.5 hp @ 6,500 rpm
  Maximum torque   3.6 ft.-lb. @ 5,000 rpm
  Maximum speed   44 mph
  Climbing ability   19.5 degrees
  Fuel consumption   212 mpg

ENGINE
  Type   Forward inclined, 2-stroke, rotary valve
  Displacement   50cc
  Bore x stroke   40 x 40mm
  Number of cylinders   1
  Compression ratio   6.8 : 1
  Starter type   Electric and kick start (U5 - kick start)

FUEL SYSTEM
  Carburetor
    Manufacturer, model   Mikuni, VM155C
    Main jet   130
    Needle jet   E-2
    Jet needle/clip position   3G9-3
    Cutaway   3.0
    Pilot jet   20
    Air screw (no. of turns out)   1.5
    Float level   22.5mm
  Fuel tank capacity   1.1 gal.

LUBRICATION
  Engine   Autolube
  Transmission   550cc
  Oil tank capacity   1.6 qts.

IGNITION SYSTEM
  Ignition type   Battery (magneto - U5)
  Ignition timing   1.8mm BTDC
  Spark plug type   NGK B7HZ

ELECTRICAL EQUIPMENT
  Generator/alternator   Mitzubishi
  Battery   6V, 2Ah
  Headlight   6V, 15/15W
  Tail/brake lamp   6V, 3W/10W
  Turn signal lamp   6V, 8W
  Neutral indicator lamp   6V, 3W
  Speedometer lamp   6V, 1.5W
  High beam indicator lamp   6V, 1.5W
  Turn signal indicator lamp   6V, 1.5W

TRANSMISSION SYSTEM
  Clutch type   Ball lock - centrifugal
  Number of speeds, type   3
  Primary reduction ratio   74/19
  Transmission gear ratios
    1st gear   37/12
    2nd gear   31/18
    3rd gear   27/23
  Secondary reduction ratio 38/15

FRAME
  Type   Step thru
  Suspension, front   Leading link
  Suspension, rear   Oil/spring shock

STEERING
  Caster   63 degrees
  Trail   3.1 in.

TIRES
  Front   2.25 x 17, 4PR
  Rear   2.25 x 17, 4PR

MODELS YJ1, YJ1K, AND MJ1

DIMENSIONS
Overall length	70.9 in. (MJ1 - 67.5 in.)
Overall width	24.8 in. (MJ1 - 27.1 in.)
Overall height	37.1 in. (MJ1 - 37.6 in.)
Wheelbase	44.8 in. (MJ1 - 44.5 in.)
Road clearance	5.1 in.

WEIGHT ———

PERFORMANCE
Maximum output	4.5 hp @ 7,000 rpm
Maximum torque	3.25 ft.-lb. @ 6,000 rpm
Maximum speed	45 mph

ENGINE
Type	2-stroke, rotary valve
Displacement	50cc
Bore x stroke	42 x 40mm
Number of cylinders	1
Compression ratio	7.1 : 1
Starter type	Kick

FUEL SYSTEM
Carburetor	
Manufacturer, model	Mikuni VM14SC
Main jet	95
Needle jet	E-0
Jet needle/clip position	3G1-3
Cutaway	1.5
Pilot jet	15
Starter jet	30
Air screw (no. of turns out)	1.5
Float level	23
Fuel tank capacity	1.4 gal.

LUBRICATION
Engine	20 : 1 pre-mix (YJ1K - Autolube)
Transmission	500cc
Oil tank capacity	———

IGNITION SYSTEM
Ignition type	Magneto
Ignition timing	2.0mm BTDC
Spark plug type	NGK B7HZ

ELECTRICAL EQUIPMENT
Battery	6V, 4Ah
Headlight	6V, 15/15W
Tail/brake lamp	6V, 3/10W
Turn signal lamp	———
Neutral indicator lamp	5V, 1.5W
Speedometer lamp	———
High beam indicator lamp	———
Turn signal indicator lamp	———

TRANSMISSION SYSTEM
Clutch type	Wet, multiplate
Number of speeds, type	4, constant mesh
Primary reduction ratio	74/19 (3.895)
Final reduction ratio	39/14 (2.786)
Transmission gear ratios	
1st gear	37/12 (3.083)
2nd gear	32/17 (1.882)
3rd gear	28/21 (1.333)
4th gear	25/25 (1.000)

STEERING
Steering angle	45 degrees
Caster	63 degrees
Trail	3.15 in.

TIRES
Front	2.25 x 17, 4PR
Rear	2.25 x 17, 4PR

MODELS YJ2 AND YJ2S

DIMENSIONS

Overall length	72.4 in.
Overall width	25.4 in.
Overall height	38.4 in.
Wheelbase	45.8 in.
Road clearance	——

WEIGHT   172 lb.

PERFORMANCE

Maximum output	5.0 hp @ 7,000 rpm
Maximum torque	3.97 ft.-lb. @ 6,000 rpm
Maximum speed	50 mph

ENGINE

Type	2-stroke rotary valve
Displacement	60cc
Bore x stroke	42 x 42mm
Number of cylinders	1
Compression ratio	6.6 : 1 (late YJ2 - 7.5 : 1)
Starter type	Kick

FUEL SYSTEM

Carburetor	
Manufacturer, model	Mikuni VM14SC (late YJ2 - VM16)
Main jet	100 (late YJ2 - 60)
Needle jet	E-0
Jet needle/clip position	3G1-2 (late - 3D1-3)
Cutaway	1.5
Pilot jet	17.5
Starter jet	30 (late - 15)
Air screw (no. of turns out)	1.5
Float level	23
Fuel tank capacity	1.4 gal.

LUBRICATION

Engine	Autolube
Transmission	500cc
Oil tank capacity	1.16 qt.

IGNITION SYSTEM

Ignition type	Magneto
Ignition timing	1.8mm BTDC
Spark plug type	NGK B7H2 (late - B8HC)

ELECTRICAL EQUIPMENT

Battery	6V, 4Ah
Headlight	6V, 15/15W
Tail/brake lamp	6V, 3/10W
Turn signal lamp	6V, 8W
Neutral indicator lamp	6V, 1.5W
Speedometer lamp	6V, 1.5W
High beam indicator lamp	6V, 1.5W
Turn signal indicator lamp	6V, 3.0W

TRANSMISSION SYSTEM

Clutch type	Wet, multiplate
Number of speeds, type	4, constant mesh
Primary reduction ratio	14/19 (3.895)
Final reduction ratio	39/15 2.600 (late - 38/15 2.533)
Transmission gear ratios	
1st gear	37/12 (3.083)
2nd gear	32/17 (1.882)
3rd gear	28/21 (1.333)
4th gear	25/25 (1.000)

STEERING

Steering angle	45 degrees
Caster	63 degrees
Trail	3.15 in.

TIRES

Front	2.25 x 17, 4PR
Rear	2.25 x 17, 4PR

MODELS MJ2 AND MJ2T

DIMENSIONS
Overall length	67.5 in.
Overall width	27.1 in.
Overall height	37.6 in.
Wheelbase	44.5 in.

WEIGHT
165 lb.

PERFORMANCE
Maximum output	5.0 hp @ 7,000 rpm
Maximum torque	4.0 hp @ 5,000 rpm
Maximum speed	45 mph

ENGINE
Type	2-stroke rotary valve
Displacement	60cc
Bore x stroke	42 x 40mm
Number of cylinders	1
Compression ratio	7.4 : 1
Starter type	Kick or electric

FUEL SYSTEM
Carburetor	
Manufacturer, model	Mikuni VM14SC
Main jet	100
Needle jet	0-2
Jet needle/clip position	3G1-3
Cutaway	2.5
Pilot jet	15
Starter jet	30
Air screw (no. of turns out)	1.5
Float level	23mm
Fuel tank capacity	.9 gal.

LUBRICATION
Engine	20 : 1 pre-mix
Transmission	500cc
Oil tank capacity	—

IGNITION SYSTEM
Ignition type	Battery/generator
Ignition timing	2.2mm BTDC
Spark plug type	NGK B7H

ELECTRICAL EQUIPMENT
Generator/alternator	Generator
Battery	12V, 5.5Ah
Headlight	12V, 25/25W
Tail/brake lamp	12V, 3/10W

TRANSMISSION SYSTEM
Clutch type	Wet, multiplate centrifugal
Number of speeds, type	3, constant mesh
Primary reduction ratio	74/19 (3.895)
Final reduction ratio	38/14 (2.715)
Transmission gear ratios	
1st gear	37/12 (3.083)
2nd gear	31/18 (1.722)
3rd gear	27/23 (1.174)

STEERING
Steering angle	47 degrees
Caster	63 degrees
Trail	3.54 in.

TIRES
Front	2.25 x 16, 4PR
Rear	2.25 x 16, 4PR

MODELS JT1, JT1L, JT2, AND JT2M

DIMENSIONS
Overall length	62.4 in.
Overall width	27.6 in.
Overall height	36.6 in.
Wheelbase	41.5 in.
Road clearance	6.3 in.

WEIGHT   132 lb.

PERFORMANCE
Maximum output	4.5 hp @ 7,500 rpm
Maximum torque	3.6 ft.-lb. @ 5,500 rpm

ENGINE
Type	2-stroke, rotary valve
Displacement	60cc
Bore x stroke	42 x 42mm
Number of cylinders	1
Compression ratio	6.4 : 1
Starter type	Kick

FUEL SYSTEM
Carburetor	
Manufacturer, model	Teikei, Y16P
Main jet	84 (JT2 - 80)
Needle jet	2.085 (JT2 - 2.080)
Jet needle/clip position	032-2 (JT2 - 0.35-3)
Cutaway	1.5
Pilot jet	38
Starter jet	50
Air screw (no. of turns out)	1.5 (JT2 - 1.75)
Fuel tank capacity	1.1 gal.

LUBRICATION
Engine	Autolube
Transmission	600-650cc
Oil tank capacity	1.1 qt.

IGNITION SYSTEM
Ignition type	Magneto
Ignition timing	1.8mm
Spark plug type	B7HS

ELECTRICAL EQUIPMENT
Generator/alternator	Magneto
Headlight	6V, 15/15W (except JT1)
Tail/brake lamp	6V, 10/3W (except JT1)

TRANSMISSION SYSTEM
Clutch type	Wet, multiplate
Number of speeds, type	4, constant mesh
Primary reduction ratio	74/19 (3.895)
Final reduction ratio	41/13 (3.154)
Transmission gear ratios	
1st gear	40/13 (3.077)
2nd gear	34/18 (1.889)
3rd gear	30/23 (1.304)
4th gear	27/26 (1.038)
Overall reduction ratios	
1st gear	37.80
2nd gear	23.20
3rd gear	16.02
4th gear	12.75

STEERING
Steering angle	47 degrees
Caster	63.5 degrees
Trail	2.7 degrees

TIRES
Front	2.50 x 15, 4PR
Rear	2.50 x 15, 4PR

MODELS YG1 (S and T) AND YG1K (S and T)

DIMENSIONS
Overall length	71.5 in.
Overall width	24.6 in.
Overall height	37.8 in.
Wheelbase	45.1 in.
Road clearance	5.9 in.

WEIGHT
161 lb.

PERFORMANCE
Maximum output	8.0 hp @ 7,000 rpm
Maximum torque	5.1 ft.-lb. @ 5,000 rpm
Maximum speed	50-55 mph

ENGINE
Type	2-stroke, rotary valve
Displacement	80cc
Bore x stroke	47 x 42mm
Number of cylinders	1
Compression ratio	6.8 : 1
Starter type	Kick

FUEL SYSTEM
Carburetor
Manufacturer, model	Mikuni VM15SC
Main jet	100
Needle jet	E-0 (E-2 = YG1K)
Jet needle/clip position	3G1-3 (3G9-2 = YG1K)
Cutaway	1.5
Pilot jet	20 (17.5 = YG1K)
Starter jet	20 (40 = YG1K)
Air screw (no. of turns out)	1½ (1¾ = YG1K)
Float level	20mm
Fuel tank capacity	1.7 gal.

LUBRICATION
Engine	20 : 1 pre-mix (Autolube = YG1K)
Transmission	400cc

IGNITION SYSTEM
Ignition type	Magneto
Ignition timing	1.8mm BTDC
Spark plug type	NGK B7HZ

ELECTRICAL EQUIPMENT
Battery	6V, 4Ah
Headlight	6V, 15/15W
Tail/brake lamp	6V, 3/10W
Turn signal lamp	6V, 8W
Neutral indicator lamp	6V, 3W
Speedometer lamp	6V, 1.5W
High beam indicator lamp	6V, 1.5W
Turn signal indicator lamp	6V, 3W

TRANSMISSION SYSTEM
Clutch type	Wet, multidisc
Number of speeds, type	4
Primary reduction ratio	74/19 (3.894)
Final reduction ratio	37/15 (2.467)
Transmission gear ratios	
1st gear	37/12 (3.083)
2nd gear	32/17 (1.882)
3rd gear	28/12 (1.333)
4th gear	25/25 (1.000)

STEERING
Steering angle	45 degrees
Caster	63 degrees
Trail	3.54 in.

TIRES
Front	2.50 x 17, 4PR
Rear	2.50 x 17, 4PR

MODEL YG5T

DIMENSIONS
Overall length	70.9 in.
Overall width	31.7 in.
Overall height	40.0 in.
Wheelbase	46.3 in.
Road clearance	6.3 in.

WEIGHT
203 lb.

PERFORMANCE
Maximum output	6.6 hp @ 7,000 rpm
Maximum torque	5.2 ft.-lb. @ 6,000 rpm
Maximum speed	50-55 mph
Fuel consumption	140 mpg

ENGINE
Type	2-stroke, rotary valve
Displacement	80cc
Bore x stroke	47 x 42mm
Number of cylinders	1
Compression ratio	6.8 : 1
Starter type	Kick or electric

FUEL SYSTEM
Carburetor	
Manufacturer, model	Mikuni VM16SC
Main jet	120
Needle jet	E-2
Jet needle/clip position	3G9-4
Cutaway	2.5
Pilot jet	25
Starter jet	30
Air screw (no. of turns out)	1½
Float level	20.5mm
Fuel tank capacity	1.6 gal.

LUBRICATION
Engine	Autolube
Transmission	650cc
Oil tank capacity	1.5 qt.

IGNITION SYSTEM
Ignition type	Generator
Ignition timing	1.8mm
Spark plug type	NGK B7HZ

ELECTRICAL EQUIPMENT
Generator/alternator	Generator
Battery	6V, 4Ah
Headlight	6V, 15/15W
Tail/brake lamp	6V, 3/10W
Turn signal lamp	6V, 8W
Neutral indicator lamp	6V, 3W
Speedometer lamp	6V, 1.5W
High beam indicator lamp	6V, 1.5W
Turn signal indicator lamp	6V, 1.5W

TRANSMISSION SYSTEM
Clutch type	Wet, multidisc
Number of speeds, type	4, constant mesh
Primary reduction ratio	74/19 (3.895)
Final reduction ratio	41/15 (2.740)
Transmission gear ratios	
1st gear	40/13 (3.077)
2nd gear	34/18 (1.889)
3rd gear	30/23 (1.304)
4th gear	20/27 (0.963)

STEERING
Steering angle	45 degrees
Caster	63.5 degrees
Trail	3.1 in.

TIRES
Front	2.50 x 17, 4PR
Rear	3.00 x 17, 4PR

MODELS G5S, G6S, G6SB, AND G7S

DIMENSIONS

Overall length	71.3 in.
Overall width	31.1 in.
Overall height	39.2 in.
Wheelbase	45.9 in.
Road clearance	5.3 in.

WEIGHT   186 lb.

PERFORMANCE

Maximum output	4.9 hp @ 7,500 rpm
Maximum torque	4.1 ft.-lb. @ 5,500 rpm
Maximum speed	50-55 mph
Fuel consumption	190 mpg

ENGINE

Type	2-stroke, rotary valve
Displacement	80cc
Bore x stroke	47 x 42mm
Number of cylinders	1
Compression ratio	6.8 : 1
Starter type	Kick

FUEL SYSTEM

Carburetor	
Manufacturer, model	Mikuni VM16SC
Main jet	100
Needle jet	E-2
Jet needle/clip position	3G9-3
Cutaway	2.5
Pilot jet	25
Starter jet	30
Air screw (no. of turns out)	1¾
Float level	20.5mm
Fuel tank capacity	1.6 gal.

LUBRICATION

Engine	Autolube
Transmission	650cc
Oil tank capacity	1.5 qt.

IGNITION SYSTEM

Ignition type	Magneto
Ignition timing	1.8mm BTDC
Spark plug type	NGK B7HZ

ELECTRICAL EQUIPMENT

Battery	6V, 4Ah
Headlight	6V, 15/15W
Tail/brake lamp	6V, 5.3W/17W
Turn signal lamp	6V, 1.5W
Neutral indicator lamp	6V, 3W
Speedometer lamp	6V, 3W
High beam indicator lamp	6V, 1.5W
Turn signal indicator lamp	6V, 1.5W

TRANSMISSION SYSTEM

Clutch type	Wet, multiplate
Number of speeds, type	4, constant mesh
Primary reduction ratio	74/19 (3.894)
Final reduction ratio	37/14 (2.643)
Transmission gear ratios	
1st gear	40/13 (3.077)
2nd gear	34/18 (1.889)
3rd gear	30/23 (1.304)
4th gear	26/27 (0.963)

STEERING

Steering angle	45 degrees
Caster	63.5 degrees
Trail	3.07 in.

TIRES

Front	2.50 x 17, 4PR
Rear	2.50 x 17, 4PR

MODELS YL2 AND YL2C

DIMENSIONS
Overall length	75.4 in. (YL2C = 74.8 in.)
Overall width	28.1 in.
Overall height	41.7 in. (YL2C = 42.5 in.)
Wheelbase	46.8 in. (YL2C = 47.2 in.)
Road clearance	5.5 in. (YL2C = 6.7 in.)

WEIGHT
220 lb. (YL2C = 240 lb.)

PERFORMANCE
Maximum output	9.5 hp @ 7,500 rpm
Maximum torque	6.8 ft.-lb. @ 5,500 rpm
Maximum speed	65-70 mph
Fuel consumption	140 mpg

ENGINE
Type	2-stroke forward inclined
Displacement	100cc
Bore x stroke	52 x 45.6mm
Number of cylinders	1
Compression ratio	7.2 : 1
Starter type	Kick (YL2C = electric)

FUEL SYSTEM
Carburetor	
Manufacturer, model	Mikuni, VM18SC
Main jet	120
Needle jet	0-0
Jet needle/clip position	4J11-3 (4J11-4 = YL2C)
Cutaway	2.0
Pilot jet	20
Starter jet	40
Air screw (no. of turns out)	1¼
Fuel tank capacity	2.2 gal.

LUBRICATION
Engine	Autolube
Transmission	650cc
Oil tank capacity	1.7 qt.

IGNITION SYSTEM
Ignition type	Generator (YL2C = generator/starter)
Ignition timing	1.8mm ATDS
Spark plug type	B7HZ

ELECTRICAL EQUIPMENT
Generator/alternator	Magneto (YL2C = generator/starter)
Battery	12V, 5.5 Ah (YL2C = 12V, 7Ah)
Headlight	12V, 25W/25W
Tail/brake lamp	12V, 7W/23W
Neutral indicator lamp	12V, 2W
Speedometer lamp	12V, 3W
High beam indicator lamp	12V, 3W

TRANSMISSION SYSTEM
Clutch type	Wet, multiplate
Number of speeds, type	4, constant mesh
Primary reduction ratio	74/19 (3.895)
Final reduction ratio	35/15 (2.335)
Transmission gear ratios	
1st gear	40/13 (3.077)
2nd gear	30/23 (1.304)
3rd gear	26/27 (0.963)
4th gear	45 degrees

STEERING
Steering angle	45 degrees
Caster	63.5 degrees
Trail	3.3 in.

TIRES
Front	2.50 x 18, 4PR
Rear	2.58 x 18, 4PR

MODELS L5T AND L5TA

DIMENSIONS
- Overall length — 70.9 in.
- Overall width — 31.7 in.
- Overall height — 40.2 in.
- Wheelbase — 46.3 in.
- Road clearance — 6.3 in.

WEIGHT — 198 lb.

PERFORMANCE
- Maximum output — 8 hp @ 6,000 rpm
- Maximum torque — 6.9 ft.-lb. @ 5,000 rpm
- Maximum speed — 55-60 mph

ENGINE
- Type — 2-stroke, rotary valve
- Displacement — 100cc
- Bore x stroke — 52 x 45.6mm
- Number of cylinders — 1
- Compression ratio — 6.8 : 1
- Starter type — Kick and electric

FUEL SYSTEM
- Carburetor
  - Manufacturer, model — Mikuni, VM20SC
  - Main jet — 180
  - Needle jet — O-8
  - Jet needle/clip position — 4D2-3
  - Cutaway — 2.0
  - Pilot jet — 20
  - Starter jet — 40
  - Air screw (no. of turns out) — 1¾
  - Float level — 22mm
- Fuel tank capacity — 1.8 gal.

LUBRICATION
- Engine — Autolube
- Transmission — 650cc
- Oil tank capacity — 1.5 qt.

IGNITION SYSTEM
- Ignition type — Generator/starter
- Ignition timing — 1.8mm BTDC
- Spark plug type — D8HC/0.5-0.6mm

ELECTRICAL EQUIPMENT
- Generator/alternator — Generator
- Battery — 12V, 7Ah
- Headlight — 12V, 25/25W
- Tail/brake lamp — 12V, 7/23W
- Neutral indicator lamp — 12V, 2W
- Speedometer lamp — 12V, 2W
- High beam indicator lamp — 12V, 2W

TRANSMISSION SYSTEM
- Clutch type — Wet, multiplate
- Number of speeds, type — 3, constant mesh, plus hi/lo range
- Primary reduction ratio — 74/19 (3.895 : 1)
- Final reduction ratio — 37/18 (2.313 : 1)
- Transmission gear ratios
  - 1st gear — 34/12 (1.647 hi, 2.702 lo)
  - 2nd gear — 28/17 (1.647 hi, 2.702 lo)
  - 3rd gear — 23/23 (1.000 hi, 1.640 lo)

STEERING
- Steering angle — 45 degrees
- Caster — 63.5 degrees
- Trail — 3.2 in.

TIRES
- Front — 3.00 x 17, 4PR
- Rear — 2.75 x 17, 4PR

NOTES

INDEX

A

Air filter 70
Autolube system
    Bleeding the pump 32
    Minimum pump stroke 31
    Pump cable adjustment 31
    Service 30

B

Backfiring 7
Battery/coil ignition system
    Breaker point adjustment 78
    Breaker point maintenance
        and replacement 79
    Condenser inspection and replacement . 79
    Ignition coil 79
    Ignition coil resistance specifications . 80
    Ignition timing 79
Bearings 25
Brake, front
    Adjustment 95
    Inspection 94
    Shoe replacement 94
    Troubleshooting 8, 9
Brake, rear
    Inspection and adjustment 111
    Shoe replacement 111
    Troubleshooting 8, 9
Breaker points 73-74, 78

C

Carburetor
    Basic principles 60
    Disassembly and assembly, Mikuni VM . 64
    Disassembly and assembly, Teikei Y16P 62
    Exploded view, Mikuni VM 65
    Exploded view, Teikei Y16P 62
    Float level adjustment 67
    Idle mixture and idle speed 68
    Periodic maintenance 61
    Reassembly 69
    Starter jet system 61
    Throttle cable free-play 68
    Throttle cable replacement 69
Chain, drive
    Adjustment 114
    Inspection 112
    Maintenance 113

Chassis
    Brake, front 94-95
    Brake, rear 111
    Chain, drive 112
    Forks, front (JT1, JT2, 80cc, 100cc,
        YJ1, and YJ2) 95-100
    Forks, front (MJ1 and MJ2) 101
    Forks, front (U5 series) 101
    Frame 121-124
    Front end 102
    Shock absorbers, rear (JT1, JT2, 80cc,
        100cc, YJ1, and YJ2) 116
    Shocks, rear (MJ1 and MJ2) 116
    Shocks, rear (U5 series) 114
    Sprocket, rear 112
    Steering head 102
    Swing arm, rear 116
    Swing arm, rear (MJ1 and MJ2) 117
    Tires and tubes 111
    Wheel, front 90-94
    Wheel, rear 104-111
Clutch
    Adjustment 50
    Exploded view, JT1 and JT2 46
    Exploded view, late MJ2 48
    Exploded view, MJ1 and early MJ2 47
    Exploded view, MJ2T 49
    Friction plate inspection 50
    Housing inspection 50
    JT1 and JT2 45-46
    Metal plate inspection 50
    MJ1 and MJ2 47
    MJ2T 47
    Plate inspection 47
    Plate specifications 44
    Primary gear retaining collar inspection .. 50
    Sectional view, U5 series 42
    Slip or drag 7
    Spring length 50
    U5 series 42-43
    YJ1, YJ2, 80cc, and 100cc 43-45
Crankcase
    Cover removal, inspection, and installation 19
    Maintenance and assembly 23
Crankshaft
    Crank width specifications 25
    Exploded view 24
    Removal, inspection, and installation . 23
Cylinder
    Inspection and installation 15
    Removal and installation 14
Cylinder head 14

E

Electrical system
  Battery/coil ignition 78-80
  Lighting/charging system (generator)....84-87
  Lighting/charging system (magneto).....80-84
  Magneto ignition system.................73-78
  Wiring diagrams........................88-89
Engine
  Autolube service 30-32
  Bearings and oil seals 25
  Crankcase cover 18
  Crankcase splitting 21-23
  Crankshaft 23-25
  Cylinder 14-16
  Cylinder head 14
  Drive sprocket 21
  Installation 14
  Noises, abnormal...................... 7
  Operating requirements 6
  Piston, pin, and rings 16-18
  Removal 10-14
  Rotary valve 19-21
  Transmission oil quantity 14

F

Flat spots............................... 7
Forks, front (JT1, 80cc, 100cc, YJ1, and YJ2)
  Disassembly and assembly............... 99
  Exploded view, JT series 96
  Exploded view, YG1 series 97
  Exploded view, 80cc and 100cc (except JT and YG1 series) 98
  Inner tube inspection 100
  Oil change............................ 100
  Removal 95
  Seal replacement 100
  Spring inspection 100
Forks, front (MJ1 and MJ2) 101
Forks, front (U5 series)................ 101
Frame
  Exploded view, all except JT1 and JT2 122
  Exploded view, JT1 and JT2 series........ 121
  Exploded view, MJ2 123
  Exploded view, YJ1 and YJ2 124
  MJ2 121
  YJ1 and YJ2 124
Front end (MJ1 and MJ2) 102, 103
Fuel system
  Air filter 70-71
  Basic principles 50
  Carburetor adjustments................67-70
  Fuel tank 71-72
  Mikuni VM carburetor 64
  Periodic maintenance 61
  Teikei Y16P carburetor 62
  Throttle operation 61
Fuel tank 71-72

G

Gearshift mechanism
  Exploded view, MJ2 (late) 41
  Exploded view, U5, MJ1 (early), and MJ2 40
  Exploded view, YG5T, G5S, G6S, G6SB, G7S, JT1, and 100cc 35
  Exploded views, YJ1 and YJ2 37-38
  Removal and inspection, U5 series, MJ1, and MJ2 39-41
  Removal/inspection, YG5T, G5S, G6S, G6SB, G7S, JT1, JT2, and 100cc series 33-36
  Removal/inspection, YJ1, YJ2, and YG1 36-38

I

Identification, model 2
Idling, poor 7
Ignition coil 80
Ignition system (see Battery/coil ignition system or magneto ignition system)
Ignition timing 74, 79

K

Kickstarter
  Exploded view, G5S, G6S, G6SB, G7S, L5T, L5TA, JT1, JT2, and YG5T 29
  Exploded view, U5, YG1, YJ1, MJ1, and MJ2 series..................... 27
  Exploded view, YL2 series 30
  Removal and installation, G5S, G6S, G6SB, G7S, L5T, L5TA, JT1, JT2, and YG5T...................... 28
  Removal and installation, U5, YG1, YJ1, YJ2, MJ1, and MJ2 series 26
  Removal and installation, YL2 series...... 28

L

Lighting/charging system (generator)
  Armature inspection 85
  Battery 87
  Generator output test 84
  Voltage regulator inspection 86
  Wiring diagram 85, 86
  Yoke inspection 84
Lighting/charging system (magneto)
  Battery charging circuit tests........... 82
  Early type 80

Late type	82
Lighting problems	80
Lighting voltage maintenance	80
Silicon rectifier	84
Wiring diagrams, early type	81, 82
Wiring diagram, late type	83

M

Magneto ignition system
    Breaker point maintenance 73
    Breaker point replacement 74
    Condenser inspection 77
    Exploded view 75
    Ignition timing 74
Maintenance, periodic 3-4
Misfiring 7
Model identification 2-3

O

Oil seals 25
Overheating 7

P

Piston, pin, and rings
    Pin fit 18
    Piston/cylinder clearance 15, 16-17
    Piston installation 18
    Piston removal and reconditioning 16
    Piston seizure 7
    Ring carbon removal 17
    Ring end gap and side gap 18
    Ring identification and removal 17
    Ring installation 18
Power loss 7, 8
Primary drive gear.......................... 51

R

Rotary valve
    Removal, inspection, and installation 19
    Timing 20

S

Safety hints 2
Service hints 1
Shock absorbers, rear (JT1, JT2, 80cc,
    100cc, YJ1, and YJ2) 116
Shocks, rear (MJ1 and MJ2) 116
Shocks, rear (U5 series) 114
Specifications, model
    G5S, G6S, G6SB, and G7S 133
    JT1, JT1L, JT2, and JT2M 130
    L5T and L5TA 135
    MJ2 and MJ2T 129
    U5, U5E, and U5L 126
    YG1(S&T) and YG1K(S&T) 131
    YG5T 132
    YJ1, YJ1K, and MJ1 127
    YJ2 and YJ2S 128
    YL2 and YL2C 134
Specifications and data, general
    Carburetor float level settings 67
    Clutch plate specifications 44
    Clutch spring lengths 50
    Crank width specifications 25
    Ignition coil resistance 80
    Maintenance intervals 4
    Models covered 3
    Piston clearance........................ 15
    Tools, Yamaha special 3
    Transmission oil quantity 14
Sprocket, rear 112
Starting difficulties.......................... 6
Steering head 102-104
Steering problems 9
Swing arm, rear
    Exploded views 118, 119
    Removal and inspection 116
Swing arm, rear (MJ1 and MJ2)
    Exploded view 120
    Removal, inspection, and installation ..117-121

T

Tires
    Pressure 111
    Removal and installation 112
Tools, special 3
Transmission
    Exploded view, JT1 and JT2............. 57
    Exploded view, late MJ2 55
    Exploded view, MJ1 and early MJ2 54
    Exploded view, YJ1, YG2, and MJ1 53
    Gearshifting difficulties 8
    JT1 and JT2 56
    Oil quantity 14
    Primary drive gear 51
    Sectional view 53
    Sectional view, JT1 and JT2 57
Sectional view, YG5T, G5S, G6S, G6SB,
    G7S, YL2, and YL2C 58
Transmission assembly, YG5T, G5S,
    G6S, G6SB, G7S, YL2, and YL2C 58
    U5, YJ1, YJ2, MJ1, MJ2, and YG1 51-56
Troubleshooting
    Backfiring 7
    Brake problems 8, 9
    Clutch slip or drag..................... 7
    Engine noises 7

Flat spots 7
Gearshifting difficulties 8
General information 5
Handling, poor 7
Idling, poor 7
Lighting problems 8
Misfiring 7
Operating requirements 5
Overheating 7
Piston seizure 7
Power loss........................... 7, 8
Starting difficulties 6
Steering problems 9
Vibration, excessive................... 7

W

Wheel, front
   Bearing replacement 93
   Description, removal, and installation 90
   Exploded view, except YG1 91
   Exploded view, YG1 91
   Runout inspection 80
   Spoke, replacement 94
   Spoke tension 93
Wheel, rear
   Bearing replacement 110
   Clutch hub cushion replacement 110
   Description and removal 104
   Exploded view, JT1 and JT2 series 105
   Exploded view, YG1, 100cc series 106
   Exploded view, 80cc 108
   Installation 109
   Runout inspection 110
   Spokes 110
Wiring diagrams
   All except U5, YJ1, YJ2, and YG1 series.. 89
   U5, YJ1, YJ2, and YG1 series 88

MAINTENANCE LOG

DATE	TYPE OF SERVICE	COST	REMARKS

VELOCEPRESS.com - MOTORCYCLE MANUALS BY MAKE

- AJS 1932-1948 SINGLES & TWINS 250cc THRU 1000cc (BOOK OF)
- AJS 1945-1956 SINGLES RIGID & SPTRING FACTORY WSM & PARTS
- AJS 1945-1960 SINGLES MODELS 16 & 18 350cc & 500cc (BOOK OF)
- AJS 1948-1956 TWINS MODELS 20 & 30 FACTORY WSM & PARTS
- AJS 1955-1965 SINGLES MODELS 16 & 18 350cc & 500cc (BOOK OF)
- AJS 1957-1966 SINGLES & TWINS (ALL) FACTORY WSM
- AJS 1959-1969 G80CS G85CS & P11 OFF ROAD FACTORY WSM
- AJS 1968-1974 STORMER FACTORY WSM & PARTS LIST
- ARIEL UP TO 1932 (BOOK OF)
- ARIEL 1932-1939 PREWAR MODELS (BOOK OF)
- ARIEL 1933-1951 (WORKSHOP MANUAL)
- ARIEL 1939-1960 4 STROKE SINGLES (BOOK OF)
- ARIEL 1958-1964 LEADER & ARROW FACTORY WSM & PARTS LIST
- ARIEL 1958-1964 LEADER & ARROW (BOOK OF)
- BMW R26 R27 (1956-1967) FACTORY WORKSHOP MANUAL
- BMW R50 R50S R60 R69S (1955-1969) FACTORY WORKSHOP MANUAL
- BMW R50/5 R60/5 R75/5 (1969-1973) FACTORY WORKSHOP MANUAL
- BRIDGESTONE 90 SERIES FACTORY WSM & PARTS CATALOGUE
- BRIDGESTONE 175 SERIES FACTORY WSM & PARTS CATALOGUE
- BRIDGESTONE 350 SERIES FACTORY WSM & PARTS CATALOGUES
- BSA SERVICE SHEETS MASTER CATALOGUE ALL MODELS 1945-1967
- BSA BANTAM D1 TO D7 1948-1966 FACTORY SERVICE SHEETS MANUAL
- BSA BANTAM ALL MODELS FROM 1948 ONWARDS (BOOK OF)
- BSA BANTAM D14 FACTORY SERVICE MANUAL
- BSA DANDY FACTORY WORKSHOP MANUAL (COMPILATION)
- BSA SINGLES & V-TWINS UP TO 1926 inc. 1927 SUPPLEMENT (BOOK OF)
- BSA SINGLES & V-TWINS UP TO 1930 (BOOK OF)
- BSA SINGLES & V-TWINS UP TO 1935 (BOOK OF)
- BSA SINGLES & V-TWINS 1936-1939 (BOOK OF)
- BSA C10, C11 & C12 1945-1958 FACTORY SERVICE SHEETS MANUAL
- BSA OHV & SV SINGLES 250-600cc 1945-1959 (BOOK OF)
- BSA C15 & B40 1958-1967 FACTORY SERVICE SHEETS MANUAL
- BSA OHV & SV SINGLES 250cc (ONLY) 1954-1970 (BOOK OF)
- BSA B31, B32, B33 & B34 1945-60 FACTORY SERVICE SHEETS MANUAL
- BSA OHV SINGLES 350 & 500cc 1955-1967 (BOOK OF)
- BSA M20, M21 & M33 1945-1963 FACTORY SERVICE SHEETS MANUAL
- BSA TWINS A7 & A10 1948-1962 FACTORY SERVICE SHEETS MANUAL
- BSA TWINS A7 & A10 1948-1962 (BOOK OF)
- BSA TWINS A50 & A65 1962-1965 FACTORY WORKSHOP MANUAL
- BSA TWINS A50 & A65 1962-1969 (SECOND BOOK OF)
- BULTACO 125cc to 37cc SINGLES 1968-1979 WORKSHOP MANUAL
- CZ 125cc to 380cc SINGLES 1967-1974 WORKSHOP MANUAL
- DOUGLAS 1929-1939 PREWAR ALL MODELS (BOOK OF)
- DOUGLAS 1948-1957 POSTWAR ALL MODELS FACTORY SHOP MANUAL
- DUCATI 160cc, 250cc & 350cc OHC MODELS FACTORY SHOP MANUAL
- HODAKA 90cc,100cc, & 125cc SINGLES 1964-1978 WORKSHOP MANUAL
- HONDA 50cc ALL MODELS UP TO 1970 INC MONKEY & TRAIL (BOOK OF)
- HONDA 90cc ALL MODELS UP TO 1966 (BOOK OF)
- HONDA TWINS & SINGLES 50cc THRU 305cc 1960-1966 (BOOK OF)
- HONDA TWINS ALL MODELS 125cc THRU 450cc UP TO 1968 (BOOK OF)
- HONDA C100 50cc SUPER CUB O.H.C. 1959-1962 FACTORY WSM
- HONDA C110 50cc SPORT CUB O.H.C. 1960-1962 FACTORY WSM
- HONDA 50-65-70-90cc O.H.C. SINGLES 1959-1983 WSM
- HONDA 100-125cc SINGLES CB/CD/CL/SL/TL 1970-1984 FACTORY WSM
- HONDA 125-150cc TWINS C/CS/CB/CA 1959-1966 FACTORY WSM
- HONDA 125-160-175-200cc TWINS 1965-1978 WORKSHOP MANUAL
- HONDA 250-305cc TWINS C/CS/CB 1961-1968 FACTORY WSM
- HOHDA 250-350cc TWINS CB/CL/SL 1968-1973 FACTORY WSM
- HONDA 250-360cc TWINS CB/CL/CJ 1974-1977 FACTORY WSM
- HONDA 350F & 400F 4-CYLINDER 1972-1977 FACTORY WSM
- HONDA 450cc TWINS CB/CL 1965-1974 K0 TO K7 WORKSHOP MANUAL
- HONDA 500cc & 550cc 4-CYL 1971-1978 FACTORY WORKSHOP MANUAL
- HONDA 750cc SHOC 4-CYL 1969-1978 K0~K8 WORKSHOP MANUAL
- HUSQVARNA 125cc to 450cc SINGLES 1965-1975 WORKSHOP MANUAL
- INDIAN PONYBIKE, BOY RACER & PAPOOSE ILL PARTS LIST & SALES LIT

VELOCEPRESS.com – SCOOTER MANUALS

- BSA SUNBEAM SCOOTER WORKSHOP MANUAL 1959-1965
- BSA SUNBEAM SCOOTER 1959-1965 (BOOK OF)
- LAMBRETTA 1947-1957 ALL 125 & 150cc MODELS (BOOK OF)
- LAMBRETTA 1957-1970 LI & TV MODELS (SECOND BOOK OF)
- NSU PRIMA 1956-1964 ALL MODELS (BOOK OF)
- TRIUMPH TIGRESS SCOOTER WORKSHOP MANUAL 1959-1965
- TRIUMPH TIGRESS SCOOTER (BOOK OF)
- VESPA 1951-1961 (BOOK OF)
- VESPA 1955-1963 125 & 150cc & GS MODELS (SECOND BOOK OF)
- VESPA 1955-1968 GS & SS (BOOK OF)
- VESPA 1963-1972 90, 125 & 150cc (THIRD BOOK OF)

VELOCEPRESS.com - MOPEDS & MOTORIZED BICYCLES MANUALS

- CYCLEMOTOR (BOOK OF)
- NSU QUICKLY 1953-1963 ALL MODELS (BOOK OF)
- PUCH MAXI N & S MAINTENANCE & REPAIR (3 MANUAL COMPILATION)
- RALEIGH MOPEDS 1960-1969 (BOOK OF)

www.VelocePress.com

- J.A.P. ENGINES 1927-1952 & MOTORCYCLES 1934-1952 (BOOK OF)
- KAWASAKI TRIPLES 1968-1980 ALL MODELS 250cc to 750cc WSM
- MAICO 250cc to 501cc 1968-1978 WORKSHOP MANUAL
- MATCHLESS 1931-1939 ALL MODELS 250cc THRU 990cc (BOOK OF)
- MATCHLESS 1945-1956 RIGID & SPRING FACTORY WSM & PARTS
- MATCHLESS 1945-1956 SINGLES G3 & G80 350cc & 500cc (BOOK OF)
- MATCHLESS 1948-1956 TWINS G9 & G11 FACTORY WSM & PARTS
- MATCHLESS 1955-1966 SINGLES G3 & G80 350cc & 500cc (BOOK OF)
- MATCHLESS 1957-1966 SINGLES & TWINS (ALL) FACTORY WSM
- MONTESA 1962-1978 125cc to 360cc ALL MODELS WORKSHOP MANUAL
- NEW IMPERIAL ALL SV & OHV FROM 1935 ONWARDS (BOOK OF)
- NORTON 1932-1939 PREWAR MODELS (BOOK OF)
- NORTON 1932-1947 (BOOK OF)
- NORTON 1938-1956 (BOOK OF)
- NORTON 1945-1963 MODELS 16H, Big4, ES2, 19 & 50 WSM'S & PARTS
- NORTON 1955-1963 MODELS 19, 50 & ES2 (BOOK OF)
- NORTON 1948-1970 DOMINATOR TWINS FACTORY WSM'S & PARTS
- NORTON 1955-1965 DOMINATOR TWINS (BOOK OF)
- NORTON 1960-1970 TWIN CYLINDER FACTORY WORKSHOP MANUAL
- NORTON 1970-1975 COMMANDO 850 & 750cc FACTORY WSM
- NORTON 1975-1978 MK 3 COMMANDO 850 cc FACTORY WSM
- OSSA 1971-1978 125cc, 175cc, 250cc, 310cc WSM
- PANTHER 1932-1958 LIGHTWEIGHT MODELS 250 & 350cc (BOOK OF)
- PANTHER 1938-1966 HEAVYWEIGHT MODELS 600 & 650cc (BOOK OF)
- PENTON-KTM-SACHS 1968-1975 100cc & 125cc WORKSHOP MANUAL
- PENTON-KTM 1972-1975 175cc, 250cc & 400cc WSM & PARTS MANUALS
- PENTON-KTM 1972-1979 125cc to 400cc ENGINE WSM & PARTS MANUAL
- RALEIGH MOTORCYCLES 1919-1933 (BOOK OF)
- ROYAL ENFIELD 1934-1946 SINGLES & V TWINS (BOOK OF)
- ROYAL ENFIELD 1937-1953 SINGLES & V TWINS (BOOK OF)
- ROYAL ENFIELD 1946-1962 SINGLES (BOOK OF)
- ROYAL ENFIELD 1948-1962 350cc & 500cc PRE-UNIT BULLET WSM
- ROYAL ENFIELD 1948-1963 500cc TWINS FACTORY WORKSHOP MANUAL
- ROYAL ENFIELD 1952-1963 700cc TWINS FACTORY WORKSHOP MANUAL
- ROYAL ENFIELD 1956-1966 250cc CRUSADER & 350cc NEW BULLET WSM
- ROYAL ENFIELD 1958-1966 250cc & 350cc SINGLES (SECOND BOOK OF)
- ROYAL ENFIELD 1962-1970 INTERCEPTOR WSM'S & PARTS (Compilation)
- RUDGE 1933-1939 (BOOK OF)
- SACHS 1968-1975 100cc & 125cc ENGINES WSM & M/CYCLE PARTS LIST
- SUNBEAM 1928-1939 (BOOK OF)
- SUNBEAM 1946-1957 S7 & S8 (BOOK OF)
- SUZUKI 50cc & 80cc UP TO 1966 (BOOK OF)
- SUZUKI T10 1963-1967 FACTORY WORKSHOP MANUAL
- SUZUKI T20 & T200 1965-1969 FACTORY WORKSHOP MANUAL
- SUZUKI TWINS 1962 ONWARDS 125-500cc WORKSHOP MANUAL
- TRIUMPH 1935-1949 SINGLES & TWINS (BOOK OF)
- TRIUMPH 1937-1961 SINGLES SV & OHV 250cc-600cc + TERRIER & CUB
- TRIUMPH 1945-1955 PRE-UNIT 350cc, 500cc & 650cc TWINS WSM No.11
- TRIUMPH 1945-1959 TWINS (BOOK OF)
- TRIUMPH 1956-1969 TWINS (BOOK OF)
- TRIUMPH 1956-1962 PRE-UNIT 500cc & 650cc TWINS WSM No.17
- TRIUMPH 1957-1963 UNIT CONSTRUCTION 350-500cc WSM No.4
- TRIUMPH 1963-1974 UNIT CONSTRUCTION 350-500cc FACTORY WSM
- TRIUMPH 1963-1970 UNIT CONSTRUCTION 650cc FACTORY WSM
- TRIUMPH 1968-1974 TRIDENT T150 & T150V FACTORY WSM
- TRIUMPH 1971-1973 650cc OIL-IN-FRAME FACTORY WSM
- TRIUMPH 1973-1976 BONNEVILLE & TIGER FACTORY WSM
- TRIUMPH 1979-1983 750cc T140, TR7 & TR65 FACTORY WSM
- VELOCETTE 1925-1970 ALL SINGLES & TWINS (BOOK OF)
- VELOCETTE 1933-1952 MOV-MAC-MSS RIGID FRAME FACTORY WSM
- VELOCETTE 1953-1960 MAC SPRING FRAME WSM & ILL PARTS LIST
- VELOCETTE 1954-1971 MSS-VENOM-THRUXTON-VIPER FACTORY WSM
- VILLIERS ENGINE UP TO 1959 INC. 3 WHEELERS (BOOK OF)
- VILLIERS ENGINE UP TO 1969 (BOOK OF)
- VINCENT 1935-1955 (WORKSHOP MANUAL)
- YAMAHA 1961-1967 YA5 & YA6 (WORKSHOP MANUAL & ILL PARTS LIST)
- YAMAHA 1963-1976 50cc to 100cc ROTARY VALVE SINGLES WSM
- YAMAHA 1968-1971 DT1 & MX SERIES Inc. GYT WORKSHOP MANUAL
- YAMAHA 1971-1972 JT1 & JT2 (WORKSHOP MANUAL & ILL PARTS LIST)

VELOCEPRESS.com - THREE WHEELER MANUALS

- BOND MINICAR THREE WHEELER 1948-1967 (BOOK OF)
- BMW ISETTA FACTORY WORKSHOP MANUAL
- BSA THREE WHEELER (BOOK OF)
- RELIANT REGAL THREE WHEELER 1952-1973 (BOOK OF)
- VINTAGE MORGAN THREE WHEELER (BOOK OF)

VELOCEPRESS.com – MOTORCYCLE TECHNICAL BOOKS

- 1930'S BRITISH MOTORCYCLE CARBS & ELEC COMPONENTS (BOOK OF)
- 1930'S BRITISH MOTORCYCLE ENGINES (OVERHAUL & MAINTENANCE)
- 1930'S BRITISH MOTORCYCLE GEARBOXES & CLUTCHES (BOOK OF)
- CATALOG OF BRITISH MOTORCYCLES (1951 MODELS)
- LUCAS ELECTRONICS BRITISH M/CYCLES REPAIR & PARTS (1950-1977)
- MOTORCYCLE ENGINEERING (P.E. Irving)
- MOTORCYCLE ROAD TESTS 1949-1953 (Motor Cycle Magazine UK)
- SPEED AND HOW TO OBTAIN IT (Motor Cycle Magazine UK)
- TUNING FOR SPEED (P.E. Irving)
- WIPAC (COMBO) MANUAL NUMBER 3 + M/CYCLE & SCOOTER MANUAL

www.ingramcontent.com/pod-product-compliance
Lightning Source LLC
Chambersburg PA
CBHW080740300426
44114CB00019B/2641